OMNICIDE II

JASON BAHBAK MOHAGHEGH

Omnicide II
MANIA, DOOM,
AND THE FUTURE-IN-DECEPTION

URBANOMIC

sequence

Published in 2023 by

URBANOMIC MEDIA LTD
THE OLD LEMONADE FACTORY
WINDSOR QUARRY
FALMOUTH TR11 3EX
UNITED KINGDOM

SEQUENCE PRESS
88 ELDRIDGE STREET
NEW YORK
NY 10002
UNITED STATES

All rights reserved.

No part of this book may be reproduced or transmitted in any form or by any means, electronic or mechanical, including photocopying, recording or any other information storage or retrieval system, without prior permission in writing from the publisher.

US Library of Congress Control Number: 2022918809

BRITISH LIBRARY CATALOGUING-IN-PUBLICATION DATA

A full catalogue record of this book is available
from the British Library
ISBN 978-1-7336281-6-7

Printed and bound in the UK by
Short Run Press

Distributed by the MIT Press,
Cambridge, Massachusetts and London, England

www.urbanomic.com
www.sequencepress.com

CONTENTS

Mania Tabula	XII
Foreword *by Robin Mackay*	XV
Introduction: Book of the Eleventh Hour (Philosophy of Doom)	1

Part 2

I. Selamania (Light Flashes)	21
II. Neuromania (Nerves)	25
III. Tremomania (Trembling)	31
IV. Ataxomania (Disorder)	35
V. Eruptiomania (Explosions)	39

Part 3

I. Uranomania (Heaven, Divinity)	45
II. Vatomania (Premonitions, Prophecies, Prophetic Figures)	47
III. Apeiromania (Infinity)	51
IV. Zeusomania (Fate)	55
V. Hademania/Stygiomania (Hell)	59
VI. Daimonomania (Demons)	63

Part 4

I. Pyromania (Fire)	69
II. Fumimania/Capnomania (Smoke)	73
III. Pyrexiomania (Fever)	75

IV. Frigomania/Cheimatomania (Coldness)	79
V. Crystallomania (Crystals)	85

Part 6

I. Graphomania (Writing)	91
II. Linguomania (Language)	95
III. Bibliomania (Books)	99

Part 7

I. Chromatomania (Colour)	107
II. Leukomania (Whiteness)	111
III. Melanomania (Blackness)	115

Part 8

I. Ombromania/Pluviomania (Rain)	121
II. Antlomania (Floods)	125
III. Thalassomania (Oceans)	129
IV. Bathymania (Deep Water)	133
V. Aquamania (Drowning)/Kymomania (Waves)	137
VI. Ablutomania (Washing, Bathing)	141

Part 9

I. Dysmorphomania (Physical Deformity)	147
II. Decapomania (Headlessness)	149
III. Teratomania (Monstrosity)	153

Part 10

I. Eremiomania (Stillness)	159
II. Clinomania (Staying Bedridden)	163

CONTENTS

III. Somnemania (Sleep)	167
IV. Insomnemania (Sleeplessness)	171

Part 11

I. Typhlomania (Blindness)	177
II. Achluomania (Darkness)	181

Part 12

I. Aeromania (Air)	185
II. Animania (Soul)	189
III. Respiromania (Breath)	193
IV. Anemomania (Winds, Drafts)	195
V. Etheromania (Sky)	199
VI. Nephomania (Clouds)	203
VII. Aviomania (Flight)	209
VIII. Basimania (Falling)/Trypomania (Holes)	213

Part 13

I. Phonomania/Acousticomania (Sounds, Voices, Noise)	221
II. Questiomania/Erotetomania (Questions)	225
III. Silentomania (Silence)	231

Part 14

I. Gymnomania (Nakedness)	237
II. Ommatomania (Sight, Eyes)	241
III. Faciemania (Faces)	245
IV. Iconomania (Images, Portraits, Icons)	249
V. Idolomania (Idols)	255

Interlude: Book of the Opium Den
(Philosophy of Smoke) — 259

Part 15

I. Praecidomania (Mutilation) — 281

II. Tomomania (Surgical Operations) — 285

III. Stauromania (Crucifixion) — 289

IV. Xyromania (Razors, Knives) — 295

V. Trypanomania (Needles) — 301

VI. Cicatromania (Scars) — 305

Part 16

I. Agromania (Open Spaces, Holes, Abysses) — 313

II. Clithromania (Confined Spaces, Caves)/Claustromania (Enclosure) — 317

III. Anginomania (Extreme Tightness) — 321

Part 17

I. Atelomania (Imperfection) — 329

II. Peccatomania (Sins, Crimes) — 333

III. Subteromania (Undergrounds) — 337

Part 18

I. Algomania (Pain) — 343

II. Pathomania (Disease) — 347

III. Molysmomania (Contamination) — 351

IV. Narcomania (Drugs) — 354

V. Iomania (Poison) — 354

CONTENTS

Part 19

I. Necromania (Death)	357
II. Thanatomania (Death-Magic)	363
III. Coimetromania (Cemeteries)	367
IV. Klaiomania (Weeping)	373

Part 21

I. Choreomania (Dancing)	379
II. Melomania (Music)	383

Part 22

I. Dendromania (Forests, Branches)	389
II. Nebulamania (Fog, Mist)	393
III. Brontomania (Storm, Thunder, Lightning)	397
IV. Spectromania (Ghosts)	401
Interlude: Book of Poor Games (Philosophy of Play)	409

Part 23

I. Chronomania (Time)	433
II. Atemania (Ruins)	439
III. Petramania (Ancient Monuments)/ Geomania (Stones)	443
IV. Osmomania (Smells, Odours)	447

Part 24

I. Politicomania (Power Structures)	453
II. Misomania (Hatred)	457

III. Haematomania (Blood)	461
IV. Phobomania (Fear)	463
V. Polemomania (War)	465

Part 25

I. Geumomania (Taste, The Mouth)	471
II. Aceromania (Sour Things, Bitterness)	479
III. Limomania (Hunger, Thirst)	483
IV. Geliomania (Laughter)	489
V. Zoomania (Animality)	493

Part 26

I. Haphemania/Chiraptomania (Touch)	507
II. Dermatomania (Skin)	511
III. Amychomania (Claws, Fangs, Horns)	515
IV. Mechanomania (Machines)	517
V. Ergomania (Work)	521

Part 27

I. Nihilomania (Nothingness)	525
II. Eremomania (The Desert)	529
III. Taphemania (Being Buried Alive)	531
IV. Athazagoramania (Forgetting)	533
Epilogue: Book of the Liar (Philosophy of Deception)	537
Select Bibliography	567

Mania Tabula

Part 1
See volume I*

Part 2
Selamania (light flashes)
Neuromania (nerves)
Tremomania (trembling)
Ataxomania (disorder)
Eruptiomania (explosions)

Part 3
Uranomania (heaven, divinity)
Vatomania (prophecies)
Apeiromania (infinity)
Zeusomania (fate)
Hademania/Stygiomania (hell)
Daimonomania (demons)

Part 4
Pyromania (fire)
Fumimania/Capnomania (smoke)
Pyrexiomania (fever)
Frigomania/Cheimatomania (coldness)
Crystallomania (crystals)

Part 5
See volume I*

Part 6
Graphomania (writing)
Linguomania (language)
Bibliomania (books)

Part 7
Chromatomania (colour)
Leukomania (whiteness)
Melanomania (blackness)

Part 8
Ombromania/Pluviomania (rain)
Antlomania (floods)
Thalassomania (oceans)
Bathymania (deep water)
Aquamania (drowning)
Kymomania (waves)
Ablutomania (washing, bathing)

Part 9
Dysmorphomania (physical deformity)
Decapomania (headlessness)
Teratomania (monstrosity)

Part 10
Eremiomania (stillness)
Clinomania (staying bedridden)
Somnemania (sleep)
Insomnemania (sleeplessness)

Part 11
Typhlomania (blindness)
Achluomania (darkness)

Part 12
Aeromania (air)
Animania (soul)
Respiromania (breath)
Anemomania (winds, drafts)
Etheromania (sky)
Nephomania (clouds)
Aviomania (flight)
Basimania (falling)
Trypomania (holes)

Part 13
Phonomania/Acousticomania (sounds, voices, noise)
Questiomania/Erotetomania (questions)
Silentomania (silence)

---

* J.B. Mohaghegh, *Omnicide: Mania, Fatality, and the Future-in-Delirium* (Falmouth and New York: Urbanomic/Sequence Press, 2019).

Part 14
Gymnomania (nakedness)
Ommatomania (sight, eyes)
Faciemania (faces)
Iconomania (images, icons)
Idolomania (idols)

Part 15
Praecidomania (mutilation)
Tomomania
(surgical operations)
Stauromania (crucifixion)
Xyromania (razors, knives)
Trypanomania (needles)
Cicatromania (scars)

Part 16
Agromania (open spaces, abysses)
Clithromania (confined spaces)
Claustromania (enclosure)
Anginomania
(extreme tightness)

Part 17
Atelomania (imperfection)
Peccatomania (sins, crimes)
Subteromania (undergrounds)

Part 18
Algomania (pain)
Pathomania (disease)
Molysmomania (contamination)
Narcomania (drugs)
Iomania (poison)

Part 19
Necromania (death)
Thanatomania (death-magic)
Coimetromania (cemeteries)
Klaiomania (weeping)

Part 20
See volume I*

Part 21
Choreomania (dancing)
Melomania (music)

Part 22
Dendromania (forests)
Nebulamania (fog, mist)
Brontomania (storm, thunder)
Spectromania (ghosts)

Part 23
Chronomania (time)
Atemania (ruins)
Petramania (ancient monuments)
Geomania (stones)
Osmomania (smells, odours)

Part 24
Politicomania
(power structures)
Misomania (hatred)
Haematomania (blood)
Phobomania (fear)
Polemomania (war)

Part 25
Geumomania (taste, the mouth)
Aceromania (sour things)
Limomania (hunger, thirst)
Geliomania (laughter)
Zoomania (animality)

Part 26
Haphemania/Chiraptomania
(touch)
Dermatomania (skin)
Amychomania (claws, fangs)
Mechanomania (machines)
Ergomania (work)

Part 27
Nihilomania (nothingness)
Eremomania (the desert)
Taphemania (being buried alive)
Athazagoramania (forgetting)

Foreword:
In Praise of Perpetual Imminence

Robin Mackay

We're all doomed. Every morning it looks more certain that the world will end badly in one way or another, and imminently so. Once in thrall to the cackling fanatic who unwound dusty scrolls to disclose portents and prophecies, we now furtively peer into our private scrying tablets where ceaseless foretellings silently unfurl, personalised to our own predilections yet expressive of a collective malaise of apprehension. Terminal catastrophes that were once the purview of bombastic prophets have been brought under the regime of probability and management, existential risk is now the business of expert panels, thinktanks, and mitigative public policy. Their relentlessly pessimistic findings are transmitted daily, and still the feeds only stimulate our appetite for the end.

Omnicide II challenges this terminal mode of Western contemporaneity by opposing to the generalised dread and despair induced by 'doomscrolling' a hyperfocalised mania, by setting against the dull paralysis of a condemned present the unbearable lightness of no future.

A series of controlled combustions fuelled by fragments drawn from the poetry and literature of the Middle East, *Omnicide II* introduces us to a cast of manic visionaries, from the Selamaniac to the Crystallomaniac, from the Bibliomaniac to the Aeromaniac—all the parts listed in the *Mania Tabula* that were left as intriguing promises in the preceding volume. Whereas *Omnicide* charted the many ways in which a micro-obsession can ripen into the desire for all-encompassing annihilation, this second collection—but needless to say there is no order in this disordered treasury, one could start anywhere, we are always *in medias manias*—is placed under the general heading of *doom*, and highlights how the most vigorous campaigns of intensity sometimes flourish exclusively under the shadow of certain extinction.

To be doomed is to enter into a relation to time in which one is by definition too late, but does that necessarily mean that in the last moments we are condemned to craven contemplation, merely looking on as everything crumbles? What might the phenomenological tonality and the aesthetic timbre of such moments be, were they entered into with wholehearted will? What abilities might they confer upon one who, in losing all hope, gains in acuity of perception, perhaps even developing new sensitivities and preternatural capacities for action? Jason Bahbak

FOREWORD

Mohaghegh's wager is that fully opening the 'exceptional window of consciousness' afforded by the prospect of inevitable demise exposes us to an anticipative form of mania that reaps analeptic quickening from certain doom.

The last moment is of course the very space within which unfold the *Thousand and One Nights*, whose yarns measure out the space between now and the end, postponing execution of the inevitable, buying time at the price of learning to live at the limit of the perpetually condemned. And like Sharhzad, Mohaghegh is a consummate storyteller—here you will encounter fantastic fates and magical curses, assassins and emperors, murders and suicides, falconers and luxury Persian Gulf hotels, cat-octopuses and bleeding lions, retellings of Mesopotamian fables and urban legends…the common thread being that the ending never arrives, but is always infinitesimally deferred by the telling of some other anecdotal detail. Such is the secret of Mohaghegh's mad method: it is by insistently worrying at an ultraparticular fixation that the maniac produces an entire alternate regime of being and a renewed thirst for life. The tiniest crack in the order of things expands to reveal a new world, another night passes without the Vizier realising he has been fooled again—and then another, and another….

Looking beyond 'doomscrolling' to other new entries into the common lexicon, we draw closer to the oblique contemporaneity of this technique, for the devices of

Mohaghegh's 'book of wonders' operate like dark twins of the clichéd forms of the doomed present. Where enumerated 'listicles' and punctual 'factoids' target the time-poor with their optimised rundowns and digests of must-have info, arresting shallow attention with definitive but soon-forgotten data, Mohaghegh's tales-within-litanies-within-tables-within-lists extract inexhaustible riches from the tiny sliver of time remaining by employing a single empirical detail as a prism through which a vain reality, on the other side of a narrow defile, can blossom into an expansive polychromatic sheaf illuminated by the unreasonable intensity of the incurably obsessed.

In pulling one singular bouquet after another from the same black hat, Mohaghegh resumes the offensive of those writers, artists, and thinkers for whom the fiercest blooms open only in the shade of certain doom, those whose creativity flourishes on the brink of imminent catastrophe, whether that of a condemned individual or that of a whole people, whether in personal intimacy or collective political struggle (the two of course being indistinguishable when it comes to Forugh Farrokhzad before her 'Window' or Mahmoud Darwish speaking of 'A Lover from Palestine', for example).

Scanning the cut flowers of his chosen array of Middle Eastern poets, Mohaghegh examines their vocabulary, metaphors, and images as if they were omens or signs: a literary radiologist spreading out the spectra of their ambiguities before us, analysing it to procure models for the maniacal inflammation of an isolated poetic gesture. Mobilising the narrative, the conceptual, the phenomenological, the poetic, and the associative, proliferating meanings through multiple readings, hyperparaphrasis and interpretosis, molecular decomposition and nuclear fission, his precision instruments reveal every verse to be a stem of latent budding-points, with alternate universes or parallel dimensions bifurcating at the juncture of every line and sometimes even within one word. Multiple conclusions drawn from a single interpretation of an image or phrase; an enumeration of alternative readings each harbouring its own dire consequences; a series of oblique associations that lend vastly different colourings to one and the same image…each a glimpse of a potential new madness, the germ of a new mania.

All of these riches once laid out before them, there is no question of commending any one interpretation to the reader as the 'truth'. Instead, we are given to understand that in these last hours what is most important is to muster the strength to *lie* realities into being (what has been called 'hyperstition'). Hence the importance of deception, of those operators—crafty, cunning, duplicitous, underhand—that permit writer and criminal alike to slide imperceptibly from one thing to another, to equivocate, to forge instrumental alliances and conduct illicit commerce, to mesmerise others and even themselves—in short, to do everything possible to forestall and repel truth's tendency to nullify in advance the capacity for further play.

To we the *truly* doomed, then, this work says: *Deceive!* By whatever ruse is necessary, by seizing upon whatever inessential trifle seizes you and pursuing it through the prism of mania, continue to exacerbate the extravagance that characterises what is most essential to the intensity of the life of thought, however long it has left to live.

Although the entry of 'doomscrolling' into the dictionary indexes a certain collective *jouissance* in our mesmerised contemplation of the end, this dissolute inward-spiralling pathology is really remarkable only for its dilution and its pale democratic character. We have each become our own prophet of a miasmic terror at once anxiety-inducing (the urgency of multiple insoluble predicaments) and etiolated (the scrolling never stops, the feed is continuous, no one figure holds the attention). It is something different to open these pages and to experience in each of them the infinitely expansive and infinitesimally condensed time of omnicide, its rhythm beat out by the music of stanzas sampled, transformed, fanned out into manifold possibilities. To enter the variegated terrain they project, in search of 'the intense, the impossible, the delirious, the no man's land', is both to finally unshackle the potency of last-days thinking, and to discover an unexpected antidote to the oppressive paralysis and lethargy of the chronic doomscroller.

Introduction: Book of the Eleventh Hour (Philosophy of Doom)

> *For the force of the aether chases them toward the sea,*
> *The sea spits them out toward earth's surface, the earth toward the rays*
> *Of the bright sun, and the sun hurls them into the eddies of*
> *the aether.*
> *Each one receives them from another, but all hate them.*
> *Of them, I too am now one, an exile from the divine and a*
> *wanderer,*
> *I who relied on insane Strife.*
>
> EMPEDOCLES[1]

Doom is always a matter of unfinished business. And this book, an attempted philosophy of doom, also addresses a kind of unfinished business: a second volume to settle affairs and leave things done; a last decisive stab at formulating the once-and-for-all. And yet concluding a line of thought is no easy task: it requires both the overpayment of debts (to bad gods) and the overkilling of consciousness

---

1 Empedocles, 'Purifications', in D. O'Brien, 'Empedocles: The Wandering Daimon and the Two Poems', *Aevum Antiquum*, NS 1: 2001 (B 115 = D 10).

(through bad turns of language, image, and possibility). The writing on the wall; the blood on the wall.

Behind this contraption of doom there is a certain physics, at once theoretical and performative, that can only be set in motion after rigorous calibration. No doubt a sensitive dynamic is required to realise states of breakdown and the never-mind. Doom being both temporal-spatial and spatial-temporal, one must determine the right time to ensure that it covers all space, just as one must select the right space to ensure it lasts for all time.

Moreover, a philosophy of doom compels us to ask highly precise questions about vengeance: Does the doomsday event culminate in a climactic instant (the split-second) or is it a gradual process of slight victories (the long-drawn-out)? Does one seek revenge on behalf of the already-dead (ghostly futility) or that of the still-living (desperate last chance)? Is it authored cruelty (requiring an overlord's cautious wrath) or a faceless exploit (reckless, anonymous devastation)? The answers to such questions vary across a vast spectrum, reflecting the many faces potentially worn by the doomsday composer: let us call them

the figure of calmness,
the figure of attraction,
the figure of translucence,
and the figure of peril.

INTRODUCTION

1. RAISED BY WOLVES (FIGURE OF CALMNESS)

37.0200° N, 4.5594° W

Among the Antequeran ranges of southern Spain one finds those jagged limestone formations that thrust themselves upward from beneath the sea millions of years ago. There they stand like ominous geological guards at the mouths of expansive valleys today inhabited only by rare fox species, griffon vultures, the Spanish ibex (mountain goat), and the now near-extinct Eurasian and tundra wolves. One can spy these doomed creatures—some scavenging, some preying, some resting idly—on adjacent rock ledges while carving through the chasms one after another. They maintain their ideal distance from the intruder; they keep close watch, and stare directly back into one's eyes.

Tranquility is horrifying. After all, is not the tranquil gaze the intermediary between the poised mind (that knows too much) and the steady hand (that carries out the deed)? Unflinching beings always signal an awful advantage.

The figure of calmness is the bearer of this same incredible serenity, as if descended from some halcyon sphere of carelessness attained only by living on borrowed time. For this remains an essential, unexplored existential question: What happens when someone's self-image includes an absolute conviction that they are the last of their kind? A thousand manic answers (but no universal explanation) ensue, each tied to the highly specific nature of a particular rendition of the figure: the last queen, the last archer, the last basket-maker, carpenter, cliff-diver, insomniac, or fire-starter. Survival is both a horrendous and enraptured commerce, and even more intriguing than the last members of a race, land, dynasty, or species are those that represent the final remaining practitioners of a craft, gesture, or outlook. A startling creative eeriness accompanies those whose teachers, allies, codes, and temples have been lost forever, and with it, a simultaneously minimalist and maximalist apocalyptic sensitivity. What turns of thought, deep or shallow, occupy the last philosopher; what deafening or delicate linguistic registers are the sole province of the last poet? What experimental materials or proportions consume the last architect's drawings, and what unprecedented colours emerge only in the visual universe of the last painter? What unsound artifacts provoke excavation by the last archaeologist, looter, or pirate, and which precarious objects are worthy of being gathered by the last collector? Each will have their own vantage in the eleventh hour (that of futility and terminal solitude), striking at the unforeseen ceilings of omnicidal imagination only when it matters both most and least of all.

2. DANCING ON GRAVES
(FIGURE OF ATTRACTION)

37.8882° N, 4.7794° W

In the mediaeval era of southern Spain, two different Arab polymaths were credited with the alleged authorship of a compendium of ritual chants, cosmological drawings, and alchemical prescriptions called the *Ghayat al-Hakim* (Latin *Picatrix,* or *Aim of the Sage*). The first figure proposed as its writer (al-Majriti) was an astronomer, mathematician, and chemist who experimented with mercury oxide, edited the *Encyclopedia of the Brethren of Purity* (a mysterious secret society of tenth-century Baghdad), and founded (with his daughter, Fatima of Madrid) a school of Astronomy and Mathematics devoted to perfecting the observation of eclipses, calendrical tables, and lunar visibility. The second figure who could conceivably have authored the work (al-Qurtubi) arrived over two centuries later, a more elusive master of esotericism known mainly as a 'man of charms and talismans'. But whether composed in the daughter's palace solarium or in the hidden quarters of an occultist's sanctum, whether describing spells that keep one hostage within a city, spells of temporary amnesia, or spells to mute speech, above all else we note in this volume the dramatic rise of a methodology of Alignment:

Mars is the source of attractive power. He governs an aspect toward knowledge of nature. He rules surgery and the taming of wild beasts, extracting teeth, bloodletting, and circumcision. From the languages, he governs Persian. From the external appendages, he governs the right nostril. From the internal organs, he governs the gallbladder whence comes yellow bile and heat. From the instincts, he governs those that cause anger and war. From the religions, he governs heretical sects and those people who switch from one religion to another. From cloth types, he governs linen, the pelts of rabbits and dogs, and other various pelts. From the crafts, he governs ironworking with fire, warfare, and banditry. From the tastes, he governs the hot, the dry, and the bitter. Among locations, he governs army camps; forts; defensible places; battlefields; places where fires are lit; where animals are beheaded; where wolves, bears, and wild beasts gather; and places of judgment. From the stones, he governs carnelian and all dark and red stones. From the metals, he governs arsenic (i.e., a red pigment of gold), sulfur, naphtha, glass, and red bronze. From the plants, he governs every hot plant, such as pepper, pine, scammony, cumin, caraway, laurel, euphorbia, hemlock, and trees that are good for burning. From the spices, he governs all those with a poor balance of humors which kill all those who eat them due to an excessive heat within. From the incenses, he governs red sandalwood. From the animals, he governs red camels, all animals with large red teeth, and dangerous wild animals. From the small animals, he governs those doing harm such as vipers, scorpions, mice, and similar things. From the colors, he governs bright red.[2]

There is unparalleled beauty in the feverish parallelism at work here, in those whirling conceptual combinations that ascribe to a remote planetary body (Mars) such raw conspiratorial influence over distinct colours, climates, textures, sensory responses, animal or insect species, anatomical organs, vegetal and culinary formations, affective disorders and destinies. This is an astonishing gesture of the mind (whether it is ultimately accurate or simply absurd), for it requires the elaboration of the most intricate diagrammatic webs and the precise differentiation of forces across a segmentary existential terrain. Not everything rules everything here; we are dealing with a theory of universal partiality in which each sliver colludes with only certain other miniature enclaves (and only under the most precise conditions). This micro-alertness to the sheer situational complexity of will, fate, perception, and power demands of the practitioner a great

---

2 Abu al-Qasim Maslama al-Qurtubi, *Picatrix: A Medieval Treatise on Astral Magic,* tr. D. Attrell and D. Porreca (Philadelphia: Penn State University Press, 2019), 133.

thing: namely, a constant willingness to switch loyalties. The figure of attraction is thereby born, in this matrix of fluctuating devotions: at first one perhaps plays favourites, selecting those genealogies that command intrigue for whatever reason, but soon enough the more developed consciousness will realise the necessity of learning all of the attractive permutations at stake. One gradually seeks acquaintance with each coordinate, altar, or foundry, for all harbour tempting notions and instructive languages of persuasion, albeit in cut-throat competition with one another (thresholds of mutual exclusivity). And how does this highly arranged derangement relate to doom? Suppose that on one strange night, the alchemist-astronomer arrives at the final dream (of the knot): namely, the simultaneity of all forces in supreme eruption, strung together at the fullest extent of their respective irradiation. Apocalyptic turmoil as a side-effect of that multiverse whose thousand fractured parts have somehow succeeded at the exact same moment: a philosophy of doom as trans-infuriation, guiding the exacerbation/release of whatever traits in order to lift the world's saga to untenable registers.

Nevertheless, such a manic showcase (the bonfire, the drunken song) requires someone with expertise in luring forces toward their combustive temperatures (she who sets alight). The figure of attraction comes to draw out all capacities, gently urging them into omnicidal exposition—the grave-dancer par excellence.

3. KEEPER OF VOWS (FIGURE OF TRANSLUCENCE)

36.5271° N, 6.2886° W
36.7167° N, 4.4260° W
36.7462° N, 5.1612° W
42.8125° N, 1.6458° W

In the nineteenth and early twentieth centuries, there were several ports across the Mediterranean coastline of Andalusian Spain where writers of mixed styles, genres, and philosophical-aesthetic inclinations arrived in search of escape from their home countries. These authors would roam in exilic territory for a while, indulging the geoscapes of foreign seas, islands, forests, caves, and deserts while gaining inspiration for their respective masterworks at the greatest distance from their origins. Little did they know that this extraneous wonderment would carry with it an undercurrent of doomed imagination, obliging them to recognise clearly the hand of demise wherever they trod, each then left mouthing its master-tongue of the incidental in their own unique literary fashion. The first figure was a legendary melancholic romantic who found inspiration along the coastlines of Cadiz for his rich allusive works about tormented wanderers, seducers, and rebels (those doomed by space, desire, and power), but who himself would meet a bizarre early death by fever while fighting a foreign war in some faraway gulf. The second figure was a lively, eccentric composer of fairy tales who delighted in loitering at nightfall among the Muslim ruins of Malaga, in labyrinthine alleys, alongside street children and so-called gypsy (Roma) performers—and yet who populated his later stories with the doomed silhouettes of nude emperors, shipwrecked princes, deformed birds, frozen orphan girls, and mutilated child dancers. The third figure was an introverted elegiac poet whose writer's block was cured only by the immense ravines of Ronda, which freed him to weigh existentialist and metaphysical questions in the 'immeasurable strangeness' of a hotel overlooking the deathly slopes below, pouring himself into the troubled mindsets of shepherds (doomed by solitude) and resurrected saints (doomed by immortality) only to die young himself from the haemophiliac effects of a hand wounded by rose thorns. The fourth figure developed a renowned nostalgic fascination with the violent arenas of the bull-fights and festivals of Pamplona, manoeuvring between descriptions of the doom-facing consciousness of the bull-fighter and the beast's doom-facing movements, mutually entangled in their choreography of lethal grace—but who later suffered severe physical ailments (concussions, ruptured liver and spleen, haemochromatosis) and mental deterioration (paranoia, delusion, electroshock treatment) leading to suicide attempts by walking into aeroplane propellers, jumping from flying planes, and finally gunshot. Aristocrat, bohemian, contemplative, daredevil:

all were beneficiaries of a momentary reenchantment while travelling adjacent longitudes and latitudes, and in each case they gravitated toward characters consumed by pain, misfortune, or despair. Are doomsday visions born only in such instances of exceptional euphoria on the part of outsiders, an eloquence of macabre formulations purchased through pleasurable vulnerability while in the elsewhere?

What unknown combination of restlessness and disillusionment makes of one the hand of the absolute moment (executor of doom's inevitability)? A specialised subjectivity built upon the quadrangulation of (1) the 'gone too far'; (2) the 'point of no return'; (3) the 'good as dead'; (4) the 'lost cause'. Further adding to its complexity, doom also combines the nihilistic courage of the 'nothing to lose' with the apotheosised exhilaration of the 'everything to lose'. This is how we fathom the unfathomed stations of omnicidal becoming.

Doom is one of those terrific concepts that partakes of both fatality and infinity. 'To decide' shares an etymological root with 'to kill'. Infinity can be etymologically interpreted as pertaining to 'the unfinished'. Thus the omnicidal will to constitute an infinite decision implies one of two things: either to kill the unfinished, or to let the unfinished kill.

This stance is called the figure of translucence. Above all else, such figures are masterful technicians of both intuition and anticipation: like a person talking to themselves, they split their identities into two alternate subjectivities: a questioning subject and an elder, counsellor, overseer, or wise one; like a person with the rushed feeling of falling on the stairs before actually tumbling downward, they split their bodies into the immediate pulsation and the autonomic grasping of the forthcoming reaction. Thought can move faster than the event; sensation can move faster than the event. Whomsoever comprehends this presentiment and disquiet in the chest (five steps ahead) is gifted with two peculiar further attributes of discernment: (1) that of summoning moods (intimidation, affinity, obsession); (2) that of animating involuntary impulses in oneself and others (laughter, weeping, spasm).

4. THROWN FROM TOWERS (FIGURE OF PERIL)

41.8934° N, 12.4828° E
41.8936° N, 12.4837° E
40.5532° N, 14.2222° E

Almost countless modes of execution have been invented over time (beheading, starvation, drowning, suffocation, burning, poison, pestilence, blood eagles), and yet only one recurs reliably since the early years of doomed empires: throwing from towers. While examples of purging by this method abound in ancient and even modern

INTRODUCTION

periods, the most infamous cruelties of this type occurred during the Roman Empire, with its varied use of hills, balconies, spires, windows, or columns from which to fling high-level dissidents, dishonoured nobles, persecuted minorities, physically deformed and mentally disabled infants, murderers, and disobedient slaves. Three sites in particular were selected for this condemnation of hurled bodies: (1) the Tarpeian Rock, a high cliff overhanging the Forum from which onlookers could witness the final drop of those most notorious traitors and criminals fallen into disfavour and stigma; (2) the Gemonian Stairs, where paranoid rulers first strangled victims and cast the lifeless torsos downward, before compounding their disgrace by leaving their decaying corpses to rot for days on full public view while stray animals feasted on the carrion; (3) the isle of Capri, where the Emperor Tiberius entertained in watching enemies being tossed from steep precipices into the sea coves below (survivors of the impact would be bludgeoned by the oars of waiting boatmen). The conceptual fusion of altitude, shame, punishment, and mortal delectation is something to consider here, for the omnicidal figure seeks the limitless extension of this affair: to throw the world from the heights of its own summit (all-defenestration).

Let us clarify this book's title, which seems to define it as being concerned with the perfection of doomed thought (lightning within darkness). 'Omnicide' must not be seen as a nihilistic fixation with destruction, but rather as a gamble that certain elevations of creative instinct (the visionary's last gift) are reached only on the doorstep of universal collapse. A search for that sacred geometry of intensity and becoming attained only in the last throes, and with it an avant-garde of scorched-earth potentiality: that much sought-after synchronicity of philosophical, poetic, narrative, aesthetic, and existential properties. It would seamlessly braid the threads of speculation, originality, craft, sensation, and will. It would align in one pandemoniac blast the otherwise fractured particles of mind, body, desire, movement, utterance, perception, and event. The housing of the sage, the liar, the storyteller, the blacksmith, the mystic, the sculptor, the acrobat, the child, the animal, and the assassin all under one roof—each with an eye to forging the impending finale.

Accordingly, the radical imaginaries that emerge here in the wake of doom's shadow and storm prove innumerable and unbound, though any given fantasy of a too-late world is enough to build first camp (where we should not stay). There is a neglected strain of traumatic dream that persists with no reality referent (ex nihilo turbulence) where we are met only by unfamiliar, outlandish appearances: here it is the dream that infects the real, not the other way around. A dream, then, that arrives from somewhere beyond the psyche. The figure of peril is therefore best described as one who glimpses an atrocity for which there is no intrinsic wellspring in their head—and yet swears allegiance to this sight of epic misgiving.

Omnicidal doom must be dreamed, traced, and walked into worlds. The multidimensional force of an idea is revealed only as it travels through the crucial levels of abstraction (the philosophical), expression (the aesthetic), and embodiment (the existential). For there are certain adaptations that can only be made in the climes of the imaginative, others exclusive to the artistic or fictive spheres, and still others that belong only to the performative, visceral, and incarnational stages. To conceive or hallucinate it, to tell or draw it, to enact or swathe it across the shoulders. These are the three strata of design at which the omnicidal will operates upon experience most fatefully.

Early human civilisations made a crucial decision when they determined to depict their first gods as unreal (whether with partial resemblances to actual living beings or in total dissimilarity to the known). Cosmic serpents and beast-headed hybrids, all bursting with alien features, extraordinary proportions, and bizarre physiologies. Why choose to worship that which is entirely unlike the real? Why store fear in an image of something that one will never actually confront (and which therefore makes fear impossible to overcome), or instil desire in a likeness that one can never actually touch (and therefore renders satisfaction of that desire impossible)? Interestingly, among the five generic questions surrounding any phenomenon—*what, where, when, why, how*—with respect to divine beings, the ancients granted two of these categories perfectly clear answers, while leaving another two categories shrouded in grand obscurity. The question of *where* the ancient gods resided was flagrantly obvious: within everything (immanence). The question of *when* the gods acted was equally manifest: always and instantaneously (immediacy). Thus the pagans existed among visceral deities that would move, breathe, feed, and strike in full proximity and everpresence. Nevertheless, in their ponderous approach to unrealities, these ancient thinkers left the question of *what* essentially these gods were and *why* they wrought creation suspended in enigmatic half-tellings. This was the nature of their anti-definition of unreal power: beings that devoured or aided, in the absence of any true correspondence to the human form or any explanation of their intent. One could not reason with such mechanisms of indifferent foreignness, could not plead for mercy or establish certain base rules of reciprocal action (even tributes, temples, and sacrificial rituals were recognised in their own time as largely pathetic attempts to negotiate with the purely pathological).

The transition into monotheistic worship is subject to a different trade-off: with the figment of an exclusive, totalitarian, and transcendently invisible god, these new belief-systems deigned to resolve the pagan mystification of the *what* and the *why*. Those once-vague particles are now fixed by the anchoring similitude of a figure in whose image we ourselves are made (an idealised mirror-reflection of sorts), and who continually tests earthly beings in order to distribute their souls to a moral eternity (thus revealing a redemptively-integrated endgame). And yet to purchase the illumination of these two alternative categories (through whatever new mythologies) is also to problematically bury the two former pagan categories in dark perplexity. The location of the omniscient source falls into irreconcilable distance or even abandonment (*where* is the promised saviour?), just as the timescape of its pursuit now stretches out into a lost continuum (*when* will the One arrive?). Thus the monotheist finds their own transaction with half-lit epistemologies plagued by desperate inadequacy.

Doom, however, is a matter of the ever-discounted *how*; it is the secret of the world's unmaking; it is the long-elided rite through which entities are undone, which is why this *how* remains a threateningly lingering question-mark in either predilection of faith (monotheistic or polytheistic). For the one who purposefully deliberates on the methodological levers and chambers of unreal power soon finds themselves straying into omnicidal provinces. Such is the price of allowing the mind to enter cosmic-level unreality. Entire domains of knowing are necessarily forfeited (thrown from towers), leaving only the mad forest of contemplation. Consider this philosophical point: Doomsday seers personify the restoration of all five categories to the paradoxical simultaneity of sheer radiance and bewilderment. The *what*, *where*, *when*, *why*, and *how* of both physical and metaphysical experience are cast into aspirational delirium through their blind eyes—which, by our current definition, is the very act of manifesting illusions that drag reality high and low (into breathless impossibility). Another name for this overture toward convening gloriously mistrustful and uninhabitable states: the figure of peril.

Part 2
Selamania (Light Flashes)
Neuromania (Nerves)
Tremomania (Trembling)
Ataxomania (Disorder)
Eruptiomania (Explosions)

Selamania (Light Flashes)

> *Even the stars seem bloody.*
> *A boy sees blood in every star*
> *and whispers to his friends:*
> *'The only holes left in the sky*
> *Are stars.'*

ADONIS[3]

The selamaniac impulse rightfully configures itself in the doomsday imagination of children, gathering light speed in terminality's wonderment, for it uses a lullaby structure to project forth semblances of soft, intermittent violence that enable a subtle reflex of transubstantiation (turning stellar luminescence into blood). Like the irregular appearance of stroboscopic flashes, the short rhythmic bursts of the lullaby channel a certain will to the occasional whereby perception pays close heed to fleeting incendiary violations of the night sky: the lullaby is therefore not a 'dark' genre, but more exactly a genre that involves destructive envoys of flickering within darkness. They neither unify nor fill the void, but rather rend the fabric of space, creating 'holes' that resemble dripping

---

3 Adonis, *The Pages of Day and Night*, tr. S. Hazo (Evanston, IL: Northwestern University Press, 2000), 96.

puncture wounds (an amazing gesture: to anthropomorphise universes only to render them fatally stabbed), all the while affording listeners the paradoxical strategy of taking comfort in discomforting associations, achieving rest within restless imagery.

Note: If the selamaniac lullaby escorts an omnicidal dream of irradiation and laceration into our midst, smuggling malignant gaps through otherwise enchanted narrative layers and vice-versa, then we can connect its 'whisper' to another practice of gentle sleep-induction and surgical incision: that of anaesthesiology. A covert multi-civilisational tradition unfolds here between pain, stupor, and somnolescence: from the Renaissance doctors Valerius and Paracelsus's refinement of oils and ethers to the earlier Muslim-world polymaths Zakkariya Razi (discoverer of sulphuric acid and alcohol compounds, inventor of flasks and distillation mechanisms), Jorjani (the great diagnostician who first set apart the anaesthesiologist as an independent physician contributing to operating procedures), Aghili Khorasani Shirazi (whose pharmaceutical encyclopaedia, *Makhzan al-Advieh* ('Container of Medicines') outlines myriad herbal-vegetal potencies), and the unparalleled Ibn Sina (Avicenna) whose *Canon* outlined fifteen typologies of pain including itching, pulsating, coarseness, prickling, stretching, tearing, fracturing, tenderness, piercing, stabbing, heaviness, numbing, disintegrating, fatigue, and biting; from the ancient Chinese Hua Tao's inscrutable *mafeisan* potion to the later Japanese Hanaoka Seishu's *tsutensan* remedy to the modern Joseph Priestley's experiments with nitrous oxides and written work on the *Different Kinds of Air*; from methods of ingestion, injection, inhalation, skin absorption, and sonic suggestion to sensorial incorporations of ice, music, oxygen, and soft cloth to postures of reclining, floating, and fainting to the accessory technical devices of syringes, IVs, masks, tables, heart-rate monitors, and pillows; from the varied mythologies of lotus and opium eaters, including the Greek god of sleep Hypnos—son of Erebus (darkness) and Nyx (night), brother to Thanatos (death), husband to Pasithea (relaxation, hallucination) with whom he lived by the side of the river Lethe (forgetfulness) and produced the three child deities of the Oneroi (dream) named Morpheus (shape), Phobetor (fear), and Phantasos (fantasy)—to the Egyptian gods of sleep and pain-relief Tutu (protector of sleepers from bad dreams and demonic influence, human-faced, cobra-tailed, with the heads of crocodiles and hawks protruding from its torso) and Bes (bearded, long-tongued dwarf god of war and dance, warder-off of evil spirits, diseases, and injury for women in childbirth), to Native American theories of how the Great Spirit created the world in their sleep, to the parasitical devouring of dreams by the chimerical Japanese Baku (elephant-trunked, rhinoceros-eyed defenders against pestilence and eaters of nightmares), and countless mythic depictions of dragons in states of deep slumber; from any number of literary-folkloric accounts of *The Thousand and One Nights* (where storytelling itself adopts anaesthetic effects) to the tales of the extended unconsciousness of sleeping beauties and cave-nappers, including Endymion, the Sirens, Rip Van Winkle, the Sandman, etc. Every particular iteration links slumber to rampant subconceptual arrangements, including those of bliss, numbness, eternity, punishment, distraction, time-travel, idleness, horror, innocence, revenge, magicality, seduction, and mischief.

Light flashes and stars; blood; the boy; the whisper; holes

Neuromania (Nerves)

> *Only networks! Skeins of nerves! Nerves, nerves, and nothing but nerves! Modern painters have painted everything, yes, everything, except for nerves! They missed the nerves, botched the nerves of our age!... I paint nerves, my dear friend, what nobody can stand!*
>
> RÉDA BENSMAIA[4]

The Neuromaniac reverses the misfortunes of the neurotic, for whom nerves become mere psychological arbiters of paralysis and repression, by restoring them to their immediate bodily affiliations with sensation and movement. In the neurotic domain, nervous hyper-sensitivity is made an accomplice to abstract conceptions of identity, resulting in debilitating pangs of guilt, doubt, sadness, and shame; in the neuromaniacal domain, nerves become channels, slits, or raceways devoted to the perfect synchronisation of speed and impulse. For this to occur, however, we must first wrest the nerves back from any indenture to the ponderous kingdoms of ontology (angst) and psyche (anxiety) in order to house them in a more drastic alternate realm: the aesthetic. To speak of nerves instead

---

4   R. Bensmaia, *The Year of Passages*, tr. T. Conley (Minneapolis: University of Minnesota Press, 1995), 3.

as streaming aesthetic 'networks' is to allow them their autonomous circulatory dance without presuming to connect them to any final sovereigns of mind or spinal cord: they then become reticulated forces of interlacing, propulsion, convolution, and entanglement whose transmitted signals go nowhere in particular ('nothing but nerves'). Like messages in a bottle thrown out into an indifferent sea, they carry themselves with a lightness granted by pure artistic futility. No longer the phobic-depressive avoidance of distress (personality disorder), but rather the impersonal reconstitution of feeling as free-flowing 'skeins' in the hands of a great seamstress: to picture the nimble fingers at the loom, spinning silk threads in a fury of coils, knots, or braids is now the only comprehensive image of sense and stimulation. Here pleasure and suffering abandon their binary distance and instead form indistinguishable waves, lattices, or displays of forked lightning; here even consciousness follows a stylistics of electrostatic charge borne by cylinders and rivulets. This is how the false walls of interiority and exteriority are demolished: by freeing neuronal cables to twist outer environments into inner manic temperaments, and vice-versa. 'What nobody can stand,' because only the nobody invites such radical betrayal of the nerves' allegiance to Being, and thereby discovers the link between rapture and the unbearable (endurance of many things at once), like the painter grasping fibres of a brush whose motion follows no rhyme or reason beyond the minefield of its own proprioception.

Note: Mania and kinaesthesia often share a locomotive destiny, refining that sixth sense of position-movement which allows one to walk through dark rooms without losing balance, or to detect raised limbs without the aid of the other five senses, though here it would instead mean some receptive signal in the limbs, joints, and neuromuscular spindles that could foretell the end of worlds..

Note: There is a delicate connection between our neuromaniacal postulate above and the hypersusceptibility sought by early practitioners of hypnosis and magnetic healing. One can travel as far back as those Egyptian papyrus scrolls of 1550 BCE that document the dream temples of the Old Kingdom (already established thousands of years before), including instructive diagrams for the hanging of calmative lanterns, auditory shock treatments, oral chants, and soothing hand gestures—these first manual practices later forming the basis for the Greek cult sites of Asclepius (god of medicine), the Roman healing caves of Velia, and the physician-conjurers of later centuries. From the Hungarian astronomer-priest Maximilian Hell to the surgeon James Braid's ideo-motor principle (movement without free volition), to the exceptional showman Franz Anton Mesmer, whose theories of animal magnetism, mysterious invisible fluids, and gravitational forces led him to hold private sessions in dimly lit salons filled with iron rods and vats, opulent drapes and wafting incense, where he himself, cloaked in purple robes and gold slippers, would use varied gazes or the passing of hands over patients' afflicted bodies to send them reeling into catalepsy, seizure, or trance; from nineteenth-century doctors such as Jean-Martin Charcot, the famed neurologist who presided over the Salpêtrière Hospital for decades, a diagnostician of hysterical syndromes whose photographs of asylum women betrayed a personal iconographic interest in exaggerating mental states through performative-theatrical suggestion (and who was himself prone to producing apocalyptic drawings while under the influence of drugs) to his students Pierre Janet and Sigmund Freud's further development of hypnotherapy as a tactical complement to psychoanalysis. The eccentric tales surrounding this experimental trend were also accompanied by a belief in creative paranormal faculties, as in the aristocrat magnetist the Marquis de Puységur's documentation of dramatic personality-switching, audio-visual hallucinations, and various telepathic abilities (the competencies of those under hypnosis to read others' thoughts or extemporaneously diagnose their ailments, and even experience a 'community of sensation' in which feelings of touch, smell, and localised pain were shared remotely between hypnotiser and subject). Certain now-dismissed studies recount tales of subjects convinced of negative illusions (missing limbs, paralysis, blindness); others tell of the hypnotised instantly absorbing new talents, persuaded into believing themselves great musicians only to then actually produce compositions of adroit quality and scope; still others speak of subjects allegedly endowed with a certain attunement to strangers (the bizarre incident of a hypnotised painter placed below the gallows of a criminal condemned to decapitation and instructed to identify intensely with the accused, only to writhe and shriek in transferred agony at the exact moment when the beheading took place above). Thus we come upon the primary neuromaniacal asset of importance here: the dimension of extensive *trespass*, which fuses elevated sensitivity to infinitised outer traversal.

Nerves and networks; skeins; the botched age; painting; the nobody

Tremomania (Trembling)

> *In the door's lock a key turned*
> *A smile trembled on his lips*
> *like the image of water dancing along the ceiling*
> *from the reflection of the shining sun*
>
> AHMAD SHAMLU[5]

The Tremomaniac here is an incarcerated rebel amid a process of catastrophic preparation: the prison guards have arrived at dawn to inform their target of the execution hour—set for later that afternoon—leaving him in a compressed temporality of anticipation. To be shot against a stone wall is no insignificant prospect, and the prisoner is tormented further by the countdown effect of those few hours preceding his final appointment. Through what intense bravery or trickery, then, does the tremomaniac face the unspeakable (head-on or obliquely), initiating the swiftest rituals to transform fear into delight? Is it by purging terror or by hyper-accentuating it (scaring oneself to death) that one endures this front-row seat in the end-of-the-world auditorium? Let us assume that training has occurred far in advance of the guards'

---

5 A. Shamlu, *Born Upon the Dark Spear*, tr. J.B. Mohaghegh (New York: Contra Mundum Press, 2015), 12.

actual announcement, and that all kinds of pre-emptive arrangements, groundwork, and qualifications have been completed before the moment of the awful turning of keys. Indeed, the guards enter to find someone who has already taken desperate measures to convert the tremor itself into an alchemical instrument capable of channelling all accumulated dread into an indecipherable smile. Is it so outlandish to seek out the pathway via which one may use horror to become horrifying, turning the victimised self into the machinic producer of agitation? For this a certain incubation period is necessary, in which disquiet is amassed and then pumped through the martyr's veins and skin, affording them disastrous intuition, in order to store provisions for the coming winter night of their murder.

Simple denials or idealistic justifications are of no use here; one must walk straight through the heart of the trembling, going beyond even the masochist's logic of acquired taste (savouring unpleasure) in order to manifest a grim smile that combines satisfaction and the insatiable. The shivering bones form tightropes to the foreboding; the quake and the shudder are high-accuracy radars bringing the condemned figure into contact with the incident. This is how one overcomes the awaiting shadow: by wrenching the affective universe of chill anticipation beyond mere presentiment and into the befallen (the same poet elsewhere found himself 'trembling [...] before the horizon ablaze').[6] For if messiahs always arrive too late, we may also imagine madmen and madwomen who can will events to happen too early, such that the guards arrive at the carceral door to collect nothing more than an already-expired form (an 'image' or 'reflection' of the long-since-passed) whose smile is but the signature of an aftermath immune to killing. To surpass the last-breath expression in isolation, rocking back and forth, allowing the head to pound relentlessly, eyes darting in sync with the ceiling's flitting light-patterns, using unsupervised moments to pace in well-choreographed traversals of arc and circle, crossing the vibratory bridges of the tremor over and again whenever the guards are not looking, and thereby building an affinity with the palpitation's excess from stolen sunset to sunrise. The velocity of the maniac works to their advantage in the state of grand emergency, allowing them to pay the tragic price on their own terms and according to their own inviolable deadline, and thus eluding the pathology of the victim through a counter-pathological resonance, a rush to the stopping-place: this is how the once-shaken one beats the slow metallic sound of the lock, etching upon his face that amused grin which is nothing but the echo of a victory won long beforehand.

Note: Post-revolutionary Iranian society saw a dark enigmatic phrase creep into the language: *seh-bar edam*,

---

[6] Ibid., 45.

meaning 'triple execution'. The exact meaning remains shrouded in tense para-official confusion, with some opting for a merciful reading and others a more sinister one: in the former case, the term is believed to refer to a forgiveness clause whereby, if a death-row inmate survives execution three times, they are exonerated of capital punishment altogether; in the latter case, the term is suspected to refer to a grave totalitarian technique of imposing the death penalty three times over upon the condemned (by repeatedly reviving the victim). Thus the first interpretation of triple execution occupies a nebulous theo-juridical site between absolution and acquittal, whereas the second interpretation hints at an absurd proliferation of violence that serves to exponentially increase the rewards of revenge. The question remains: How would the tremomaniac adapt to these bouts of cruel awakening (defibrillation, chest compression) which torment both body (mal-resuscitation) and spirit (mal-resurrection) by administering artificial jolts and shocks to the system?

Trembling and the door; the lock; the key; the smile; the image; the ceiling; the reflection

Ataxomania (Disorder)

> *Then something strange happened. Into the room came a foreign body—a being possessed of a hot vitality and terrifying strength. I heard the sound of it striking the wooden door, then the chair, the bed and finally the other door* [...] *Splinters of wood covered the floor, the bed and my hair, as well as the magazines scattered all over the floor, and I stared in horror at the places where the object had been. It had dug into the wood to a depth of at least ten centimeters. And as for the low chair it had struck, some pieces of melted, broken nails were now scattered throughout its splintered remains, just exactly as if it had been pounded by some infernal hammer.*
>
> GHADA SAMMAN[7]

The Ataxomaniac stands in a room awestruck by the cascade of metal (bullets, spikes) threatening them from every window and wall, every narrow aperture. A mechanism of devious potentiality makes its incursion from multiple angles, invading all lower and higher planes of this closed space: it is that of the makeshift bomb or improvised explosive device. The poet describes it as an almost godlike force of disorder, endowed with

---

7   G. Samman, *Beirut Nightmares*, tr. N. Roberts (London: Quartet Books, 1976), 17.

ancient attributes—heat, vitality, terror, strength—but also with technological proficiency in that it strikes acutely (minimalist chaos measured in 'centimeters'). Above all else, though, it is an agent of impersonal wrath based in powers of refraction: the projectile burns the house down through a scattershot effect, sending 'splinters' indiscriminately across surfaces and objects (door, chair, bed, skin). No hierarchy of impacted sites, it penetrates into floor beams and human hair and flesh alike, for it typifies a primordial paradox: that of being a *high-precision instrument of chance*. The pagan cosmos, inasmuch as it cleaved existence by introducing internal boundaries, also made secret pacts with certain anarchical principles, ensuring the persistence of instances of impunity/gambling that could break apart creation itself. The detonative contraption partakes of this same crafted aimlessness: it is built specifically to wager with unpredictable trajectories; it binds invention to randomness (contriving volatility) and slides consciousness toward the qualm; it approximates the spontaneous movements of 'a billiard ball or frightened cat' and seeks only a destiny of rubble, fragment, ruin, and detritus; it weaponises frailty and charge, marrying older deities of smoke and thunder with the more modern phenomena of gunpowder and shrapnel. Such is the essence of 'the infernal hammer' that swings with intended wildness, prime mover of debris, its byproducts melting sanctuaries and spitting nails into both ground and upper air; it leaves in its wake only the frenzied gaze of the ataxomaniac who trusts in nothing solid to hold—neither soil, cement, plaster, rock, sinew, nor glass—and hence walks with scurrying steps (barely touching the ground) in the suspicion that the entire world is riddled with such armaments of disarray.

Note: For nearly a thousand years, legends have circulated about the superior blades of Damascene Steel (named for the city of Damascus, Syria), a most rare accomplishment of metallurgy and swordmaking which resulted in weapons known for their lethal sharpness, hardness, lightness, super-plasticity, and unique alloy patterns resembling waves, rippling water, teardrops, or ladders. Their shatter-resistant edges were said to cut through silken scarves or strands of hair simply by touch, and to be flexible enough to bend ninety degrees without breaking, thus presumably giving Islamic armies a crucial material advantage during the Crusades. Furthermore, weapon masters' guilds across the Middle East concealed their exact hammering methods and thermal cycling processes, giving rise to outlandish rumours according to which the metalsmiths would douse the finished red-hot blades in obscene liquids or plunge them into the intestines of muscular slaves. Recent discoveries, however, have finally identified the principal secret component to be a trace impurity of vanadium (found in a .003% concentration in Damascene sabres), which the subtle skills of the blacksmiths succeeded in forming into the microscopically-thin nanowires and nanotubes that create these weapons' stunning visual patterns. Thus, a single ataxomaniacal imperfection (the slightest chemical impurity) becomes the source of a priceless, envied formulation that rules in mid-air.

Disorder and the foreign body; heat; vitality; terror; strength; splinters; scattering; horror; remains; infernal hammer

Eruptiomania (Explosions)

> *The eye of a horse*
> *Doesn't know where to land*
> *Explosion in the living flux*
> *Returns at a gallop*
> *An explosion in the flux lived by*
>
> JOYCE MANSOUR[8]

The Eruptiomaniac here explores the nature of the outburst by way of the percussive sound of a horse's gallop and its fitful, unresting eye. A number of questions surface from this poetic image of the beast: Why does it run (is it fleeing from danger or chasing after something)? Is it bred for war or for racing? Is it untamed or does it carry an unnamed rider, and why does it sprint endlessly? Apparently, the author conceives of an imaginative manic solution to a scientific limitation: namely, the impossibility of an explosion of ceaseless duration. No longer beholden to the impermanent phases of enkindling, smouldering, and fumes, the horse's explosive will discovers an inexhaustible energy source (permanent paroxysm). This is perhaps the 'flux lived by' alluded to in the final line,

---

8   J. Mansour, *Essential Poems and Writings*, tr. S. Gavronsky (Boston: Black Widow Press, 2008), 281.

one that promises a singular alternative to the ebbing or dying-down of the convulsion and the roar.

Note: There is an outlying political dimension at stake here as well, for rioting crowds also inescapably proceed through successive stages of expansion and escalation—the concentrated clamouring in streets; the smashing of public buildings, symbols, monuments, effigies, and statues; the setting of fires; the overthrow, arrest, or revenge-killing of former leaders—which then almost always devolve from their delirious apex into the consolidation of a new authoritarian regime of meaning and a new archetype of collective reality. Thus the recurring political challenge: How to sustain the short-lived torridity of revolutionary openness and stave off the downward spiral into another banal order of things? Can sedition perpetuate its explosive meantime (if even by cyclical self-immolation)?

The poet offers us some semblances of keywords in other verses, for elsewhere she divulges that '*I have troubles in my mind. They live near the lake of my sunken eyes.*'[9] Note the central importance of the eyes again (as if tumultuous capacities reside in the oculus alone), in addition to the reiteration of the word 'live' to describe inanimate or even affective matters (a new definition of *the living*): these are indicators to interpret eruptiomaniacal perception as that

---

9   Ibid., 83.

which sees everything always in an incandescent condition. It is an alternative visionary outlook that blankets being with immanent radioactivity and nitroglycerine. Just as the Decadents envisioned all lived experience in terms of states of ever-present decay, thereby eliciting a literary style fixated on morbidity, decline, and loss, so does the eruptive figure allow us to speculate on an aesthetic touch linked to the dominion of boiling, gushing, venting, and seething temperatures. The careening motion of the horse is born of this same effervescence and rampancy, its black hooves resembling the churning of volcanic lava, its reddened eye-sockets marking the perpetuation of an incinerative glare. Together these form a phosphoric approach, one of world-inflammation, for which all experiences must enter the great furnace and for which all thought, language, or sensation amount to nothing more than the lit matches of a cremator's oven.

Explosion and the eye; the horse; the unlanding;
the gallop; the living flux

Part 3

Uranomania (Heaven, Divinity)

Vatomania (Premonitions, Prophecies, Prophetic Figures)

Apeiromania (Infinity)

Zeusomania (Fate)

Hademania/Stygiomania (Hell)

Daimonomania (Demons)

Uranomania (Heaven, Divinity)

> *One can genuflect a whole lifetime*
> *with bowed head at the foot*
> *of a saint's cold sarcophagus.*
> *One can find God in a nameless grave.*
> *One can find faith with an insignificant coin.*
>
> FORUGH FARROKHZAD[10]

The Uranomaniac becomes a scavenger of divine experience in the most unusual locations: she searches the vacuous, the unsettled, the dilapidated reaches of non-dwelling. Nevertheless, the sarcophagus or nameless grave is not such a far cry from that sacred delirium which for millennia found its meeting-places in imponderable realms: deserts, jungles, occulted caves, whale bellies, rotted gardens, crucifixes, mountaintops, leper colonies. Thus we stumble upon a geo-metaphysics in which gods surface only in the most inhospitable sectors, and heaven itself is an unkempt, decrepit radius. The Firmament is uncared-for; the Afterworld built with tattered scaffolding; the Kingdom raised upon dampened, moldy earth (where nothing grows). The implications of

---

10 F. Farrokhzad, *A Lonely Woman: Forugh Farrokhzad and Her Poetry*, tr. M. Hillmann (New York: Three Continents Press, 1987), 82.

this unconventional mapping (from transcendent paradises to barren or crumbling territories) are far-ranging, though best demonstrated by the poet's line elsewhere in which she asks herself 'Will I again climb the stairs of my curiosity to greet the good god pacing on the roof of my house?'[11] Here once again we are faced with the prospect of a uranomaniacal encounter that can only be staged in an improper, rickety space: the slope of the rooftop (prone to accident), as slippery as the slick metallic surface of the 'insignificant coin' the flipping of which consigned faith to mere chance. Moreover, the grandiosity of theological belief is now supplanted by its overlooked stepsister 'curiosity' as both prime axis of confrontation and badland compass; it is only the one of minor leanings who wins access; it is only the figure of inquisitive mood and peripheral vision (drawn sideways toward marvel or trifle) who discovers an ambulatory god strolling along the rafters. Nomadic eyes alone can spot nomadic deities.

Divinity and genuflection; bowing; the sarcophagus; the nameless grave; the coin; rotting; the precinct

---

11 Ibid., 124.

Vatomania (Premonitions, Prophecies, Prophetic Figures)

We are the folk of the abandoned temple, abandoned atop our white horses—the reed sprouts over us and meteors flash above us, we search for our final station.
[…] Are these the words that brought us to the court of vision in the underworld?

MAHMOUD DARWISH[12]

The Vatomaniac negotiates the worst twists and turns of prophetic enunciation, finding themselves the beneficiary of a certain distasteful wisdom: namely, the ability to extract the ulterior motives behind premonitory words and thereby to penetrate into the true augural score to be settled. Indeed, the manic current takes prescience beyond the teasing, enigmatic play of the prediction and instead strips naked the violence hiding behind the decorative symbolic surface of 'temples' and 'white horses'. Once cast aside from these distractions, the 'abandoned' prophet gains piercing, accursed eyes that see farther than the realm of regular soothsaying could ever conceive ('the court of vision'): to a place where cosmic forces no

---

12 M. Darwish, *If I Were Another*, tr. F. Joudah (New York: Farrar, Straus and Giroux, 2009), 46.

longer conceal their dire orientations, but populate the empty space of speculation with hollow stems, grasses arching overhead, and meteoric ruptures that lead like signs to the 'final station'.

What do we know of those endowed with divinatory powers? That they typically gather followers from the dejected strata, mobilising the enslaved, the diseased, and the suffering through marshes and slender creases of safety; that they are typically gifted tidings of a mission that convenes a new perception of the end.

Note: The above poet is surrounded by others in our omnicidal literary configuration who use vatic resources for alternative purposes: whereas one writes 'and may the wind blow black and with pestilence on the day of the debacles',[13] another asks 'Who stilled the prophecies of havoc? Come then. Invade us.'[14] The former expels (gushing outward); the latter summons (inhaling inward). But this leader of the devastated populace recites articulations that follow another direction altogether: toward the 'underworld' (straight downward). All words are then maledictions of subterranean design, leading to the understanding of an increasingly total movement of existence itself below (the universal beneath).

Note: We should find a supplementary interest here

---

13 Bensmaia, *The Year of Passages*, 34.5.
14 Adonis, *The Pages of Day and Night*, 39/43.

in the histories of dark monks (Rasputin, Nostradamus) who were able to accomplish this remarkable task: to acquire prophetic powers without actually being chosen prophets. Through what occult back-channel were they able steal access to this highly exclusive prize of foreknowledge (without divine sanction), in the same way that Saint Francis of Assisi was said to receive the stigmata (spontaneous manifestation of the wounds of Christ) without himself carrying the messianic mantle? Paradoxically, all three aforementioned dark monks were prone to cataclysmic visions—floods, earthquakes, famines—while at the same time being extolled as legendary healers: Nostradamus forged good luck charms and was solicited to combat plague, Rasputin allegedly cured the Tsar's son of haemophilia, and Saint Francis pacified ferocious wolves while also being the patron saint against fire and dying alone. Still, the question remains as to how a controversial mystical propensity could supersede the entire theological hierarchy, allowing glimpses of restricted futurities without metaphysical permission. The answer, undoubtedly, lies in their shared manic approach to prognostication (moving constantly between deprivation and excess)—i.e., the willingness to writhe for the sake of second sight, accepting the often-gruesome sensory toll of the becoming-oracular.

Prophecy and the abandoned temple; white horses; reeds; meteors; the final station; the court of vision; the underworld

Apeiromania (Infinity)

> *'Every man has both a poetic obligation and a human obligation,' as the Professor used to say. But if that was true, how could I tell the difference, and easily, between the limits of the human obligation and those of the poetic obligation? [...] But why did the Professor say that we confuse the two obligations and do not recognize the diabolical element that drives them both? Because the diabolical obligations imply the capacity to stand in the face of a man when he is pushing his own humanity towards the abyss.*
>
> HASSAN BLASIM[15]

The Apeiromaniac appears besieged by a conflict between existential requirements: on the one side, the 'human obligation' to fight for survival; on the other, the 'poetic obligation' to fight on behalf of the infinite abyss. This places them squarely in the mad in-between of vitalism and extinction. And what counter-paradigm of sovereignty must we contemplate for the scarecrow, mummified walker, or living dead?

Mania offers a new theory of imagination combined with incredible suspicion (like the slow creaking of the house at night, that hour when every noise suddenly

---

15 H. Blasim, *The Madman of Freedom Square*, tr. J. Wright (Manchester: Carcanet Press, 2010), 8.

becomes an ultra-referential mark of disaster). It enlivens a creative sensing of the tempest or the invader. But let us take this mal-intuition toward its 'diabolical' conclusion (which, ironically, lies in ancient times): thousands of years ago, early Babylonian and Greek civilisations hazarded a storytelling of the world's origin based precisely on the contrast between human and poetic obligation noted above. While some envisioned an endless state of watery nothingness, and others spoke of darkness as the primary condition, Anaximander (610–546 BC) described an even more abstract concept of *apeiron* (primordial void, formlessness, indefinite space) as the force from which all creation was descended. This breaching of the limitless—which gave rise to the differentiated realm of beings—was an unwanted violation or mutilation of the vacant everything that ruled beforehand. In this schema, the spontaneous emanationist outflow that we call 'life' constitutes no more than a radical betrayal of the infinite: even worse, it wants desperately to claw us back (by what indistinct techniques?). More pointedly, it harbours an impulse, both angered and elated, to restore the unbound, to ardently recollect its lost and broken pieces and welcome all fractured particles of existence back into the waiting, ageless mouth of its sunkenness. In light of this, what is the diabolical poetic obligation, as construed by the inceptive passage? In essence, to do as another once instructed in his final notebooks: 'In the struggle between oneself and the world, back the world.'[16] Apeiromania is therefore not to be read as a mere pessimistic interpretation of Being as irreparable crime, guilt, deviation, or decline, but rather as an empathic alignment with the infinite's own relentless craving for return (the mania of the *apeiron*): to serve the arche-passion of the unbridled and the open-desolate, to compulsively embrace the perishing of our epoch's separations in order to rebalance oblivion, against oneself and all that stands apart.

Infinity and the poetic obligation; the diabolical element; the abyss

---

16 F. Kafka, *The Blue Octavo Notebooks*, tr. E. Kaiser and E. Wilkins (Cambridge, MA: Exact Change, 1991), 29.

Zeusomania (Fate)

Some blind and terrible power rides on our heads. There are some people whose fate is governed by an evil star under which they get crushed and want to get crushed [...] Fate may rule, but it is I who have made my fate, and now I can't get away from it. I can't escape from myself.

SADEQ HEDAYAT[17]

The Zeusomaniac conceives a conceptual admixture in which fatalism involves blindness, terror, evil, and inescapability as extensions of a self-inflicting will (those who 'want to get crushed'). Like hurling oneself down a flight of stairs or swimming concertedly into a whirlpool's centre, this omnicidal version of the will can be defined as an active overture toward the involuntary: it calls forth an imperative ('evil star') through which a certain generated momentum pulls even its instigator, source, or architect. A single imposition that then wheels back to possess its dreamer, to wrest them away: the initial provocation might have concentrated itself in a central figure, but very quickly sheer movement binds everything into helpless succession (lost to gravitational trajectories and atmospheric affairs). No doubt, it requires exceptional

---

17 S. Hedayat, *The Blind Owl*, tr. D.P. Costello (New York: Grove Press, 1957), 161.

power to summon that which makes one powerless, to command the utter vulnerability associated with being dragged (to will that which wills itself).

Note: The combination of fatalism and mania affords a rare philosophical opportunity to consider the overlooked history of those figures who embarked upon what might be called 'counter-destinies': namely, subjects who willingly abandoned their fortune, their status, and in some cases even their empires. What unique anti-psychology ascends to such heightened states of authority and influence only to throw it all away in a split second? In order to pursue this critical trajectory, one may examine in rotation the intriguing stories of actual elite individuals who entered this state of deliberate fallenness. From rebel princes to deviant aristocrats, from celebrated artists who disappeared into anonymity to great judges who confined themselves to remote asylums to heroic icons suddenly consumed by mysterious projects, there resides somewhere a formidable archive of examples of those who sabotaged their own affluence (inherited or earned) and strayed elsewhere. The brief outline below (with proper names omitted), like the table of contents to an unwritten anthology, may serve to commence such lines of thought:

INCINERATION. The Emperor Who Burned Down His City.
SABOTAGE. The Prince Who Joined the Rebels.

RENUNCIATION. The Aristocrat Who Disowned His Title.
ESCAPE. The King Who Built Castles in the Mountains.
CONSPIRACY. The Queen Who Protected the Sorcerer.
PERVERSION. The Marquise in the Asylum.
MARTYRDOM. The Doctor Who Became a Revolutionary.
IRRADIATION. The Heiress Who Became an Extremist.
SECRECY. The Writer Who Led the Militia.
ABJECTION. The Intellectual Among the Addicts.
FANATICISM. The Hero in the Folds of the Cult.
TREASON. The Prophet Who Led the Slaves.
DERELICTION. The Mystics Who Rejected Their God.
PARANOIA. The Judge Who Talked to Demons.
DELUSION. The Officer Lost to the Desert.
WASTE. The Philosopher Who Squandered His Fortune.
MASOCHISM. The Artist Who Willed Starvation.
ANNIHILATION. The Master Who Destroyed Mastery.

Ultimately, this assortment of abnormal players who relinquished their thrones or riches to become strangers, foreigners, nameless outsiders, or dregs leads us onto several intriguing questions: What rupture must occur for someone to contemplate forsaking an apparently tranquil existence and instead choose imperfect paths of exile or wastage? What does this teach us about ideas of glory, sacrifice, abandonment, and transformation? Does this counterintuitive strand of zeusomania alone enable us finally to contemplate the prospect of multiple destinies, competing destinies, untimely destinies, obstructed destinies, forbidden destinies, missed destinies, switched destinies, or abducted destinies?

> *Fate and blindness; terrible power; governance; the evil star; crushing; the inescapable*

Hademania/Stygiomania (Hell)

We break a hollowed almond
*   in memory of the territories*
and the acidity of hell
*   runs through every one of our veins.*

AHMAD SHAMLU[18]

The Hademaniac discovers quickly that every miniscule gesture releases Hell, that the entire matrix of potential action is formed of buttons, triggers, or keys that let loose the inferno. A labyrinth of unavoidable doors installed in the everyday practice of human experience itself (breathing, walking, feeding)—our eyes, throats, lungs, stomachs all unlock and open onto the nethermost zones. These are the sprawling tracts of perdition and brimstone whose gates rest in the most minor object—a 'broken almond' (for evil has always manipulated the scales of large and small, sneaking cosmic implications into tiny decisions). And yet here we should devote some concentration to a fascinating new portrayal of the netherworld itself implied in the crucial reference to 'veins': no longer plunging into the condemned depths of the pit or ruin, no longer restricted to the vertical spatiality of nine descending

---

18 Shamlu, *Born Upon the Dark Spear*, 101.

circles, hademaniacal affliction is here portrayed as a circulating liquid substance. Soul-loss apparently follows its own aqueduct (tied to the rich material logic of flow, secretion, and seepage): it transports itself as an acid solution that rushes across the circulatory systems of its prisoners, so that we do not so much inhabit Hell as find ourselves inhabited by it, in our own tormented interior reaches.

Note: Another significant insight may come to mind for those who spend lengths of time with this short yet haunting poetic work: that its title ('Remoteness') is followed immediately by an ominous, allusive note stating that 'the gloom of this place is not in that place.' At first glance, this line appears to be a sombre, nostalgic reflection on somewhere before or beyond the present Hell ('in memory of the territories'), but then we escape any moral-dualistic reading by conceptualising Hell as something closer to the planetary phenomenon of dayside and nightside environments. For instance, scientists recently confirmed the existence of an exoplanet (Wasp-76B) whose close orbit of its parent star results in a continual downpour of 'iron rain': since, owing to its 'tidal locking', it shows only a partial face to the host star, the exoplanet's dayside hemisphere is left perpetually roasting (at 2400°C) while the nightside's hemisphere is subject to cooler temperatures that allow the vaporised metals to condense in the atmosphere (shadows induce iron rainstorms). Here we are also reminded of those rare accounts of individuals stuck in windows while attempting to flee burning homes during the dead midwinter months: the upper halves of their bodies are flung suddenly into freezing air while their lower halves remain trapped in the flames (note: mania alone often approximates this near-inconceivable schismatic togetherness). What if Hell followed a melting pattern similar to this galaxy of iron droplets or that of the desperate escapee's body with torso and legs split across antagonistic intensities? This would reconcile the notion that 'the gloom of this place is not in that place' with the infusive influence of an elixir that also floods 'every one of our veins'—i.e., would allow us to place the variance of shadings, layers, and climates alongside a principle of wicked immanence.

Hell and breaking; memory; the territories; acidity; the veins

Daimonomania (Demons)

> *He turned, but all he could see was the mouth of the vault.*
> *So he asked, 'Who is following you?'*
> *She pulled her wrap over her face before replying: 'The*
> *demon!'*
> *'Is he a demon from the spirit world?'*
> *She nodded yes. Then he exclaimed in a defiant tone: 'Ha,*
> *ha…No demon from the spirit world will dare hide from*
> *me.'*
> *'He threatens me with his hateful fingers, tipped with blue*
> *nails.'*
> *'Know that to the demon master, every demon of the spirit*
> *world is nothing but a shadow.[…] I'll pluck him from*
> *your world the way a thorn is plucked from the foot.'*
> *Then he added as he crept toward her and took her in*
> *his arms: 'Don't you know, water girl, that Spirit World*
> *Demon is one of my names? But he's a demon who frightens*
> *only to entertain and who does evil only to do good.'*

IBRAHIM AL-KONI[19]

---

19 I. al-Koni, *The Seven Veils of Seth*, tr. W. M. Hutchins (Reading: Garnet Publishing, 2008), 188–99.

The Daimonomaniac entertains the possibility of close proximity with the nefarious, but exploits mania's routes of enchantment in order to shift villainous forms toward a concept of benevolent malevolence. The demon becomes protector, companion, lover; the demon takes midnight walks along the riverbank with the young woman to ward off his evil brethren, adopting an instrumentalist perspective on hypocrisy, injury, and deceit (as strategic means to the ends of amusement or support). Thus the demon's embrace constitutes simultaneously a mode of persecution and a mode of affection: savagery colludes with devotion; the bloodthirsty commingles with romantic concern. He reveals his depraved hidden name to soothe her fears of those who trail her each evening with 'hateful fingers, tipped with blue nails', and to escort her to her tribal home unscathed.

This peculiar scene, wherein the demon master speaks in sweet tones of assurance, and she effectively solicits his gentle nature, allows us to pursue a more acute sense of the unbearable. Indeed, the highly performative aspect of their encounter makes possible a discourse on the aesthetics of the unbearable: for thousands of years, different cultures have told threatening stories of paintings with content supposedly too hideous to behold, music whose melodies would split eardrums or lure audiences into derangement, poetry that concealed spells of annihilation for the listener. In each instance, a forbidden art form gives onto certain doom. But what is the specific criterion of such an inconsumable production, and in what particular way does it offend creation or gain the mark of inadmissibility? Does such stigma accompany pieces that are absolutely profane (intolerable throughout) or, like our demon master above, is this greatest dishonour reserved only for those artworks that somehow achieve a convolution of beauty and the grotesque? This could happen through the simple logic of vandalism (the single stain, defect, or streak): for instance, to conceive the radiant face of a saint only to fasten it with a foul grimace, to trace the profile of an immaculate symmetric body only to rake it with a thick scar or place it amid filthy quarters (the slightest marring). Or from the opposing vantage, to endow the most gnarled figure with a single saving grace (the slightest purification), so that the mangled being stands in possession of some irresistible gift (a voice, insight, craft, striking physical dimension, or limb of unparalleled quality). For what would one do if the most entrancing melodies emanated from a devil's slit throat, or the most vile shrieks from an otherwise angelic mouth? Is this not the presumed nature of both the name of the monotheistic God (fatal to pronounce) and the lamented wailings of those female spirits known as banshees (fatal to hear)? To despoil supremacy; to crown the appalling: the collapse of dualities into aberration. This is perhaps what it means to meet one night the demon with exquisite eyes or flawless words: to discover the caress of the unbearable itself, an exercise in contaminative style whereby a massive inversion of the perceptual order is waged through a lone infective feature (to ingrain the ultimate semblance of what does not belong).

Demon and following; defiance; threat; hate; the master; the thorn; the name

Part 4

Pyromania (Fire)

Fumimania/Capnomania (Smoke)

Pyrexiomania (Fever)

Frigomania/Cheimatomania (Coldness)

Crystallomania (Crystals)

Pyromania (Fire)

> *The firewood comes to you throughout the night, wrapped in nightmares. When you wake up you have a bath on fire. You eat on fire. You read the newspapers on fire. You smoke a cigarette on fire. In the coffee cup you come across prophecies on fire. You laugh on fire...You dream of the final act: It goes out.*
>
> HASSAN BLASIM[20]

The Pyromaniac sees fire everywhere, and thus sets alight indiscriminately (there are tales of eastern mystics found flailing in the streets, screeching that they were enveloped by invisible flames). Still, it would be imprecise to simply assume that this searing issues from a unitary source: instead, we find evidence of many scattered ignition points, and by extension many typologies of aridity or torridity. These are the nightmares of incandescence, each written in their own distinct typescript depending on their appearance, habitat, impact, and somatic bombardments that might encompass a bath of scalding water or sheet of burning paper. Though all may bow to the same elemental

---

20 H. Blasim, *The Corpse Exhibition: And Other Stories of Iraq*, tr. J. Wright (New York: Penguin, 2014), 57.

altar, the candle, the torch, the wildfire, the bonfire, and the conflagration are experiential universes apart.

Yet what if this reveals something critical about the prospect of thinking every event as a unique vector of vying forces? More exactly, what if every phenomenon, subject, or object—whether organic or inorganic, animate or inanimate, human, animal, vegetal, mineral, thing, etc.—finds itself situated in an arena where god, destiny, will, and chance grapple with one another in cut-throat contestation? No doubt, one could imaginatively multiply the players even further, but even these four archetypal envoys can themselves be broken down into their own intriguing sub-categories: in any given scenario, we would find ourselves contending with the gods who work for us and against us, with destinies viable and prohibited, with branches of chance linked to accident, circumstance, and luck, and the iterations of conscious versus unconscious will. The ratios are in continual fluctuation: like something resembling sectarian conflict, at any given moment some gain strongholds while others reach dead ends or fall into bondage; the gods corner fate, fate eludes chance, chance is conquered by will, will overthrows the deity. Furthermore, temporary alliances may arise, forming rare circumstantial combinations (e.g., the will to chance, or the divine accident), not to mention the exponential complications generated when encountering another who brings their own colliding vectors to the forefront (for everyone is a carrier of such adversarial configurations). Hence what has always appeared to be an unpredictable existence is in fact merely the competitive complexity of these quadrangulations which shift at each turn, calculation of which is impossible, so that life itself entails just an array of ever-winning or ever-losing tactics in an amphitheatre of partisans. This would be an appropriately manic approach to a philosophy of becoming, for it excludes no potential participant in the ongoing struggle (idols, fortunes, contingencies, volitions), but rather invites all to join the field of interminable strife. Now tie this paradigm to a single object-in-delirium like the flame, so that the pyromaniacal imagination is compelled to negotiate gods of fire, destinies of fire, probabilities of fire, and the will to fire in chronic rivalry across the stadium of their own body and mind.

Note: An old rumour tells of a northern mountain range renowned for being the site of three time-worn guilds: the master blacksmiths, the master lantern-makers, and the master rug-weavers. On the western flank of the mountain chain there lay the town of the hardened blacksmiths, a dominion of metallic surplus in which all night long one could hear the sound of steel being hammered and smell the billowing smoke of the forges. On the southern flank was the town of great lantern-makers, a heaven of colour and glass where all night long one could hear the expert cracking and arrangement of shards. On the eastern flank rested the town of the elder rug-weavers, their eyes shutting and opening in perfect rhythm with the loom, where all night long one could hear the spinning of silk threads into microcosmic patterns (whether abstract geometric shapes or floral vines). But these three eminent guilds served more than just their immediate surface purpose: the fact is that that their creative traditions masked the existence of a fourth town in the valley below, that of the ancient fire-worshippers. Fire-worship having long since become an outlawed faith, the three guilds had vowed to safeguard these original keepers of the sacred flame, diverting all visitors away from the fire-temples in the lower ravines by dazzling them with their respective wares. Thus the stipulation, in this ancient narrative, that these artisans practiced their teachings 'all night long', doubling the reverse temporality of the earliest fire-cults, which would never carry out their rituals in the light of day for fear of committing obscenity before their sun-god. Nevertheless, the most fascinating element is that none of the three towns themselves, nor the masters of the guild orders who populated them, were professed followers of the pyromaniacal religion concealed in the chasms beneath. For it was never a matter of belief, but only of a sworn oath to stave off the others' 'final act': they had promised to defend (by means of iron, glass, and silk) against something's 'going out'; they had decided nothing about absolute truths, but simply that fire had its given place, and that the world had the right to burn.

> *Fire and night(mare); the bath; the paper; the cigarette; prophecy; laughter; the dream; the final act; the going-out*

Fumimania/Capnomania (Smoke)

See *Book of the Opium Den*.

Pyrexiomania (Fever)

> *My nurse says: you were raving in a fever.*
> *...I forgot how to speak, and am fearful for my language.*
> *Leave everything else as it is, but bring my language back*
>   *to my life!*
> *My nurse says: You were delirious. You were crying out to*
>   *me.*
> *I don't want to return to anyone. I don't want to return to*
>   *any country.*
>
> MAHMOUD DARWISH[21]

The Pyrexiomaniac basks in the assortment of physiological crises that occur during episodes of extreme fever—shivering, perspiration, fatigue, chills, headache, muscle aches, flushed skin, increased heart rate, dehydration—none of them, however, more compelling than the syndrome of 'raving'. For the symptomatology of language in fever proves almost identical to that of language in mania; neuropsychology has provided a partial inventory of the latter's expressive abnormalities, tying the manic subject to conditions of semantic clustering and overactivation, distractibility, rapid speech, speech

---

21 M. Darwish, *Unfortunately, It Was Paradise*, tr. M. Akash, C. Forche, S. Antoon, and A. El-Zein (Berkeley, CA: University of California Press, 2003), 144.

pressure, combinatory discourse structures, verbosity, clang associations (association via sound over meaning), crowded thoughts, brooding rumination, the flight of ideas, and the hyper-fluidity of word retrieval.[22] Correspondingly, in fever one can picture the bedridden figure torn between rambling, muttering, and long protracted bouts of silence punctured by intermittent uproar, alongside episodes of aphasia (impairment of linguistic ability) and echolalia (meaningless repetition of words). Thus the above author of elevated temperatures is found 'raving' while concurrently 'forgetting how to speak', caught slowly in a kind of muralising effect wherein thought-patterns become affixed to an impossible wall or ceiling of locution, such that it appears throughout such passages as if one is either talking to oneself or talking to no one. But in fact neither interpretation holds, nor is the nurse correct to assume that the sufferer is 'crying out to me', for this is precisely where mania enables us to consider an alternative: namely, that one is speaking to the fever itself. Many have witnessed the sad sight of elderly demented patients sitting in institutions babbling into thin air, the far-off gaze and the surrounding white walls prompting one to describe this too as a 'talking to oneself' or 'talking to no one' when it might actually

---

22 L. Weiner, N. Doignon-Camus, G. Bertschy, and A. Giersch. 'Thought and Language Disturbance in Bipolar Disorder Quantified via Process-oriented Verbal Fluency Measures', *Scientific Reports* 9 (2019), article number 14282.

manifest a more dire orientation: that of talking back to death, loss, or eventuality itself. In essence, the patient is answering the call of the force that consumes them, in a sort of cryptophasia (those invented languages developed by twins). Or even more drastically, it might indicate that death, loss, or the inescapable instant speaks through them—that it is no longer their own individual voices we hear, but rather an act of ventriloquism whereby a looming phenomenon plays puppeteer to their larynxes. Ultimately, it is not hard to fathom the idea of opening a dialogic channel with materiality, experience, mood, sensation: after all, we understand crying as a communication addressed to extreme pain, or moaning in eroticism as a sound meant not for the self or partner but as a reply to immediate pleasure. Fever, too, is omnivorous in this way: it grips and clasps unconditionally, it contrives a poetic epidemiology that demands possession (note that in all three cases—sobbing, sensuality, pyrexia—we also observe a shared tendency to close the eyes). But this language of manic fever has one key difference: the total lack of self-consciousness. The self is virtually no longer there (either in memory or sapience); only the diseased utterance persists, as if apparitionally disembodied from the identity of its host, the one lying prostrate who cannot 'come back to life' and desires 'no return to anyone'—as when the same author writes elsewhere that 'the two strangers who burned within us are those who wanted to murder us only moments ago'.[23] What remains is a thermal dialect wherein one either mimes or responds to fever's own intonations, or rather becomes a vessel for its rasping voice.

Fever and raving; forgotten speech; fear; delirium; crying; non-return

---

[23] Darwish, *Unfortunately, It Was Paradise*, 82.

Frigomania/Cheimatomania (Coldness)

*Too much accumulated resentment when you need to look
at things coldly, with a head that is cold and clear as steel,
cold as ice, when you need a will of steel...
cold-bloodedness
cold-bloodedness above all else
Let's first of all write a poem with cold blood.*

RÉDA BENSMAIA[24]

The Cheimatomaniac's proclivity for becoming ice-cold affords four pathways of conjecture on: (1) radical indifference; (2) untimeliness; (3) the caretaker; (4) the emblem. The first conceptual chamber here turns frigidity into a state of impervious concentration with respect to all things: thus we imagine the philosopher or artist staring with dilated, coal-like eyes of radical indifference at themselves, at their work, at the reader/viewer, at the world and its presumed future, indifferent even as they continue to enunciate their messianic messages. All that would concern this figure would be a kind of unmoved, superior fulfilment of the task, relying on neither subjective inspiration nor subjective imagination but rather following only the necessary progression of a

---

24 Bensmaia, *The Year of Passages*, 59.

construct: or, as an Italian avant-gardist once suggested in his remarkable manifesto on deception, it is a matter of knowing exactly what to do with something one does not understand (like an assassin piecing together the components of a multifaceted weapon). Substitution of the psychological ('accumulated resentment') for the psychro-logical ('cold-bloodedness').

This manic stoicism also furnishes us with a platform for reconsidering the discourse of untimeliness, and moreover the specific protocol by which one may generate or evaluate an untimely work. Despite the apparent vaulting ambition of such a project—i.e., to conceive the unprecedented or discontemporaneous thought—it actually begins with a degree of extreme suspicion toward oneself (questioning the validity, sincerity, and even ownership of one's own mind): indeed, it is to disown the vast majority of one's consciousness as consisting of throwaway archetypes and clichés of the era, to be rid of the dominance of the prejudices of collective wisdom, to perceive how the crowd's untruth pervades one's own internal voice, and thereby to begin isolating strands of potential meditations that evade the pre-established rules of the epoch. Is it any wonder that a mediaeval Italian author once represented the price of such infra-betrayal and inter-betrayal as the coldness of the ninth circle of Hell itself, his own reports functioning as a kind of literary spectrograph, with a six-winged devil trapped waist-deep in a frozen lake?

Note: It is excruciating to effectively launch this procedure and thereby grow unaccustomed to one's habituated assumptions, to treat the most seemingly intimate notions as dispensable matter (not of one's own); a cheimatomaniacal outlook alone might then numb this agony of disentanglement and self-rejection. Furthermore, on that faraway evening when the solitary one does perhaps forge the untimely artefact or spark an unexpected turn of ingenuity, one must still treat these gems with the same compulsive coldness, recognising their pure artifice: they are no more than uncommon fashioning implements synthesised amid a complete absence of authentic life.

Another perfect agent of manic coldness would be the humble caretaker: the keeper or custodian of temples, shrines, inns, or land. We picture them shuffling around the empty halls or fresh soil casually, attending to each minute detail with an air of serene purpose. But this nonchalance is not to be confused with passionless distance: they are in fact great watchmen and watchwomen, calm in their fanatical knowledge of what they are prepared to give in order to preserve the site or idol; the most callous protectors against invaders, they are sworn generously to a hard-heartedness that offers everything of itself (executioners of the highest order). This is the unspeakable sacrificial focus of the caretaker who goes about their daily chores in silent severity ('the will of steel').

Finally, we arrive at the apex of cheimatomaniacal study: the emblem (or how to emblazon oneself in a hallmark). For the emblem amplifies the subject by transforming it into a miraculous object: stated more aggressively, it is the augmentative prism through which 'one becomes what one already is'. While the symbol attempts to fill the glaring void of the actual (religious iconography), and the metaphor exists as a pitifully transcendent idealisation of the original (romantic fantasy), the emblem is affixed to the chest, jacket, or tattooed body of the actual proponent (warlike display). Thus the members of a royal bloodline themselves wear the embroidered insignia of their dynasty, just as the nomad etches in black kohl powder, henna, battle paint, scar tissue, or calligraphic ink the seals of their tribal fury. This insignia harnesses, in a seemingly impassive thing, the prowess of what is already there; it both contains and transmits irreproducible strength, just as the 'poem with cold blood' is no retroactive hagiography of past deeds but a flagrant attestation of the advent (presence-in-arrival). The queen's sceptre; the leader's badge; the genius's monogram; the knight's banner; the publisher's imprinted colophon. To turn oneself into a pennant or token is to render oneself fearless, pitiless, unstoppable. It is never to brandish the modern, bloated logo diffused across generic structures of consumption: for here, it is clear that one must be prepared to fight, kill, and die for the emblem. It is equivalent to the disturbing power one gains from converting self into the third person (to say 'it demands') which, like the pen name, is neither alter-ego nor inner consciousness but rather the distillation of an individual's creative touch into a single inhuman design without the barriers of subjectivity, identity, or history (to give title to the impersonal). In effect, to cryogenically freeze desire into a lone character, relic, or impression which stands for the attainment of an entire inimitable world.

Coldness and the look; the head; the will; the poem; cold-bloodedness

Crystallomania (Crystals)

> *the landscapes have grown netlike,*
> *and the walls and the gaze*
> *converge at the far-off provinces of disenchantment,*
> *and the sky*
>   *a prison*
>   *of crystal?*
>
> AHMAD SHAMLU[25]

The Crystallomaniac perceives a state of dismal entrapment in a series of reflective surfaces: while the horizontal axes of the 'landscape' form their own webs, even the vertical climes (usually antidotes to the labyrinth's extending lairs) shape themselves into deceptive snares in which the image refracts and becomes eternally locked. This is why the same poet elsewhere determines to 'plunge my voice like a dagger into the crystal of the sky', for the sky-prison's trickery (confinement in densely arranged microscopic structures of translucency) must be met with a technique of violence that shatters the very atomic, molecular, and ionic levels of world.[26] Certainly there are long-standing folkloric traditions warning against

---

25   Shamlu, *Born Upon the Dark Spear*, 61.

26   Ibid., 3.

the danger of glass and crystal spheres and their ability to forever condemn souls to their flat faces and sharp angles, like antediluvian life forms suspended in amber. Here also, then, we are warned of the superficial allure of the crystal—that iridescence of sunset fire and black galaxy opals or amethyst and fluorite purples, those dense grooves of bismuth, the rounded edges of tourmaline, the sharp milky 'daughters' of rose quartz or split-growth patterns of azurite—for fear of losing ourselves in their titanic caves and infinitesimal prisms.

Note: The author's manic challenge to the crystal atmosphere above him, his threat to burst through its barricade of fractal appearances beyond the limits of both wall and gaze, reminds one of the insane posture of Hercules, who blindly shot an arrow into the sun, or even of Genghis Khan, whose Mongol hordes avoided starvation on long campaigns by drinking blood from the narrowly-slit veins of their horses' legs or necks, and who once declared 'I am the punishment of God. If you had not committed great sins, God would not have sent a punishment like me upon you.'[27] Thus mania serves again as an ingredient for supernatural insurgent action, fuelling a subversive confidence like no other and thereby fracturing the edifices of both cosmic and human empires.

---

27 'Ala-ad-Din 'Ata-Malik Juvaini, *The History of the World-Conqueror*, tr. J.A. Boyle (Cambridge, MA: Harvard University Press, 1958).

Note: This urgent sense of alarm in facing despotic airs reminds one of an indirect aesthetic counterpart: the hall of mirrors. While the western world celebrates the Hall of Mirrors at Versailles as a preeminent example, its relatively simple flat-mirror design was long preceded by the Persian practice of *ayeneh-kari* (mirror-making), which gave rise to the most elaborate interior assemblages throughout royal palaces, shrines, and teahouses. For instance, the *Takhte Marmar* (Marble Throne Room), *Talare Bolour* (Crystal Hall), *Talare Almas* (Hall of Diamonds), *Talare Brelian* (Brilliant Hall), *Talare Adj* (Hall of Ivory), and *Talare Ayeneh* (Mirror Hall) of Golestan Palace are all enveloped by these shimmering symmetric walls and ceilings inlaid with great skill and patience. Variations of the same sparkling mirrorwork can be seen in Isfahan's *Ayeneh-Khaneh* (Palace of Mirrors) and *Chehel-Sotoon* (Forty Columns) where the magical nature of these vast polychrome galleries is again on full display, or the antechambers of Shiraz's funerary parlour *Shah-Cheragh* (King of Light) where golden calligraphy bounces off the countless green triangles, protruding rhombuses, and glittering silver domes surrounding a single tomb. All are the work of a sixteenth-century architectural school of grievous delicacy, predicated upon the handling of needles, pens, cutters, isinglass glue, and consecutively large and small pieces of carved glass to form a terrain of optical wonderment—all of which rests stylistically upon a lesser-known Sufi mystical principle: that one can glimpse divinity only through a broken mirror.

Note: The other locale where mirror-halls and mirror-mazes are customarily found is the carnival, as the ticket-holder walks carefully in ever-tightening steps, stumbling against convex, concave, or curved panes to find their way out of a puzzle-world. Hence we descend from the grand vestibules and aristocratic courts of monarchs to the localised squalor of these roving amusement parks that arrive yearly in rural locations, noting curiously how this same spatial invention (that of the mirror hall) could embed itself historically in both centralised monuments and peripheral funhouses. Perhaps what binds the two, however, is precisely the poet's inkling of the tyrannical intent behind these specular zones: the aim of both palace and carnival—the former through fear of the carceral (law, state, the political), the latter through the temptation of the carousel (pleasure, indulgence, the sensual)—is to cage the individual will in the magnifying or kaleidoscopic effect of ceaseless mirroring. So it is that 'the far-off provinces of disenchantment' are masked behind the thin crystalline veneers and facades of enchanting glass-play.

Crystal and the landscape; the net; the wall; the gaze disenchantment; the sky; the prison; the dagger

Part 6

Graphomania (Writing)
Linguomania (Language)
Bibliomania (Books)

Graphomania (Writing)

I opened your head
To read your thoughts.

JOYCE MANSOUR[28]

The Graphomaniac, by standard definition, would either be one who writes incessantly or one who wishes to consume all writing in existence. Yet here these compulsions are folded into a new composite via a theory of telepathic assault. If telepathic ability entails the vicarious transfer of information from one person to another ('to read your thoughts'), here it seemingly also requires an initial assault of vampiric brutality via an entry wound ('I opened your head'). Thus, to have the evil ear is, above all else, to hook oneself into the consciousness of the other (sinking fangs, nails) in order to imbibe their vital essence and thereby make self indistinguishable from other. It is true that for centuries parapsychologists have attempted to confirm the veracity of what they call 'extra-sensory perception' or 'anomalous cognition', and that schizophrenics often attest to 'thought-insertion' or 'thought-removal' (the sense that external entities are conspiratorially planting ideas in or deleting information

---

28 J. Mansour, *Screams*, tr. S. Gavronsky (Sausalito, CA: Post Apollo, 1995), 43.

from, their minds). But we would be better served here by concentrating on the vampiric side of this philosophical equation. For, in order to understand the author's cryptic line elsewhere—'your name shall be written on her mind's checkerboard in the blood of capital letters'[29]—we must interrogate the long-shrouded records surrounding this parasitic creature of mental extraction and physical extortion. Undoubtedly, legends of vampires have circulated in many times and places, across all continents, most often in oral traditions. The term used today is itself perhaps etymologically tied to the Turkish word for 'witch' or the Old Slavic expression for 'thrusting violently', but here we are not concerned with rehearsing the numerous beliefs as to these creatures' origins, methods, and weaknesses, but with just a single critical feature: that, according to most legendary accounts, the revenant's bite is always experienced not as painful but as pure gratification for both parties. How is this possible, unless the vampire transmits its own appetite or thirst into the other at the moment of devouring, thereby constructing a reciprocal current, a runway that makes the consumption process a mutually-sensed moment of thrill, rush, delectation, or rhapsody? To share insatiability itself, to relish sentence fragments of the mind with the same longing for bubbles of blood (text entering into states of liquefaction). In similar fashion, the above-cited poet treats the other's

---

29 Mansour, *Essential Poems and Writings*, 259.

head as a sieve through which their most intimately-reserved thoughts will be deciphered (and savoured by both), using the coercive entrenchment of the wound to rope them together in a clairvoyant bond. Perhaps it is in this same vein that we must also understand her strange graphomaniacal claims to ambidexterity: 'I'll write with both hands the day I'll no longer speak'—for she is absorbed in projects of blending, amalgamation, and coalescence (all pursued by techniques of ravishing) on almost every page of her oeuvre.[30]

Note: It is almost exclusively the purview of the child's imagination to contemplate the premise that one may exist only in the dream of a giant, or even (for those who dare venture a more megalomaniacal interpretation) that one might themselves be the dreaming giant. As such, the young will often ponder this hypothesis: that we are bred in the duration of the colossus's unconscious hours, that we awaken only when it sleeps, and that we sleep when it wakes. But then our dreams would likely be illustrative chronicles of the giant's own waking existence, the seemingly involuntary figments of our mind a telepathic looking-glass into the alternative dimension where the giant roams.

Writing and the head; thought; mind-reading; the checkerboard; the ambidextrous

---

30 Ibid., 211.

Linguomania (Language)

> *She moans as though some secret, spiritual electrons wrap her up like a cloud, as she simultaneously quarrels with herself and the ghosts within her. Moaning is a language that suffices her for dialogue. She is in no need of familiar speech to say what she wants to the spirits surrounding her and tormenting her. We gradually sink in silence like a stone that sinks to the bottom of the sea. Sometimes I speak with my sweet, tender, and bald husband's ghost, not so that he may hear me but so that I may hear my voice, which alone ties me to the world of the living or those who think themselves as such.*
>
> GHADA SAMMAN[31]

The Linguomaniac here takes prose to the absurd outer edges of a post-homicidal rhetoric—into a discourse that reaches beyond death and into the undying or undead realms (immortal language). She achieves this inexplicable traversal through her manic devotion to a lost lover, as she persists in murmuring to a man murdered in a warzone. This is the nexus where romanticism and gothicism converge, as sentiments of infatuation attach

---

31 G. Samman, *The Square Moon: Supernatural Tales*, tr. I. Boullata (Fayetteville, NC: University of Arkansas Press, 1999), 65.

themselves (in bad taste) to decomposing forms. This involves the invention of a tongue unwrecked by finitude, one that continually dispenses sensitivity and warmth even to skeletal recipients. Mad love attains true madness in this nightly 'quarrelling with ghosts', as the poet articulates her prolonged cherishing of a cadaver that 'sinks to the bottom of the sea', hinting at a vestigial necromantic faculty active only in the utterance that lasts no longer than whisper, breath, or fleeting sound. The inherent logic or illogic of this claim does not interest us here; what remains pressing is the nature of this manic language that resists defeat by putrefaction: assuredly, it must be a language of unremitting *Adynaton* (insinuations of the impossible). Every syllable of every word of every phrase in this perimeter finds itself arcing toward extreme, hyperbolic lengths and sowing covenants with the insurmountable.

Note: Intriguingly, the demographic group in old-world cultures most inclined toward the impossible recitations of *adynaton* is that of elderly women (it therefore accompanies the genres of old wives' tales, fortune-telling, and superstition). In all instances, such sayings are oriented toward the elapsed sectors of the dead or the impenetrable sectors of fate and chance, perhaps because these aged women have typically accumulated the greatest losses and suffered the greatest injustices over time. Thus the great spinsters seek a manic language of aggrandisement with which to struggle against near-immutable regimes (natural or manmade) and to win near-unattainable advantages. They devise their own unofficial mode of address, weaving riddles and preposterous suggestions to bend the otherwise immobile circumstance.

Note: Another example of something like the linguomaniacal passage above—one that 'moans [...] [through] some secret, spiritual electrons'—is that of the Japanese death poem (*jisei*), a work of last words or farewell composed by monks or disgraced samurai. Stories abound of enlightened Zen masters drafting these short verses only to die gracefully on the spot after setting down their pens, and others of stigmatised nobles setting out their sayings in fresh ink before committing ritual suicide by disembowelment. Hence one wonders: to what odd roster does this genre of release belong? One that assists simultaneously in the recusal of the esteemed, the defector, and the rogue? How can these elegiac stanzas pertain to such disparate factions and specimens of the dying? Nor does this final ceremonial act seem to follow a thematic handbook of any standardized kind, for *jisei* epithets range in content from sage-like wisdom to wistful reflection to ghoulish humour to complete emotional blankness: a note to hallow ambiguity and impermanence itself.

> *Language and moaning; the secret electron; the cloud; quarrelling; the ghost; dialogue; silence; the sea-bottom; the husband*

Bibliomania (Books)

> *When your innocent eyes glance*
> *over this confused, beginningless book,*
> *you will see a deep-rooted lasting rebellion*
> *blooming in the heart of every song.*
>
> FORUGH FARROKHZAD[32]

The Bibliomaniac recognises that the production of an insane literary work would first require the erasure of its origin ('this confused, beginningless book'). Now, there are certain genres which, purely by virtue of their peculiar circulatory nature, lend themselves to a lack of credited authorship (jokes, rumours, fables), but here we seek even rarer typologies of manic textuality: (1) the pseudonymous book or found object book, whether uncovered as an anonymous or apocryphal artefact (The Dead Sea Scrolls) or purported to be the transcription of another, metafictional author (H.P. Lovecraft's *Necronomicon*, attributed to the 'Mad Arab' Abdul al-Hazred, or Miguel de Cervantes's *Don Quixote*, attributed to a North African Moor, Cide Hamete Benengeli, allegedly encountered during his five-year captivity in Algeria); (2) the lost book, whether misplaced for centuries and therefore

---

32 Farrokhzad, *A Lonely Woman*, 34.

existing only in the references, commentaries, or selected quotations of others (Heraclitus, whose few remaining cryptic statements gained him the title 'The Obscure' and 'The Weeping Philosopher'), or the forgotten work that reaches completion in the mind only to dissipate into fragments of partial memory (Samuel Taylor Coleridge's poem 'Kubla Khan', with its exotic descriptions of the city of Xanadu, the three hundred lines of which the author claimed had come to him in their vivid totality during an opium-induced dream only to vanish for the most part when interrupted by a salesman knocking at the door); (3) the recorded book, whether compiled long after the original author's demise by strangers or adherents (most prophetic traditions) or transcribed diligently by actual protégés (Plato's recording of the Socratic dialogues) or close interlocutors (Rumi's recording of the wanderer Shams-i Tabrizi's esoteric teachings).

Of these alternative routes, it is the last-mentioned category—that of philosophical or poetic figures who themselves never or only rarely penned texts, yet persist as an influence in the disciple's catalogue—that best matches the formula outlined in our initial quote. For only the disciple brings 'innocent eyes' to the difficult charge of compilation, but even beyond this, it is the disciple alone who turns this act of impersonation into a 'deep-rooted lasting rebellion': a rebellion against origin, against temporality, against language, against memory, against world, and ultimately against the master figure themselves. In the cases of Socrates and Shams-i Tabriz, both of whom exhibited tell-tale signs of lucid madness, their own preferred modality was to speak always and everywhere, dripping words frantically along each axis of encounter, whether in marketplaces, bazaars, taverns, banquets, academies, or symposia, much like the graffiti artist who sees all surfaces and planes as potential parchments or canvases awaiting inscription. What persists of them in real time is nothing but a half-faded dye or the haze of a world view left in the hands of an acolyte who now must rise to the occasion of this master's vestige. Once again, though, why discern a 'deep-rooted, lasting rebellion blooming in the heart of every song' in what otherwise appears as pure veneration? With respect to their material contact we must recall that in most instances these disciples were either eyewitnesses or at close quarters to the untimely deaths of their masters: on the one hand, Plato's proximity to the trial and execution of Socrates, ravaged by the image of the latter's ingestion of hemlock poison; on the other hand, Rumi's suspicion that his own young followers had stabbed and discarded the body of Shams in a nearby well, out of jealousy over their kindred spiritual connection. Hence the recorded, beginningless book ('as they once said') is nothing less than a concerted will to vengeance, a spectral assault on existence in order to retaliate against its murderous deeds (to carve the unforgiven), as much as it is a revolt against textuality itself for compelling such a distasteful reliving of an event that ended cruelly (each line re-crucifies). But also a manic dissent against the master's limitations, for inevitably there occurs some distant moment years or decades later when the disciple finds themselves prompted to embellish, improve, or altogether fabricate some additional statement in the name of the absent elder (the opportunity for creative adulteration). Thereafter, spontaneity supersedes deference, and all is overthrown.

Note: The most obvious ideal setting for the bibliomaniac would be a library of immense proportions, a citadel of books with innumerable aisles comprising all subjects, languages, and authors. The *Bayt al-Hikmah* (House of Wisdom), or Grand Library of Baghdad, was founded in the late eighth century, and quickly became the epicentre of the most illustrious collection in existence, spawning a renaissance in Arabo-Persian thought across myriad scientific, philosophical, historical, theological, mystical, and aesthetic disciplines. For generations the House of Wisdom drew all curious thinkers to its quicksand of awaiting shelves, forming a precious intellectual membrane for the thriving metropolis, until the Mongol Siege of Baghdad in 1258 when, allegedly, millions of bound manuscripts were thrown into the Tigris River (making its waters run black with ink). Would the true bibliomaniacal site be that of a legendary library lost in time? Like the fictional island city of Atlantis, which attained the heights of civilisational refinement only to be banished forever into the oceanic depths, or the allegorical Tower of Babel, whose spires of human aspiration dared arrogantly to touch the heavens, only to be demolished by God, its denizens dispersed into a thousand warring clans, the House of Wisdom founded a superlative utopian structure of unrivalled resources that was to be razed. Again, an omnicidal reflex laying beneath the surface of delirium, much like the ironic end of al-Jahiz, pioneering scholar of the House of Wisdom, whose original manuscripts (over two hundred, of which thirty survive) included a seven-volume encyclopaedia titled *The Book of Animals*, and who died in the library aged ninety-two beneath a massive pile of fallen bookcases. So that today at long last, we are left with only books about this place of books, and indeed this seems closer to the logic of bibliomaniacal musing found in the passage above: the dream of a precarious maximalist archive (the exemplar) that ultimately tips over into disappearance.

The Book and innocence; eyes; confusion; beginninglessness; rebellion

Part 7
Chromatomania (Colour)
Leukomania (Whiteness)
Melanomania (Blackness)

Chromatomania (Colour)

> *I live surrounded by colors,*
> *simply,*
> *like any man.*
> *I marry the blind gods*
> *and the gods of vision*
> *for the last time.*
>
> ADONIS[33]

The Chromatomaniac appears to resist Western modernity's subliminal conspiracy against colour, its imposition of the puritanical constraints of drabness in the name of a pious New World, those formal celebrity events that privilege black suits or gowns, the insistence of luxury interior decorating upon so-called earth tones, and futuristic urban design's depictions of cities of pure white sterility—which have resulted in the brazen relegation of all vividness to so-called primitive cultures and peoples. In opposition to this neurotic chromatophobia of the imperialist project and its false civilisational hierarchies, here we find this writer 'surrounded by colors', set to

---

33 Adonis, *The Pages of Day and Night*, 25.

hatch the most ambitious of perceptual conspiracies: to wed 'the blind gods and the gods of vision' in some unholy nuptials (letting madness unseat the incommensurable). So the poetic narrator plays the role of pseudo-matchmaker, avoiding harmonious options and instead coupling the ill-suited and the extraneous, as if to favour only the admixture of pigments and thus to disseminate mixed races, to bastardise tincture and thereby end the reign of dichotomies. Furthermore, this experiment strays beyond the visual register to provoke an epistemological dilemma as well (of stained correlation), for such countermarriages necessarily upset the scales of knowing (the sighted cannot understand blindness), stranding those they bring together in mutual incomprehensibility. On the one side, gods of dreariness—anemic, ashen, sickly, bleached; on the other, gods of vibrancy—bright, variegated, prismatic: companions in disseverment alone.

Yet a series of strange questions arises upon encountering this verse: (1) Where does a mere mortal—someone who lives 'like any man'—gain the authority to pair the gods into grooms and brides (presumably against their will and contrary to cosmic law)?; (2) Why does this figure describe such a seemingly complex gesture (of the misfacing ones) as a task accomplished 'simply'? The first question calls to mind an old mythic concept whereby unassuming or weak figures (the wretch, the beggar, the crippled, the widow, the passerby) in fact boast some extraordinary capacity to bless or curse those who cross them, while the second takes us into the realms of the associative power of chromaesthesia. A subset of synaesthesia (wherein one sense is experienced simultaneously by other senses), chromaesthesia happens when a certain non-visual sense (usually sound) leads to the involuntary evocation of colour before the subject's eyes. Similarly to a manic disposition, this results in the translation of all quotidian, mundane objects and environmental noise into a condition often described by neurologists as something resembling 'fireworks', in addition to a longevity factor whereby their cortical over-stimulation can lead to abnormal latencies of coloured afterimages (prior sightings paint the next perceived thing). Indeed, if the members of a secret society of philosophers nearly a century ago could ponder the 'colour of the sacred', then we might extend their inquiry further to ask after the 'colour of the sacred afterimage' and whether it might open a fissure into some paradox of psychedelic dusk.

And then, hanging ominously like a blade overhead, there is the final line of the matchmaker's stanza—'for the last time'—which can only be read with three inferences: (1) that these tinted unions have been attempted in prior aeons but have never held for long; (2) that the chromatomaniac has finally discovered the key component to make these incompatible, unseemly pledges endure; (3) that these marriages between blindness, vision, and chroma will bring about the end of the world (and after all, what is the colour of omnicide?).

Colour and surroundings; simplicity; marriage; blindness; vision; the last time

Leukomania (Whiteness)

> *His eyeballs looked so white that they did not seem capable of seeing anything. His eyes expressed astonishment mixed with fright. This was the astonishment of an eye that had grown accustomed to darkness and that had gazed into eternity for a long time. His eye was frightened by the light marking its return. It felt perplexed at having lost space and at having been deprived of the sensation of existing in space.*
>
> IBRAHIM AL-KONI[34]

The Leukomaniac enters states of self-induced turmoil that hold all Being hostage in the milky whiteness of the eyeball. Here the opaque, ivory tissue of the sclera is no longer a protective outer coat but rather a sanctuary for 'astonishment': its paleness allows the light's devastating 'return'; it authorises disorientation to whip, siphon, and suffuse itself into the optic nerve to the extent that one perceives only spacelessness.

A recent neurophenomenological study on altered states in meditation found that expert practitioners were able to subtly alter their neural activities, particularly in the cerebellum and insular cortex, to produce senses

---

34 Al-Koni, *The Seven Veils of Seth*, 181.

of 'timelessness' and 'spacelessness' (described as a loss of bodily boundaries or an out-of-body experience).[35] Another recent study on digital memory with regard to 'virtual possessions' discovered that the rapidly-increasing use of mobile technologies and cloud storage resulted in experiences of placelessness, spacelessness, and formlessness with respect to personal objects, with the three following consequences: (1) that the sheer mobility of virtual possessions disassociated them from any specific experience of setting or context; (2) that the sizelessness of virtual possessions (i.e., that they do not clutter space) resulted in the lack of any cumulative understanding of the magnitude of one's archive, leaving collections to become ever more disorganised and unstructured over time; (3) that the total absence of touch upon virtual possessions effectively erased the sentiment of wornness, use, or impression that would lead to singular histories or memories being attached to such items.[36] As consumption takes the place of worship in modern society, this growing ambivalence of shared pseudo-space or spacelessness (amid the infinite white noise of the virtual) makes of it a pale god that does not enter, linger, or override our

---

35 A. Kovich-Ohana et al., 'Alterations in the Sense of Time, Space, and Body in the Mindfulness-trained Brain: A Neurophenomenologically-guided MEG Study', *Front. Psychol.* 4:912 (2013), 10.3389/fpsyg.2013.00912.

36 W. Odom, J. Zimmerman, and J. Forlizzi (Human-Computer Interaction Institute, Carnegie Mellon University), 'Placelessness, Spacelessness, and Formlessness: Experiential Qualities of Virtual Possessions', DIS 2014, June 21–25, 2014, Vancouver, BC, Canada.

atmosphere with material presence. What is left, then, is essentially a state of *the unpossessed* which prompts the following dangerous questions: Is there a gradual convergence between mysticism and futurism? Does the mystic's meditative encapsulation (supposed to bring about leukomaniacal enlightenment) not resemble at least partially the postmodern technological obsession with transparency, exposure, and irradiated images cast across glossy screens? Is there not a persuasive parallel between the mystic's quest for self-annihilation and the dissolution of subjective borders and personal reminiscence in the virtual world? Does the futuristic weightlessness of science fiction tales set in outer space not mirror mystical levitation, 'perplexed at having been deprived of the sensation of existing in space'? And yet, in many of those same gravity-drained stories, the surface of some approaching planet surreptitiously plays tricks on the traveller's consciousness, most often by projecting the false simulacra of memories (inauthentic past lives) and by extension the false simulacra of an unconscious not their own. Would this feeling be the manic epitome of white light described above: to be inundated by massless, ex-nihilo phantoms with zero connection to our being-in-the-world?

Note: In Siberian and Mongolian Tengerism, a long-persecuted animist religion of horse-riding tribes, White Shamans serve the fifty-five beneficent *tngri* (highest divinity class) of the pantheon, primarily conducting rites of blessing and communion with nature. They are divided according to specialisation into *ooselshen* (diviners), *otoshi* (healers, exorcists), *bariyachi* (midwives), and *barishi* (bone-setters). Originally, the White Shamans were frequently women draped in bird feathers or capes, known for carrying silk fans, bells, and wood staffs, and charged with supervising the overall health of the clan by preventing both infertile land and bodies. They were expert practitioners in the preparation of herbs and pacifiers of angry spirits, said to derive their powers from the West (White Heaven) and to learn their specialisms from various animal-helpers including mountain foxes, snakes, reindeer, wolves, owls, or ravens, while striving to maintain balance in the World Tree. This notwithstanding, the selection of a shaman followed an excruciating initiation principle: namely, they must have undergone a near-death experience during childhood, whether from severe illness or being struck by lightning. This horrific suffering presumably indicated a latent 'cocooned' potential—awaiting training by elder shamans—and their having been designated in advance for 'dismemberment' and 'rebirth' by the spirits.

Whiteness and the eye; astonishment; fright; eternal gazing; return; perplexity; spacelessness

Melanomania (Blackness)

> *Nothing has happened here!*
> *In the far distance, there is a fire though without smoke*
> *which blazes on the gaping shore of night;*
> *and here, beside us, it is a night of terror*
> *our mouths warm*
> *and well-informed of the situation.*
> *It is a grudge that, with whatever stands before it,*
> *turns the black-surfaced thing*
> *even blacker.*
>
> AHMAD SHAMLU[37]

The Melanomaniac combines three primordial fears—fear of the outside, fear of the unseen, fear of small things—in a single image of smokeless fire. Together, these phobic currents somehow gel into a manic state of *pandemic* which can be deciphered in the following terms: (1) it is cryptogenic (of obscure origin), requiring no calamitous event or source to proliferate itself ('nothing has happened here'); (2) it is experienced always as something out-there, in the wilderness, and therefore on-the-way ('in the far distance'); (3) it is opportunistic, taking advantage of all unarmed sites, holes, and vulnerabilities ('blazes

---

[37] Shamlu, *Born Upon the Dark Spear*, 22.

on the gaping shore of night'); (4) it intensifies affective circuits, inciting panic without actually touching anyone ('it is a night of terror'); (5) it incites over-speculation, with townspeople guessing incessantly at its nature ('our mouths warm and well-informed of the situation'); (6) it operates according to the principle of the vendetta, patiently taking whatever it is owed ('it is a grudge'). Indeed, the viral always persists as a minimalist reckoning, arising as a mere clandestine speck that then cuts like a scythe across entire populations, reducing nations to bare waiting and idleness (the lesson of absolute passivity) while also giving rise to black markets (the lesson of absolute criminality). And once visible, which is to say inescapable, it simply continues the pandemic's logic of exponential growth and spreading in order to reach its melanomaniacal summit ('turns the black-surfaced thing even blacker').

Note: In Siberian and Mongolian Tengerism, Black Shamans or 'Shamans of the Dark' form a priestly class thought to possess direct alignments with the forty-four *tngri* (highest divinity class) of the Terrible Ones, controllers of the Black Side of the Universe or Black Heaven. The most fearsome sorcerers in the shamanic tradition, burning wild plants and carrying ritual drums, often clad in dark robes, animal hides, antlered or horned headdresses, the Black Shamans derive their powers from the accursed energies of the North, matching cruel force with yet crueller force, and therefore considered instrumental in times of war and hunting. Their primary function: to curse enemies, to speak imprecations and bring scourge to livestock or harvests, always accompanying chieftains to battle or in diplomatic affairs as advisors. In certain rare instances, however, Black Shamans might live apart from the tribe in the Palaeolithic caves of nearby mountains, invited down only in moments of grave exception and granted payment in the form of an undeniable wish (i.e., the right to demand any price, including the taking of a child back to the valleys).

Blackness and the non-happening; distance; smokeless fire; shore; night; terror; the mouth; the grudge

Part 8
Ombromania/Pluviomania (Rain)
Antlomania (Floods)
Thalassomania (Oceans)
Bathymania (Deep Water)
Aquamania (Drowning)/Kymomania (Waves)
Ablutomania (Washing, Bathing)

Ombromania/Pluviomania (Rain)

> *The rain had spun a web about him. He was drenched, enclosed in its delicate strands. The raindrops, like slimy creatures, grasped the threads of the web as they fell. He passed like a vagrant shadow through wet deserted streets beneath the rain and disappeared.*
>
> SADEQ HEDAYAT[38]

The Ombromaniac gives us to contemplate the particular sensorial dynamics of the drenched: the feeling of wetness, encrustation, grime, ooze, or foam (that which clings to or glazes another body) alongside contact with the density of ethereal things. A well-used image sees the classical hero covered in the dirt of the forest, the mud of the swamp, or the sands of the desert, the natural residue of which forms an oppressive layer meant to symbolise hardship, adversity, and tribulation. But here the geo-existential relation shifts away from human-centric enterprise, for which sediment is always an obstacle, and instead turns toward an osmotic principle: the 'slimy creatures' instruct their wearer in their own ways (those of the rain's ever-lowering gradations), exploiting porosity

---

38 S. Hedayat, 'Dead End', in E. Yarshater (ed.), *Sadeq Hedayat: An Anthology* (Boulder, CO: Westview Press, 1979), 117.

in order to activate powerful thread-like emulations in ourselves. This is how the Ombromaniac learns to pass 'like a vagrant shadow' through the dampened alleys of the city—once again highlighting the manic capacity to absorb traits of the phenomenological world (even that of dripping), which here allows the protagonist to learn the art of disappearance and evasion. In this filmic vein, he escapes from the 'Dead End' of the short story's title by absorbing lessons of elasticity and resiliency from the 'delicate strands' that froth upon his naked skin.

Note: Arithmomania (obsession with counting, numbers). In some theological traditions, the Archangel Michael holds responsibility for calculating every single drop of rain that falls upon the earth (an unexplained sacred computation), just as in some dark folkloric traditions, vampires or demons can be distracted by being told to tally raindrops or grains.

Note: Arachnomania (obsession with spiders). Those exhibits of contemporary installation artists who preserve spiderwebs in glass cases remind us of a little-known, twin scientific observation: (1) that, according to certain astronomers, the complex interwoven network of the spider's ecosystem is the only thing in nature to accurately mirror the movement-design of star and planetary constellations; (2) that, according to certain biologists, the spider's silken spirals are the only thing in nature to accurately mirror the nuanced system of receptors found in the human brain. From a creature's small impeccable habitat to the inner workings of consciousness to the most remote cosmological stirrings, we find a manic paradigm of adhesion that binds the interior and exterior, the infinitesimal and the universal, in addition to anthropological, arthropodal, and astral forms.

> *Rain and spinning webs; drenching; strands; slime; falling; vagrancy; shadow; disappearance*

Antlomania (Floods)

My task is to exaggerate the truth. To spread panic about drought. To paint a bleak picture of the many villages that lie scattered along the banks of the River Nabi, which runs between my country and that of our hostile neighbours. We've been fighting ruinous wars with these neighbours since the dawn of history. The fragile peace we now have with them is just a dormant volcano. I'm currently contributing to a narrative that concludes with the volcano erupting once again. Without water blood will flow. Thirst will arouse that brutal, hostile memory. And it won't be just humans that will perish, but also rare birds and insects and the flocks of animals that provide the local people with their sustenance, not to mention the rhythm of their lives. This year I've toured six villages and recorded my dramatic observations on each one. Sarsara's village, which faces the River Nabi, was my last fact-finding destination. This is the great river of whose banks poets have sung countless praises. Each, in his own language, offered to its sweet waters love, reverence, rituals, fabulous stories and reports of floods and drownings...

HASSAN BLASIM[39]

---

39 H. Blasim, *The Iraqi Christ*, tr. J. Wright (Manchester: Comma Press, 2013), 101.

The Antlomaniac delineates a clear solidarity between mania and omnicide as a malicious storyteller makes his way across consecutive villages to 'arouse that brutal, hostile memory.' He defames their others; he tweaks long-lasting animosities; he dabbles in aspersion, enmity, and grievance. There are old Bedouin stories about sadistic jinn who delight in offering false choices or false hope: making deals of release only then to kill their human associates, promising ways out only to dam them between four walls again, they tease and play with their prey in cat-like fashion (as overseers of the no-win situation). But the above monologue suggests a beautifully unique alternative—a figure delighting in false reports of threat (bluffing like a gambler with no cards in hand)—for whom every new town is a chance to 'paint a bleak picture' of bloodbaths and volcanic destinies. These games, however, can yield only a masochistic outcome: for in the aftermath of the prediction's failure, this bandit will obviously suffer discredit or even fatal punishment for ringing false alarms. He gains nothing, then, for his catastrophic pranks: it is an errand likely to end with his head on a tray or spike, and yet his taste for 'fabulous stories and reports of flood' remains unslaked.

Another in this literary configuration makes his identity synonymous with torrents, writing once that 'I know him—he named me flood', and elsewhere: '"[t]he world needs a deluge," I said and wept instead of rage.'[40] What differs, though, is that this latter author wavers between cold facticity, necessity, or mourning and thereby shows no indications of the joyous tone of the earlier figure who revels in describing havoc for the 'rare birds and insects and the flocks of animals' and whose language appreciates only the halting of each place's life-rhythm. One looks scornfully ahead at what must soon come, while the other grins in merriment at the most vigorous descriptions of what will never come: he who traffics in charades and misrepresentation; he who reaps the getting-caught; he who scatters ironic omens, telling peoples of half-dry rivers that they will perish beneath excessive waters. This is the rare pleasure-principle of the liar who has discovered the supreme lie (that of the nothing's flood and the flood's nothingness).

Note: A futuristic library was built in 2017 in Tianjin, China with over 1.2 million books that stretch from floor to ceiling in uneven serous arcs, arranged in states that abandon solidity and instead resembling something closer to hovering or floating forces, whirlpool or tornado, which convey the look of a textual downpour: endless volumes being washed away in a sea with no protective ark. Similarly, a futuristic bookstore recently opened in Hangzhou, China makes use of extreme circularity

---

[40] Adonis, *Selected Poems*, tr. K. Mattawa (New Haven, CT: Yale University Press, 2010), 30; Adonis, *The Pages of Day and Night*, 67.

in order to plunge one through a wonderland of optical illusions, elliptical rooms, and coiling shelves that feel like the rotations of a Ferris Wheel or merry-go-round, and all supplemented by the halo-effect of illuminated mirrors so as to seat one in the middle of a radiant flood.

Flood and exaggeration; panic; bleakness; hostility; war; volcano; blood-flow; thirst; memory; perishing; rhythm; drama; the river

Thalassomania (Oceans)

The cafes in the center of town are deserted, everyone has emigrated in the direction of the northern edge of the city, in the heights over Algiers, at El-Biar, the Telemny, Hydra, whence the extent of the devastation can be best seen, whence the disaster can be seen coming, whence people will be in the first rows of seats to see the city get swallowed up by the sea…

RÉDA BENSMAIA[41]

For disaster is on board, the devil's our pilot
And hellish flames our beacon.
Men do not get near pale sailors
Who pass the sails with their cavernous voices.
Men, do not board my black cruiser
For disaster is on board, the devil's our pilot
And the moon our port of call.

JOYCE MANSOUR[42]

---

41 Bensmaia, *The Year of Passages*, 50.1.
42 Mansour, *Essential Poems and Writings*, 165.

The Thalassomaniac eagerly awaits the hour when oceans swallow earth, an omnicidal longing that nonetheless can take two distinct paths of action (as evidenced by the excerpts above): the first figure's instinct is to climb high to gain a superior view of the tidal destruction; the second figure gathers a crew of 'pale sailors' and procures a ship to glide into the heart of the ocean's wrath. Hence, the first manic trajectory treats apocalypse as a theatrical event, one for which the thassomaniac craves balcony seating or a terrace overlooking this one-time performance beneath the night stars. This is the ecstasy of wallowing, voyeurism, and the vista, reminding us of those great early indigenous societies that constructed architectural monuments so vast or high that their designs could only be properly beheld by an omniscient sky-entity (and thus were intended exclusively for the gods): they perceived these watchers as personalities of benevolent or malevolent neutrality who had orphaned the world. In like manner, this particular thalassomaniac holds no interventionist intent—neither to flee, save, nor resist (only to survey)—but rather sits resignedly even as the debacle makes its way to the 'northern edge of the city', overtaking his body, first the legs, then the abdomen, chest, neck, and head, lap by lap, salt water permeating every cell, as the gradual foreclosure of possibility plays itself out across his own individual physiology.

The second manic trajectory, however, does not merely pause until reached but rather reaches out to the oceanic fiasco with the rapacious will of the commander. Thus the disaster is not something arriving from beyond but rather exists already 'on board' as the vessel charges into certain peril: like the storm-chaser who pursues trouble wherever it arises, she encroaches upon the apocalyptic sea with mad attraction, infiltrating its perceived glamour while yelling 'the devil's our pilot' over and again in deranged singsong excitation. She reminds us of that character from another nineteenth-century literary masterpiece, the insane whaling captain with missing limbs and giant scar sweeping down face and thorax, caused by thunderbolt, highly learned but also having lived among cannibals, and who drags a cadre of last-resort men into the jaws of an impassable fight with the abyss. He is described perfectly as 'grand, ungodly, god-like', much like our second author above who revels in her mastery of the bad voyage and misadventure. She too is the personification of remorselessness held by the 'grand, ungodly, god-like'; she too seeks the unsweet air of the ocean pounding against her 'black cruiser's' deck, its course set for chasmal and lunar whiplash; she too makes sail only on the day of unsafe passage.

Ocean and desertion; emigration; the edge; the heights; devastation; seeing; swallowing; disaster; the pilot; the devil; the beacon; the pale sailor; cavernousness; the port of call

Bathymania (Deep Water)

> *It is the lost dimension of the Sea that both enchants and scares us.*
> *The song of the Sea: its threnody for its lost dimension.*
> *It is not the Sea depths that scare us about the Sea; what scares us is the freedom that lurks there.*
>
> IBRAHIM AL-KONI[43]

The Bathymaniac is here motivated by the rich melancholic sadness of a forlorn place ('the lost dimension') and therefore listens for all traces or signals of its potential retrieval somewhere across the ocean floor. This vivification process, however, is a source of both terror and fascination, in that it requires submergence in a fatal exercise of freedom (like stepping off a building's edge): more acutely, it perhaps approximates the feeling of those great sandbars or straits that allow one to walk kilometres in electric blue, warm, shallow pools until suddenly coming across a sallow line and bone-chilling drop in temperature (reflecting one's having fallen off a cliff under the ocean's surface). This abrupt transition of tint and degree is more awful than any moral archetype

---

43 I. al-Koni, *A Sleepless Eye: Aphorisms from the Sahara*, tr. R. Allen (Syracuse, NY: Syracuse University Press, 2014), 59.

of transgression, for it marks an amoral slip into somewhere that does not want us, hosting millions of other unrelated creatures yet offering no hospitable conditions for our survival anymore—though we emerged evolutionarily from its womb. The bathymaniac, then, is the one harassed by the thought of such irreconcilable destitution, who thereby turns sorrow into uncontainable desire: to charge beyond the inviting surf of breakwaters and re-enter the uninviting, certain that the sea depths conceal some fallen zone of perfection. Psychoanalysis often discards such idealistic fantasies as the psychotic refuse of delusion, ignoring the astounding geographies associated with this category of 'lurking' utopias and the actual expeditions that went in physical search of them throughout history: Edenic gardens, Elysian Fields, journeys to the center of the earth, cities of gold, treasure caves of the forty thieves, bardos and purgatories, island mountains of the immortals, rooms of the holy grail and fountains of eternal youth. One might recall that another nineteenth-century literary masterpiece—featuring a manic doctor and his creature sewn together from the appendages of criminals, the insane, and the dead—begins with the letters of an equally manic explorer to the North Pole, his near-starved crew debating mutiny as they drift pointlessly amidst the arctic tundra in search of their own lost dimension. We picture the poor creature's husk as he flees the laboratory of his disgusted creator and runs off into the acid rain; we follow him into the nearby hills where the one called 'wretch' or 'fiend' contemplates his abhorrence, his stitched-together countenance and birth among lime pits; we understand him as the re-animated flesh of the repellent and of sub-optimal being. He is plaintive (pleading for restitution); he wears titles of both most harmed and most harmful, and he too sings 'threnodies' (wailing odes) of the half-strangled, his atonal voice squeezing like a manacle, memorialising the delinquent father he might soon kill. Consequently, our last image of the creature is of him vaulting across the icecaps, meeting a bathymaniacal end with frost-bitten sentience, and perhaps realizing finally that, by all measures, it is he who indeed houses the lost dimension in his very galvanised skin and bones: namely, that the inhuman is nothing more than the unrepressed, self-aware error of the human itself. A different utopian story (aboard the pulverised raft): one where the requiem of the immortal depth reflects only the absolute mistake of the mortal itself.

Deep Water and the lost dimension; enchantment; fear; threnody; freedom; lurking

Aquamania (Drowning)/Kymomania (Waves)

> *Gradually the sea grew higher…The waters rolled over him and the waves slid together…A mysterious force drew him toward the waves to cleanse him of life's misfortunes and unreal desires. The voice of the waves murmured in his ear, 'Come! Come!' The dark sea summoned him.*
>
> SADEQ HEDAYAT[44]

The Aquamaniac is something like the storm-swimmer or storm-surfer who waits for the worst conceivable weather (low pressure systems, howling wind swells): they love only the overcast skies and the thought of wading into pallid or obsidian waters. The steady strokes of their arms and legs in machinic synchronicity only mask the unruliness of their manic taste for balancing the imbalance, again confirming the great contrast between annihilation (as furor, delirium) and suicide (as lack, anxiety, resentment). For instance, comparative empirical studies of global methods of suicide report substantial deviations across culture, gender, and region with respect to deaths caused by drug overdose, poison, asphyxiation, firearm

---

44 Hedayat, *Sadeq Hedayat: An Anthology*, 113.

(gunshot), or jumping from heights, and yet almost universally drowning remains among the most infrequent approaches at less than one percent worldwide. (Note that a careful forensic pathology is necessary to differentiate intentional vs. accidental drowning). Moreover, the very criterion of suicidal drowning is complicated by the customary use of other supplemental materials in order to successfully complete the act (e.g. tying weights, concrete blocks, or anchors around neck and ankles, or ingesting substances to diminish consciousness and impair motor reflexes), all of which point to the body's instinctual opposition to the mental-emotional plan for this type of self-destruction.

But then there are those periodic historical accounts of individuals who, just like our protagonist in the above quotation, march casually into waters and drown themselves without observable resistance (almost as if being 'summoned'). They have been seen fully clothed and advancing serenely; they do not scrape or claw against submersion. What is the nature of this 'mysterious force' that would render the psychoanalyst's self-preservation principle inoperable and thus make even drowning appear a literally and figuratively breathtaking experience? Does this beckoning sensibility ('Come! Come!') override the controlling ego and the equally narcissistic gestures of living and suicide? Does it even abandon the formulaic universality of the death-drive in order to direct

AQUAMANIA/KYMOMANIA

us toward an aquamaniacal stunt navigated only by the select few (those who obsolesce psyche by will)? Note the perceptual emphasis above: that it is not a matter of one's going lower but rather the sea that 'grows higher'. In some mordant sense, it is the very fastening of 'unreal desires' to an outer bank of reverberation that permits no hindrance; to consign oneself to the indisputable momentum of the deed (if even to its terrible slowness) and thereby become *the corollary*.

Note: Is this theory of becoming-corollary—i.e. aftereffect, outcome, culmination, or inference of a previously proved proposition—again visible in the related writings of Kymomania (obsession with waves)? For example, another in our literary configuration speaks of 'Generous hysteria / When war will rain down on waves and beaches', and elsewhere that 'There are green waves wavering in the blue / And the sea / There are men hung in the vineyards', and lastly that 'He preferred the waves / Wandering in the distance / Faded creatures softly deformed in their placenta vice / Victims of an immense jaw galloping on the beach.'[45] These three stanzas together enable us to reach three conclusions: (1) that drowning requires a sort of hysterical preference (to elect the waves over oneself); (2) that the hanging of men on earth or in killing fields is either met by total indifference by the sea, or is in fact

---

45 Mansour, *Essential Poems and Writings,* 199, 245, 307.

an analogic sequel to some motive of the waters; (3) that the beaches are themselves hungry for our kind, treating us as secondary functions of their 'rolling'. We are the development ('faded creatures softly deformed'); we are the ramification called in again. Corollarium, from the Latin *corolla* meaning 'small crown or garland'—given to actors as extra payment or tip for their performative services (thus are we commissioned); Corollarium, in later philosophy, meaning a supplemental position stemming from another incontrovertible one (thus do our madnesses naturally follow themselves).

> *Drowning and the gradual; growing-higher; rolling; sliding; mysterious force; cleansing; unreal desire; voice; murmur; summoning*

Ablutomania (Washing, Bathing)

Will this be the longest day in history? No one is washing the dead. Let the dead wash themselves—I mean with blood flowing more freely than water. I hoard my treasure of water and use each drop with extreme care. Every drop has a role. Five hundred for washing the hair. Two thousand for the body. One hundred for the mouth. One hundred for shaving.

MAHMOUD DARWISH[46]

The Ablutomaniac begins pacing in contexts of forced scarcity and asymmetrical warfare: the urban landscape is riven by embankments, ramparts, and roadblocks of street gangs that cause embolisms of delivered goods for non-combatants. A temporal-spatial paradox arises (common to pain) in which time feels viciously prolonged while space feels viciously compressed. Furthermore, what emerges quickly in these scenarios is a tense duel in the logic of expenditure itself between necessity (survivalist calculation) and the sacred (sacrificial excess), such that even water consumption hangs in the balance of a new algorithmic model. Waste becomes an increasingly

---

[46] M. Darwish, *Memories for Forgetfulness*, tr. I. Muhawi (Berkeley, CA: University of California Press, 1995), 32.

intolerable offence; the stockpile takes on numinous proportions, and so the question presents itself: How does this atomising gaze of the hoarder who cultivates, coddles, and enshrines each droplet in its selected fate constitute a manic practice (especially given mania's avowed tendency for squandering or overflow)? The answer lies in the author's bizarre suggestion made in the wake of the absence of corpse-washers to attend to the many uncollected, marred bodies piling in the alleys outdoors: 'Let the dead wash themselves.' What appears like an apathetic aside is actually the pathos of an amazing psychosomatic proposal: And how might mania allow us to will the psychosomatic extraordinary? We have all heard anecdotes of inflated powers rendered to someone in a life-and-death situation, referred to as 'hysterical strength', often something like a mother lifting a heavy vehicle off her trapped child, for which the tentative explanation includes hypotheses of adrenaline rush, amphetamine release, neuronal circuit overload, and fast-twitch or slow-twitch muscle activation (resulting in energy spiking, pain insensitivity, and apparently superhuman fortitude). These are typically short-lasting bouts concluding in extreme dizziness and self-disbelief, but could the manic figure train themselves to perceive the state of emergency at will ('longest day in history'), thereby converting the normal mind-body into a regimen of enhanced durability, might, agility, and dynamism?

ABLUTOMANIA

This is conceivably how the dead might wash themselves; this is how madness drives psychosomatic production toward feats of maximum capacity.

Note: Another ablutomaniacal example of this accord involves the story of a refugee in a detention center clinging to a bag of his mother's bones. He often uses a scrap of orange cloth to clean her remains, and persists with lunatic stamina toward his goal of burying her somewhere safe, all the while bathing in lachrymal fluids: 'His mother's bones, the mirror, the wooden comb, the picture of the Imam Ali and the Quran were all in place, but what was missing was her head, which used to rub cheeks with his as she watered it with her tears and tortured sobs....'[47] Once again, a lone memory (of weeping) funnels itself manically into a psychosomatic near-miracle: to brave the unspeakable toil of illegal migration, to be hounded by police patrols and sleep in harsh thickets, to work slave-like in balloon factories until the next mountain crossing, to live in one-room apartments of packed strangers, to lose the maternal skull in Greek forests and somehow adjust hysterical fear into hysterical strength, all to honour the solemn vow of carrying a travel-sack of bones to an unblemished site: that is, to fulfill the work of ablution.

Washing and the longest day; the dead; hoarding; treasure; care; the role

---

47 Blasim, *The Madman of Freedom Square*, 67.

Part 9

Dysmorphomania (Physical Deformity)

Decapomania (Headlessness)

Teratomania (Monstrosity)

Dysmorphomania (Physical Deformity)

> *He couldn't, there in the long, broad wadi, find the other remains. Whenever he found a piece of her body, he'd place it in his bag, climb up to the heights and bury it there, so that his martyred mother had five graves along the tops of the wadi. The memorial stones stood like signposts, condemning the unknown transgressor.*
>
> IBRAHIM AL-KONI[48]

The Dysmorphomaniac, above all others, understands the benefits to be derived from becoming unrecognisable—forever shunned by beauty—alongside the techniques of splitting and amorphousness. In another work by this same author, a desert-god's entire arsenal revolves around such dysmorphic expertise—'I found you coiled snake-like around her. So why deny your ability to shape-shift?'[49]—but for now we remain with the battered subject of the passage above, who collects massacred shreds of his mother's body and turns them into touchstones of the accursed. It is an unusual ritual practice, one that defies the archetypally human instinct for proper burial—no mounds, pyres, tombs, erected monuments to both

---

[48] I. al-Koni, *The Bleeding of the Stone*, tr. M. Jayyusi and C. Tingley (Northampton, NY: Interlink, 2002), 68.

[49] Al-Koni, *The Seven Veils of Seth*, 280.

separate and preserve withered forms—by establishing the disunity of 'five graves' that together function as an alarm system. Instead, this young hunter-shepherd stages the deformed pieces of the progenitor in a limbo of radars and antennae that both warn him of trespassers and transmit the hatred of ages. It turns the martyrdom of the precursor into a modality of attack: her bisected limbs form a dysmorphic array of 'signposts', crests of retribution. Multiplicity taken to the vertex of world-abuse, now closer to rage that exceeds those known to be guilty, lashing out immanently against all as 'unknown transgressor' (to haemorrhage everything). Hence, the dysmorphic figure is never allowed transcendence to any grove of the afterlife or the hereafter; rather, they remain in the manic posture of ambush. Their forked path along this non-oasis is itself a map of execration—never judgment, only chastening—attained by further amputation of the once-mishandled.

Deformity and remains; pieces; the heights; five graves; signposts; condemnation

Decapomania (Headlessness)

> *I saw others who had been decapitated, scurrying down the pavements of this grieving homeland of ours in search of their heads, which had been cut off on some dark night. I saw heads whose features had been erased, so severely had they been tortured, heads which had been cut off and were now floating on a sea of blood and darkness in search of their tongues, which had been extracted with pincers.*
>
> GHADA SAMMAN[50]

The Decapomaniac employs a fundamental shared trope of horror and dark romanticism: that of manic loss and reclamation. This is the nexus where these genres meet, often embodied by a figure in search of a lost object (the ring, the box, the picture) or a lost organ (the heart, the eye, the head), though these are rarely narratives of convalescence or attained wholeness, but tend to follow an ever-worsening decline. The longer it takes to rescue the forsaken item, the more atrophied and irate the seeker becomes: with each passing second the soul poisons itself further ('features had been erased'). On the other hand, if the misplaced or thieved aspect ('cut off on some dark night') should ever somehow be re-sutured, it will only

---

50 G. Samman, *Beirut Nightmares*, 64.

radically unfurl the evil of this being who arrives too late: evil being defined here as subversive power (to bring down the house of cards of the real).

Beheading has always been with us: its application swings across a pendulum of ancient, mediaeval, modern, and postmodern epochs; its use tempts coercive state apparatuses, paranoid emperors, democratic mobs, and revolutionary extremists alike. The favoured punishment of both royalty (the apogee of kings) and of regicidal movements (the killing of kings), it can accommodate the visceral, the symbolic, and the virtual in a manifold notion of vengeance-turned-spectacle. Nevertheless, it is mania alone that could fathom the return of the headless, 'scurrying down the pavements' in some lurid saga; it is mania alone that has caused otherwise 'normal' individuals throughout history to suffer the shared hallucination of decapitated mystics picking up their sliced heads and running off cradling them in their arms:

> They say that when 'Ayn al-Qudat was beheaded and his body was thrown into the middle of the famous square in Hamadhan, the one which is now well-known as the Charcoal Square, Baba Tahir happened to be passing by when he saw a crowd of onlookers surrounding [al-Qudat's] body. When he realized what the commotion was all about, he approached the body and with the tip of his toe struck it and said,

'men of God do not sleep like this.' 'Ayn al-Qudat instantly stood up, picked up his severed head, put it under his arm-pit, and fled. The onlookers chased after him until he reached the public cemetery of Hamadhan, known as Ahl-i Qubur ('People of the Graves'), descended into a pit and disappeared from sight. That pit to this day is known as Ayn al-Qudat pit.[51]

Upon closer scrutiny, one observes three interlinked maniacal conduits at work in the story above: the mania of the first mystic whose craniumless body suddenly bolts from the public square; the mania of the second mystic who rouses the great predecessor from his 'sleep' with a tapped foot and a disapproving statement that conceals a resurrection spell; the mania of the crowds who then chase after the headless infidel-genius and thereafter name the site after his fantastical return. Hence we verify a series of manic injunctions that backfire against the original decree of execution, revealing a paradoxical effect whereby an initial act of detachment leads to a miraculous conjoining of gestures (the lost head becoming a bridge, pipeline, or aqueduct across time and narrative history). Still, this convulsive trail does not emanate from just any decapitated frame: the original holder, no doubt, must be

---

[51] Hamid Dabashi recounts this supposed eyewitness tale regarding the death of mystic 'Ayn al-Qudat al-Hamadhani as an example of what he calls the 'subversive carnivalesque'. H. Dabashi, *Truth and Narrative: The Untimely Thoughts of 'Ayn al-Qudat al-Hamadhani* (New York: Routledge, 1999), 539.

a famed affiliate with certain strands of lunatic experience, a figure given to insurrectionary flirtations, such that others could willingly entertain their capacity to return to challenge the tiered structures of the day for the crown. Never underestimate the one who wants something back: the headless alone threaten whatever exists at the top; for the headless maintain their own axis of sovereignty.

Headlessness and scurrying; the pavement; grieving; the homeland; searching; the cut; erasure; torture; floating; extraction

Teratomania (Monstrosity)

> *For I have been made in a strange and frightening shape*
> *My bones were not hidden from you when I was being created*
> *I was molded in the bowels of the earth*
>
> FORUGH FARROKHZAD[52]

The Teratomaniac fires off a missive against the almighty while squatting in a leper colony surrounded by children with thickening skin lesions, nerve damage, compromised respiratory tracts, tissue loss, muscle weakness, and cartilage erosion. Fingers curl with the onset of paralysis; nerves enlarge around elbows and knees; feet are covered with ulcerated sores; eyes gradually stop blinking, lose their lashes, become dried out and surrender to blindness. The author herself arrives at the gates of this wasteland colony as a healthy outsider, and stares at these afflicted bodies in play, school, weddings, and religious prayer (with scriptural recitations conducted by an armless patient since no clergy will tread there). The poetic composition that emerges instinctually from her experience of clinicopathological segregation is one that convicts the divine itself (to reproach the claymaker). She manically inverts the leper's blamelessness into the creator's

---

52 F. Farrokhzad, 'The House Is Black', from the film of the same name (Tehran, 1963).

blame, and catapults line upon line of censure against the dreamer of 'strange and frightening shapes'; she forges a negative valence of contempt around her words—a statement no longer about the creation of monstrosity but rather about creation *as* monstrosity. In this sense, she echoes the dismay of another in our literary alliance who, upon entering the worst slums of a cosmopolis, once penned the following indictment: 'A Medusan spectre ascends between the shoulders. A market with slaves of every race. Humanity living like plants in glass gardens. Unseen, invisible wretches submerge like dust in the web of space spiralling victims.'[53] Both stagger among monsters awhile; both call for a vanquishing of the causal agent.

It is no slight thing to put a god on trial: indeed, there are suppressed accounts of religious clerics who convened, often during genocidal periods, to hold court and preside over such hearings and weigh up the possibility of divine negligence. Far more heretical than the accusation of the non-existence of a god is the accusation of the failure of an existent god—though one wonders whether we are referring to ontological implosion (a problem of being) or aesthetic implosion (a problem of appearance), or whether teratological awe is precisely the juncture wherein these two faults become forever inseparable.

---

53 Adonis, *A Time Between Ashes and Roses*, tr. S. Toorawa (Syracuse, NY: Syracuse University Press, 2004), 129.

TERATOMANIA

The charge is miscreation. Myriad theo-juridical problems arise here (when trying a god who does not show): How does one ascertain motive, alibi, prosecution, and defence? Are all the collective living and dead on Earth simultaneously evidence and witness? Who plays judge, jury, and executioner against the essence, or is the verdict itself a mere formality? Furthermore, is miscreation premeditated (malicious intent—'my bones were not hidden from you') or temperamental (a crime of passion—'molded in the bowels'), or is it perhaps the spontaneous action of something whose brute force supersedes its intelligence (capable of willing what should not be and does not work)? The latter finding would be a simple upward extension of Christ's diagnosis upon the cross—'they know not what they do'—into celestial precincts, to implicate the god that also *knows not what it does* (though in this case without any appeal for forgiveness). For it is altogether possible that human ignorance is mere mimicry, made in the image of its divine originator. Fortunately, however, mania surpasses all frameworks of law: it is a ferocity that turns even detestation into an ecstatic concern; its tribunal is both self-abolishing and world-abolishing; it is a mercilessness that carries out the mercy-killing of the source (while dousing itself in its abomination).

Monstrosity and strangeness; fright; shape; bones; the unhidden; creation; moulding; the bowels

Part 10
Eremiomania (Stillness)
Clinomania (Staying Bedridden)
Somnemania (Sleep)
Insomnemania (Sleeplessness)

Eremiomania (Stillness)

> *I paid vast amounts to three workers in the ministry to help dig up the soldier's grave. There he was with his decayed body and a hole in his forehead. I shook his body several times to make sure he was dead. I whispered in his ear, then shouted and insulted him. I challenged him, if he could, to open his mouth or move his little finger. But he was dead enough. A worm came out of his neck chasing another worm, then the two of them disappeared inside again somewhere near his shoulder.*
>
> HASSAN BLASIM[54]

The Eremiomaniac offers us an excellent opportunity to examine two new philosophical variations on mania: (1) the transmission of intensity from one subject or object of compulsive desire to another; (2) the anticipation of potential fervour in something completely dormant. Before addressing these forms of manic wherewithal, let us set the scene for the short story from which the above is excerpted: One day, the editor of a military newspaper receives a mysterious package of manuscripts sent by a soldier on the front line, and is shocked to find five elementary school notebooks full of tales unrivalled in

---

54 Blasim, *The Madman of Freedom Square*, 19.

both style and content (the finest ever read). He remarks that the unknown author has attained the elusive 'tenth rank of language, the rank from which fire is created, and from which, in turn, devils are spawned' and tries to locate him, to no avail, until he receives notice that the soldier was killed in the latest air raids. The editor quickly takes advantage of this by publishing the stories in his own name, gaining an international reputation and becoming a celebrated figure among dignitaries, cultural ministries, and the global intelligentsia, until several months later he receives three new parcels of manuscripts and then countless more, presumably from the same deceased soldier. The volumes fill entire warehouses, each newfound text a grenade of escalating brilliance; this rate of sublimity terrifies the editor, leading to the scenario recounted in the quote wherein he exhumes and shakes the dead soldier's body, and later builds a 'special incinerator' in which to burn the corpse, the notebooks, and ultimately himself. A manic finale in which subject, object, and other all go up in flames.

Given this ingenious plot, we can posit many theoretical questions on the paradox of eremiomania (mad stillness) which circle back around to the original two points. Most important among these is whether mania can be decanted into a non-manic subject (relegation) or given from one to another (virulence). Note that the editor is no visionary: he is an intelligent technocrat with just enough sensitivity to recognise another's genius, a figure who some combination of ambition and admiration allows to steal the soldier's manic legacy—or is it that the stranger deliberately wired the stories to him as mechanisms of incantatory persuasion? This is not the classical paradigm of the muse: the texts themselves are chalices, and the nightly readings constitute a form of tangential initiation rite, an intoxication by the wines of a certain faraway mania. Nothing is inchoate, then; none of this is spurred by an intrinsic psychological property, but rather by incidental exposure of the lukewarm and the slothful to some inclement draft from the outside. The true author incentivises burglary of his own talent by a non-productive figure; he encourages beautiful greed, envy, and avarice and makes them grow voluptuously into insane behaviours; he seizes upon the editor's listless routine as a perfect infrastructure or breeding ground wherein stillness can mature into eremiomania; he stokes the pure cyclicality of pages to form a convection oven or a rapidly-congealing, associative paste that reassigns his mad assets, redeploying them from the warzone back to the stalled human world.

Secondly, we wonder how it is that mania can shift its object of concentrated desire, and with the same degree of ultra-investment, for in the course of this short story the editor goes from an all-consuming interest in the books to an all-consuming interest in the corpse:

he taunts the half-decomposed body; he watches the movement of other creatures passing through its orifices—confirming its inability to defend itself against violation by creeping things—but still suspects a lingering animus beneath its quietude (thus the eremiomaniacal turn). And in fitting omnicidal fashion, the editor takes active responsibility for bringing all facets to the point of combustion. The original mania of battle had become the mania of storytelling, which itself intercepted the mania of the hapless reader, who injected it catalytically into a comatose world. A logic of deportation whereby madness thrives in the fallow, in the interim, in the slack life of inertia. Thus, if the first question is a matter of identity-theft, the second is about nothing less than energy-theft (or rather donation).

Stillness and payment; the grave; decay; the hole; whisper; insult; challenge; movement; disappearance

Clinomania (Staying Bedridden)

> *Ever since I have been confined to my bed people have paid little attention to me…My condition grew worse. Only my old grey-haired nurse…attended me, bringing me my medicine or sitting beside my bed, dabbing cold water on my forehead.*
>
> SADEQ HEDAYAT[55]

The Clinomaniac affords us insight into two instrumental performers of madness: the figure who is *their own* worst enemy, and the manic companion. The natural inclination of the former is to damage themselves without the slightest exertion; they lift not a single finger but rather allow consciousness to ruin itself while reclined horizontally in a large bed. Note that, left to his own devices, the above protagonist has purposely entered retrogressive states, has permitted the false atmosphere of rest to facilitate a devious minimalist decline. That others 'paid little attention' to this process is merely a sign that they have correctly understood this figure as a lost cause, and as one whose mind-body takes on a backbiter's or inquisitor's function (the treasonous within). His dream is nothing more than to master dwindling and the art of destruction through

---

55 Hedayat, *The Blind Owl*, 66.

immobility, like another in our literary configuration who writes 'Embrace me, creator of fatigue, give me your hammocks, test me'.[56] Both pray to the same god of weariness; both defile themselves amid blankets and pillows; both find some vitalist tingle in the immense dulling of self and room; and both send their own timelines in reverse by turning beds into anti-cradles that will inevitably weaken them unto death.

The second figure dwells in what is perhaps a more subtle conceptual province: for the manic companion ('my old grey-haired nurse') is at once ingénue, pantomime character, and stage director; she changes covers, flips mattresses, or brings soothing water. Like the second in a duel, her job is one of embodied neutrality: never to attempt saving but rather to remain gracefully attendant to the other's fatal practice, intervening only to bring requested accessories to the pallet. She is aware that the medicine on her tray is but a hollow placebo (it inoculates against nothing). It is not clear, then, whether she serves the clinomaniacal subject or the clinomaniacal drama itself, since both are collaboratively intertwined, but her understated presence in the wings is a supplement of great value in reaching the extreme limit of the bedridden. She remains voiceless so as not to drown out the sounds of his wheezing; she adopts the humble pose of the ancillary in

---

56 Adonis, *A Time Between Ashes and Roses*, 85.

honour of the collapsing centre. Above all else, she keeps him company along the euthanistic path ('sitting beside my bed'); she does not allow him to quit this radical self-quitting; she places cooling rags across the fevered head and thereby makes things vaguely better so that they might become far worse.

Note: The term 'Quarantine' (from mediaeval Latin/Italian *quarentena*, meaning 'forty days') follows a crooked track that cuts through the provinces of trade, science, and religious mythology: (1) a fourteenth-century maritime policy of forced isolation whereby ships arriving from plague-struck lands would be kept waiting in port for forty days; (2) a medical concept devised by the iconic Persian polymath Ibn Sina (Avicenna, 980–1037) whose suspicion of contamination spread by microorganisms (particularly tuberculosis) led him to institute a protocol called *al-Arba'iniya* (the fortieth) in the Islamic World, from which some say Venetian transcontinental merchants later adopted the same practice of sanitary distancing; (3) a theological reference to Mount Quarantania (Arabic *jabal al-qarantal*) or the Mount of Temptation, a steep hill near the Palestinian city of Jericho, 1200 feet above sea level and affording panoramic vistas over the Judean Desert, Jordan Valley, and Dead Sea, where Christ supposedly fasted in the wilderness for forty days and nights while visited by three of the Devil's temptations (to turn stones into bread, to jump from the sheer rock face and have angels break his fall, and to accept dominion over all the kingdoms of the world), before which the famished prophet showed unshaking hermetic restraint. In all three instances, however, we detect a shared logic of asceticism born of the manic imagination, for all are consumed by the notion of pre-emptive combat against invisible or unprovable foes: that of the contagious sailor or foreigner arriving from far-spread shores; that of the microscopic particle working its way through lungs; and that of the demonic voice rustling in messianic heads.

Staying Bedridden and confinement; attention; worsening; the nurse; attendance; dabbing

Somnemania (Sleep)

It will teach me how to seduce
Men, deer, angels with double wings,
It will take away my thirst, my clothing, my illusions,
It will sleep,
But my sleep runs across roofs
Murmuring, gesturing, violently making love
With cats.

JOYCE MANSOUR[57]

The Somnemaniac yields a state that somehow fuses lucid dreaming (awake in the sleeping world) and sleepwalking (asleep in the waking world) in a relay-race of seductions. Seduction here, however, achieves the coveted goal of an ability to seduce all things ('men, deer, angels with double wings'), constructing a mosaic of indiscriminate attraction by either (1) generating something universally irresistible, or (2) turning chameleonesque in a way that unlocks the specific code of endearment of whatever it meets. Nevertheless, it is a promiscuity worn bare—for this mistress of the somnambular herself forfeits all 'thirst' and 'illusions' in order to shoot herself like rays across the rooftops of the human, animal, and divine orders.

---

57 Mansour, *Essential Poems and Writings*, 147.

Thus we ask: What kind of manic figure is desired by all? Furthermore, what kind of manic figure can lull all into gentle sleep?

She is the *raconteur* (figure of skilful recounting) whose 'murmuring, gesturing' conceals a will to amorous cruelty in the feline realm of alley cats: in this sense, the pairing of violence with lovemaking in the final line once again mirrors the intimacy between mania and omnicide that runs through the heart of this book. Her nudity ('it will take away my clothing') is precisely her costume; her language is a poetics of feigning that makes all castes languish, drowse, and swoon. She retires the knowing subject, just as she brings predatory organisms into hibernation, and even the beneficent messengers above will cut off their wings for her and take intermission. She is the most gutted-out and bereft, and therefore the most tantalising at every level (like a gutter that gathers all blown debris).

She is also the *snake-charmer* par excellence, whose wiles confirm this important tendency: mania often drapes itself in softness. Does this puzzle rely on blankness (the clean slate onto which all conceivable fantasies can be projected) or fullness (the jungle of congested forms whose vines attach to every potential becoming)? Or do these strategies blend in the self-altering visage of one who possesses no face and therefore a thousand masks:

a repose brought on by the collusion of presence and absence?

Note: Given that conventions of beauty/attraction are obviously governed by differences in particular cultural-temporal customs and trends, traditional psychoanalysis might situate the premise of something 'universally desirable' only in forms that tap into supposedly primordial drives (sexuality, aggression): that is, dreams of libidinal energy including disguised symbols of balloons, knives, fountains, reptiles, boxes, jewels, sweets, fruits, falling or sliding motions. Accordingly, the same holds for phobic forms whereby something universally frightening would necessarily derive from ancient fears contained in the most originary psychic recesses (death, humiliation, separation, pain): that is, dreams that might include symbolic experiences of being chased, teeth falling out, long journeys, immobility, insect swarms, or threatening strangers. In either instance, however, classical psychoanalytic dream theory holds that the content of both types of sleep imagery is consistent with wish-fulfilment, another cornerstone forever agitated by the arrival of the mad dreamer.

The somnemaniac figure above never alludes to any such inherent, archetypal source of universal attraction or repulsion: instead, she refers explicitly to procedures of taught seduction in which one abandons archaic signifiers for novel encounters of the unforeseen (like no other). Hence mania reorients the wish toward learned whimsicality, exoticism, and surprise: never a deep-seated root-theory but one of numberless idiosyncratic petals delicately attached only to extemporaneous, preternatural, or incongruous satisfaction (one of a kind). It is these alone that give rise to dream-imageries of things that have never existed before.

Sleep and taught seduction; roofs; murmur; gesture; love

Insomnemania (Sleeplessness)

A sleeping child in my arms sick...
did not rest from the pain until midnight...
o stars absorbed in staring,
this is my child who is sick...

FORUGH FARROKHZAD[58]

The Insomnemaniac compels us to contemplate a breakdown of the sleepless night into three acute chambers: the mania of the vigil; the mania of the vigilant; the mania of the vigilante. The link between disease (physical brokenness), unease (existential brokenness), and appeasement (solace through breaking) evinces itself palpably in the figure of the mother rocking her unwell child. No respite: she will stay awake incessantly even as the infant drifts in and out of consciousness, atoning for its every breath in perfect lockstep while striving to leverage her individual endurance against this state of misrule. Mania of the vigil: she sits in a low-lit room half-illuminated by candles, eating nothing, turning her own chest into a bastion as her thoughts become lookouts for the undebatable. Mania of the vigilant: she will not tear her unblinking eyes for one second from the face of the

---

58 Farrokhzad, *A Lonely Woman*, 15.

weak child—whether singing, praying, or crying—for such sentinels of the highest order have gazes always on 'the eve' of things. Like those knights in chapels who wore white robes (to symbolise purity) beneath red robes (to symbolise the willingness to be wounded) beneath black robes (to symbolise readiness to die for the king), she too dresses herself in the raiment of devotional watching and would gladly trade her death for the young one's life. Mania of the vigilante: she turns radically choleric in the last line, promising eviction for eviction, drawing down the attention of the night skies to her aching offspring and declaring again that 'this is my child who is sick' as if in warning: if the child dies in her arms, there will be a counter-onslaught. Here she becomes the wild card, at once riled and livid, making sleeplessness an apprentice to the vindictive and thereby scheduling the prospect of a great experiment in wrath: if for thousands of years it was believed that the stars could curse human lives, then is it so far-fetched to consider conditions where humans could curse the stars in turn? So it is that the site of a failed vigil transforms the vigilant into the vigilante (and god help the world thereafter).

Note: Doomsday costumes are among those rare instances where we see sensibilities so clearly manic and apocalyptic occupying a shared visual space: it is here alone that the mimetic gameplay of fashion is directed toward the end of all things. During the second wave of the Black Death, a French seventeenth-century medical doctor named Charles de Lorne designed a birdlike mask with protruding beak whose image to this day remains synonymous with terror in the collective imagination. The garment was initially modelled on the armoured look of soldiers—with a long-hanging waxen coat and round glass spectacles affixed to the bird-mask—to shield doctors against contraction when examining those dying of bubonic plague. The curved beak was filled with scented herbs, spices, and dried flowers in accordance with the 'miasma theory' of the times (preceding the later germ-theory) whereby it was believed that noxious smells such as rotting garbage or infected flesh could transmit the fatal substance. Thus the awful pointed mask protected physicians from inhaling the foul airs of those to whom they administered treatment, though we can only speculate on the wide eyes of those sick children visited by such ministers of care, the last image they beheld before death being that of a thing clad in leather boots, gloves, and overcoat with a wooden stick (to fend off the clutching hands of the sick) and a face of bird-like features. Thus the manic hypothesis of airborne tainting gives rise to an elaborate mimetic outfit of those night-walking birdmen healers who will not leave our memories.

Note: The increasing rise of dystopian literature and cinema in modernity often involves the concept of *waking in someone else's game*: more exactly, of being caught in another's scheme (killer mazes, competitions, contraptions), for which our primary strategies of play (skill, chance, role-playing, sensation) are rendered useless by virtue of the obvious fact that another decides the rules and that we ourselves have not assented voluntarily by free will. In these rare circumstances (those of an anonymous virus, natural disaster, or unreachable overlord), we are not players but rather reductively move along as playthings on another's checkerboard or turning wheel. Ultimately, this leaves only one strategic option: that of an alternative definition of imitative role-play, much like the moment in horror stories when the monster shrieks and the victim shrieks reactively, or when the fiend claws and the victim raises their hands. This is often incorrectly understood as a defensive reflex or even as a negation of the feared entity; rather, it is pure mimicry that is at stake here, the last desperate resort of joining or succumbing to becoming-alike. It motions, we motion; it screams, we scream (surrendering to resemblance). Such mimicry also betokens the inventive facet of mania whereby consciousness playacts its own object of compulsion, like the delirious patchwork sewing of a crow's mask when confronting a pathogen that swoops down from the upper airs.

Sleeplessness and the child; the arms; sickness; pain; midnight; the stars; absorption; staring

Part 11
Typhlomania (Blindness)
Achluomania (Darkness)

Typhlomania (Blindness)

> *The moment when the dark night returns, not a trace of my blind readings, not a trace of my blind wanderings, not a trace of my blindest memory, not a trace of my tracks left blindly behind me, not a trace of my blind larceny, of my fears, of my falls, not a trace of my oblivion, not a trace of the blood of the blindman within me...*
>
> RÉDA BENSMAIA[59]

The Typhlomaniac raises the disturbing proposition of the 'blindman within': at first glance this seems to justify the almost groping nature of the language itself, the staggered clauses resembling an unsighted person knocking around a room and clasping for objects on all sides. Then again, this cannot be the case: for the blindman leaves 'not a trace' (tracelessness being the conceptual criterion for perfect crimes), which makes us revise the interpretative image into a figure of extreme grace, perhaps even one who turns sightlessness into its own refined lens. Note the impressive row of expressions in which 'blindness' repeats itself insistently, although with highly inconsistent conceptual branches: blind spot (occlusion); blindsided or blind luck (accident); blind drunk (oblivion); blind

---

59 Bensmaia, *The Year of Passages*, 62.3.

alley (danger); double-blind (testing); stone-blind (totality); blinded by the light (revelation); blind faith (fanaticism); swearing blind (insistence); turning a blind eye (mercy); robbing blind (mercilessness). Would the typhlomaniac, then, be precisely this seer-like blindman capable of turning a supposed perceptual void into all these many techniques of influence?

We may enlist four examples of willed blinding: (1) those martial artists of 'no-mind awareness' who practiced with eyes shut, offering training demonstrations of both offensive and defensive forms that favoured grappling, holding, and push-hands styles; (2) those executed rebels who chose blindfolds (where only the eyes are covered) in defiance of the executioner's hood (where only the eyes are uncovered), the two garments duelling before the firing squad or axe; (3) the obscure avant-garde movement of four French youths whose 'great game' included ingesting poisonous leaves, anaesthetics, strychnine, or carbon tetrachloride (a cleaning fluid and insect killer), focusing their sight on mirror surfaces until shapes blurred toward uncanny motion or attempting paroptic vision (registering visual phenomena without use of the eyes), and running or bicycling through their rural town blindfolded, a group whose prodigious leader once wrote 'I hate you, mask of gold, mist and fire, circular / Blind monster blinding all the prey around';[60] (4) those Oedipal kings and monks who blinded themselves, thereafter becoming like nomadic bicephalous beings with the reputed power to curse or bless cities through simple touch or word. All four cases have a touch of mania within, but our blindman above adds yet another existential slant: he waits for 'the dark night' (temporality of universal blindness) to move others cleverly to his cause, leaving no fingerprints of his memories, no footprints in blood, while making time and sensation matters of territorial advantage.

> *Blindness and the moment; night; the return; reading; wandering; memory; tracelessness; larceny; fear; falling; oblivion; blood; the blindman*

---

[60] R. Gilbert-Lecomte, *Black Mirror: The Selected Poems of Roger Gilbert-Lecomte*, tr. D. Rattray (Barrytown, NY: Station Hill Press, 2010).

Achluomania (Darkness)

> *And if his expectations turn out to be true, this Eastern region will in a short while be under siege by two types of priests of darkness. I agree with his forecast, deeming it the final stage of the ongoing disintegration and one of the forms of the coming catastrophe. But we differ endlessly about his claim that such an outcome is all that can save us, because one darkness can triumph over another and leave the dawn for us.*
>
> MAHMOUD DARWISH[61]

The Achluomaniac is caught between two peddlers of *the forecast*: the first cleric tells a story of full amplitude wherein darkness overruns the world and takes universal control, while the second tells of a darkening tied sequentially to bounty, windfall, and voluminous gain. This is how the conceptual cinderblocks of 'catastrophe', 'triumph', and 'dawn' find a common masonry built into the above excerpt: they form a cube-like theory of *the reward* that arises only from deepest privation. The victorious age (of plentiful harvest) thus follows the long night, like a dynamo (that which cannot stop once started) whose coils are wound by the torsion of a world-eclipse. This is the mania of the crepuscular, the tenebrous, and those

---

61 Darwish, *Memories for Forgetfulness*, 156.

penumbra-terminologies that have fallen out of use in an era of fluorescent neon signs but which carry their own arcane logic of friction and voltage. This is also the mania of the night-raid, which converts darkness into an instrument of guerrilla war against those who entitle themselves to relaxation without first wearing veils of denial and detriment. If a supreme twentieth-century thinker once juxtaposed the violence of being tied to train tracks (equated with reason's limits) with that of the spider or snake (equated with the sacred inhuman), giving the latter alone the title of sovereignty (pure indifference, serving no means or goals) alongside rights to a 'solar economy', then we can certainly also fathom a nocturnal economy that would shower with generosity those who first survive 'ongoing disintegration' into the pitch-black. This priest of 'expectation' is therefore a harlequin character of the first order: a servant of nimble dislocations who foils his master's plan (the human masses), decked out in diamond-chequered suit and bright trickster's mask, and most importantly carrying a magic wand capable of one dramatic function: changing the scenery. He comes as an auxiliary figure preaching salvation through suspension, drawing the transitional curtain and thereby introducing us to the last act of the 'final stage', all the while waving his cane at leaden skies, bidding them to descend in their mad entirety.

Darkness and expectation; siege; the priest; forecast; the final stage; disintegration; catastrophe; saving; triumph; dawn

Part 12

Aeromania (Air)

Animania (Soul)

Respiromania (Breath)

Anemomania (Winds, Drafts)

Etheromania (Sky)

Nephomania (Clouds)

Aviomania (Flight)

Basimania (Falling)/Trypomania (Holes)

Aeromania (Air)

> *Prepare your heart like a recording device*
> *so that I might sing my anthem:*
> *the anthem of the pressed guts of the orange*
> *in the dank air of the prison...*
> *in the burning air of torture...*
> *in the air of the suffocation of the hanging-place,*
> *and which has not yet vomited the bloody names*
> *in the pain-coated fever of confession*
>
> AHMAD SHAMLU[62]

The Aeromaniac here speaks of that mercurial oxygen found only in the cell or dungeon, beneath the boundary layer of the troposphere where the tortured and the hanged await their confiscation. All the unwritten histories of the world are presumably kept in this air's ledger (especially those of treachery and bile); all silenced testimonies compiled in 'anthems' sung into the ether as the noose tightens around the windpipe's meridian. This is the opposite of both apology and apologia: here the punished remain unrepentant, expressing no regret; here the punished offer no formal defence, justifying nothing before their accusers. The tablets of their fatal sincerity

---

[62] Shamlu, *Born Upon the Dark Spear*, 6.

are stored in the 'recording device' of this pressurised aeromania like a time-release capsule: the conviction that, amid the staleness, must, and moth-eaten cellars of the prison, there will someday be 'vomited the bloody names' that once filled their serpentines. Thus, as suggested by another in our poetic configuration who writes: 'Air is now blowing like a cough in the throats of space/—Let me create a talisman for my condition', there is a necessity to convert subterranean gaseous space into a microphonic speaker whose broadcast is also an amulet against mortification.[63]

Note: The Persian *siyah-chal* (literally 'black pit'), among the worst conceivable modes of incarceration in past centuries, was a windowless vault near the king's palace where condemned heretics were collared by heavy chains and led down three flights of stairs into a huge cistern permitting not a single ray of light. They say that these denizens of the rank, uncirculated air below would often sing together in chorus to pass the time.

Note: The ancient Egyptian Thoth, lunar god of writing, wisdom, magic, equilibrium, and the calendar, arbitrator of conflicts, self-created at the outset of time, worshipped by scribes, he to whom ink-drop sacrifices were made, considered the great persuader and counsellor, consort of Seshat (goddess-keeper of the books), was

---

63 Adonis, *Selected Poems*, 283.

believed to author an ever-infinitising compendium upon whose parchments were recorded all the names of the dead and all the disputes of the living. The mythologies warn that whomsoever reads this book will become the most invincible sorcerer alive but will also be accursed for gaining knowledge from 'The Lord of Divine Words'. Although Thoth is a deity of underworld treatises who rarely intervenes except as 'Master of the Balance', he is typically represented in the form of an ibis—a creature of the air, millions of which were found mummified around the centre of the god's cult—pictured with palette and stylus, and whose papyrus documents are thought to play some unknown enforcer's role in the act of final reckoning (for the neutral and the omnicidal share important paths).

Air and the recording device; the anthem; pressure; guts; dankness; burning; suffocation; vomiting; pain; fever; the name; the confession

Animania (Soul)

I stuffed a dead man's nose
And his soul kept on knocking, knocking
Waiting to get away from the body of his past
Begged for my pity for his hour in flight
Waned as a tired God waited for him.

JOYCE MANSOUR[64]

The Animaniac is one whose mad dream consists in becoming a *soul-strander*: that is, one with special powers to seal the traditional escape-routes of the spirit toward its final exospheres. She plugs the nostrils of the dead man; she blocks all elevation; she will not let his soul sign the register of the afterlife's hotel. Rather, it must become *the unleaving* and *the remnant*. As such, the soul grows increasingly foetid and jaundiced: it slams itself in desperate gyrations; it bangs against interior walls of ligaments and tendons for release ('knocking, knocking'). Meanwhile, the patron-client relation between heaven and earth is obstructed, as god and corpse sit in shared meekness, a simple childish gesture having been enough to render metaphysical processes defunct. The transcendent hand apparently cannot reach into the crypt's puddles;

---

64 Mansour, *Essential Poems and Writings*, 137.

it cannot extricate the stifled form that she has lodged there, thereby making both human and divine players supplicants who knock at her door to beseech permission ('begged for my pity'). Accordingly, the reference to 'waning' souls and 'tired' gods simultaneously belies another crucial secret: that even the eternal can be forcibly exhausted.

Note: An accompanying figure to the soul-strander is *the soul-stealer*, who traps pieces of the enemy's vital force within themselves, either to derive animistic power from them or to torment the other's marrow. Either way, it requires a sort of pneumatic hostage-taking, the prime example being the great Arabian figure Hind bint 'Utbah, a seventh-century aristocratic woman whose father, son, uncle, and brother were all killed in battle by the rising Islamic forces of her time, and who thereafter swore revenge and famously opposed their armies through acts of graphic degradation. In effect, Hind became legendary for taking legions of women into the high hills surrounding the battlefields to hound, jeer, dance, and pelt the incoming Muslim armies with stones: fabulous stories are told of her singular ability to shriek at the top of her lungs and rocket ululations at the fighters below. According to oral traditions compiled by the early hagiographer Ibn 'Ishaq, her grating squeals were surpassed only by her predilection for leading women to mutilate the fallen bodies of Muslim warriors, carving ears and noses into necklaces and anklets, and even fondling livers and cooking ripe hearts to be ingested in public view. This sensory manipulation of sound (shrillness), touch (anatomisation), and sight (bloody salivation) remains a performance art unrivalled for all time: against a new theology's obsession with *tawhid* (sacred unity) stands a soul-stealer's manic segmentation and reabsorption of enemy organs into her own unwholesome body (thus forever denying oneness).

> *Soul and stuffing; the dead man's nose; knocking; past; begging; pity; waning; tiring; waiting*

Respiromania (Breath)

> *He heard the specter exhale and inhale. He heard his heavy breathing, the beat of his heart, his certainty, his yearning, and his choked voice, which resembled the rattling of a snake: 'The spirit world granted me life the day it banished me. You killed me the day you saved me. Why? For what reason?'*
>
> IBRAHIM AL-KONI[65]

The Respiromaniac is a figure of ghostly immortality, one who has been rescued in the very midst of the last breath. The story's setting is captivating in itself: a spectral man stands at the entrance to a tent speaking with a desert god, known here as the Master Tactician, who once wrested him from death's hands (and to whom he is now forever indentured). Over time, the man does the bidding of the Tactician as ongoing payment for his deliverance centuries before when he was plucked back from the verge of death. This highlights the insidious conceptual link between salvation and enslavement, although clearly these many passing years have aroused the anger of his 'heavy breathing': note that breathing loudly is almost always experienced as an annoyance by those in hearing

---

65 Al-Koni, *The Seven Veils of Seth*, 263.

range, as if it transfers onerousness onto the other; note also the bizarre coupling of the spectre (that which is itself air) with breath. In any case, the two figures speak in riddles to one another: when accused of profanation (for challenging fate's claim), the Master Tactician answers that 'bringing the dead back to life is a sin, but to save a person on the brink of annihilation is a duty for the elite'; when asked why he would reopen the dying man's eyes only to gouge them for millennia, the Master Tactician answers 'Don't you know that I kill only those I love and revive only those I hate?' Thus we have two respiromaniacal points of inflection along the axis, the first being that delicate tipping-point between inhalation and exhalation where life hangs in the balance and may be stolen back by greedy forces, the second being the laboured, rattlesnake-like breath of the spectre's growing ingratitude. One does not trifle with those who hold the knife in their grip, and who can ransom the incipient (first gasp) into the insipid (tasteless or flavourless existence). And so one continues the work of bracketed fortune, from plateau to plateau, from dune to dune, at once soloist and fatal diplomat, as breath itself becomes pure vexation.

Breath and the spectre; heaviness; the beating heart; the choked voice; certainty; yearning; banishment; salvation; the reason

Anemomania (Winds, Drafts)

> *King Mihyar*
> *lives in the dominion of the wind*
> *and rules over a land of secrets.*
>
> ADONIS[66]

The Anemomaniac prompts us to inquire after the special relationship between madness and tyranny, though here with particular reference to those lunatic sultans who become like chimes amidst the 'dominion of the wind' (those of fitful majesty). This quicksilver nature may refer to the erratic changing of ideologies, but more likely brings us face-to-face with empires ruled by pure mood: to be sure, we are not interested in those who increasingly grow mad with power, but rather those whose preexisting mania by some fluke finds itself elevated to the highest echelons of licence. Consequently, we can again distinguish between neurotic sadism (power) and apocalyptic mania (will to power) in terms of punitive versus indeterminate violence: while the former is always a paranoiac calculation made to negate a hypothetical negative, the latter obeys the paroxysmal suddenness of peak wind-bursts. It projects the shadow of doom with

---

[66] Adonis, *Selected Poems*, 25.

an almost ticklish unpredictability—another in our literary configuration writes of '[g]reat aspirations of wisps of smoke! Great expectations sent to the winds! An assassinating mood this morning!'[67] Thus the anemomaniac is the tyrant of cyclonic tendencies for whom all concepts of vertical jurisdiction are supplanted by horizontal impulses that resemble breezes, gales, or typhoons.

Note: The philosophy of wind-like mood among leaders (that which comes from nowhere) is chronicled in various political anecdotes and court stories. Cicero famously tells the tale of the Sword of Damocles: a Sicilian courtier in the palace of Dionysius II of Syracuse lavishes praise on the ruler for his magnificent lifestyle, at which point Dionysius suggests that the two trade places so that the flatterer might experience the king's position. The courtier is told to recline upon a golden couch and is pampered with perfumes and feasts only then to watch Dionysius hang a gigantic razor-sharp blade above him, its hilt suspended by only a single strand of horsehair. Obviously, this is meant to signify the tyrant's perpetual vulnerability, always evading coups and plots, always looking over their shoulder for those many enemies (within and without) who crave opulence and acclaim and may at any moment strike out of resentment or jealousy, and hence living always beneath the dangling sickle ('hanging by a

---

[67] Bensmaia, *The Year of Passages*, 98.9.

thread') whose lethal ballet plays out overhead. Gluttony, indulgence, entourage: all could be brought crashing down by the fickle blowing of the wind that makes the Sword of Damocles sway. This is perhaps what is meant by 'the land of secrets' in the above passage: the navigation of worlds of the shaken and of the chute where iron-fisted authority knows all too well that it is merely a bluff before the reality of a windswept existence, forever fighting off insolence and pretenders to the throne who arrive like hurricanes from all sides.

Note: Another Persian account tells of a cruel Shah Anushirvan whose ministers reported the growing discontent of his people, to which he responded by ordering a bell to be hung in the centre of the city outside the palace gates, which any individual with a complaint could ostensibly come and ring to seek personal audience with the king and voice objections. According to legend, the Shah then stationed his best archer upon a neighbouring tower with commands to shoot anyone through the heart who dared approach the bell. These are not narratives of royal vanity or conceit, but rather hymns to all-encompassing vagary: whether cut down by a pendent sword or pierced by a deadshot's arrow flying through winds, the point is to let calcify this realisation of the imminent peril and fragility that gusts across the everything (for only the manic tyrant perceives their own chaos in all guests or callers).

Wind and the king; dominion; the land of secrets

Etheromania (Sky)

> *With thoughts like this running through my mind, I lay down alone in the heart of darkness. Meanwhile, there was an astounding spectacle coming in through the moon windows. The rockets and bombs going off in the sky were illuminating the night like lightning, flashing through the tiny windows like a hellish thunder storm that refused to abate. I felt extremely afraid. But in spite of everything, I couldn't help but be impressed with the beauty of the sight.*
>
> GHADA SAMMAN[68]

The Etheromaniac takes us into a controversial ozone where perception is compelled to admit that relations of beauty, wonderment, and attraction are to be discovered in devastating phenomena. Here we must focus on the skylight: a distorting optical prism through which awful technological systems start to resemble awesome naturalistic occurrences. Just as we possess historical accounts of those first eyewitnesses to aerial bombing in the early twentieth century who described the fire-dropping planes as something both hideous and otherworldly, like contemporary Palestinian, Yemeni, and Afghani poets who describe drone strikes as something akin to alien

---

[68] Samman, *Beirut Nightmares*, 20.

hovercrafts or giant birds of prey or some pagan spear from the cerulean ('the drone eats with me', one says), so we can picture our author laying down on her apartment floor to stare at the pyrotechnic exhibition through her upper window. Through this single polyhedron cleft in the ceiling, whatever catastrophic illuminations may be occurring above are torn from all larger contexts and inserted in a momentary artistic sky without meaning. In fact they induce a kind of rupture of the otolith (the inner ear segment that detects gravity) whereby the spectator cannot find balance or understand linear acceleration, but can only follow the spectacle of an artificial 'storm'. Rather than become a partisan, she becomes show-stealer and accomplice. But what is the nature of this entertainment, and of this complicity, especially given its blood-stained outcomes? Here Armageddon takes on an irrefutable aesthetic quality or cinematic effect, despite all of reason's attempts at non-cooperation ('in spite of everything'): like those magnificent photographs of rainforest wildfires, glacial melting, and geological erosion that capture ecological depletion, such showcases nevertheless produce a manic splendour wherein the imagination escapes banal connections and freelances in a blank-canvas sky. Never transcendent, but rather immersive. Still, does this alter-aviary always require a mediating lens or translucent aperture of some kind (the looking-glass or vinyl screen) in order to impress us with 'the beauty of the sight'? Or is there something phenomenologically distinct about the skylight—perhaps its ability to form a parenthetical enclosure that blocks out all knowledge of the sky's connection to earthly matters? Lastly, does this counter-intuitive affirmation of the scene (as virtuoso exposition) not slingshot the entire foundation of inside and outside, self and other, friend and enemy, upon which most human collectivities limp along? Here all technics become stroboscopic accompaniments. So it is that the missile-shredded sky becomes the nerve centre of amoral vision, bringing uncomfortable lyricism to a steel-dome world, if only for an instant (to see just one thing at the expense of all else).

> *Sky and laying-down; the spectacle; the moon-window; illumination; storm; the unabated; impression; beauty; the sight*

Nephomania (Clouds)

Even while I say this
I see a cloud necklaced with fire.
I see people melting like tears.

ADONIS[69]

The Nephomaniac lays claim to its own partial share in a philosophy of misanthropy, like those great schizophrenic painters throughout history whose growing obsession with clouds always ran in parallel with an increased distaste for drawing the human form, or those ancient philosophers who were satirically alleged to have advocated worshipping clouds rather than anthropomorphic deities (and were later killed by the masses). Thus the cloud-necklace above results in 'people melting like tears'—with the poet taking on the conceptual persona of cosmic jeweller—and indeed another piece makes a similar connection between nephomania and anthrocide (the wiping out of the human race) by positing an alternative telling or second coming of the flood story entitled 'The New Noah'. Although the original Noah is himself a figure of great convolution: he participates both in the grand-scale extermination of humanity and in

---

69 Adonis, *The Pages of Day and Night*, 67.

its meticulous preservation; he is a known drunk tasked with the most critical task of concentration imaginable; he is a father to three sons of both anointed and damned races; he labours throughout his nine hundred and fifty years for both reversal (of creation) and futurity, and is the prophetic embodiment of protection who is nonetheless often found naked and unconscious in his tent. Perhaps we might even speculate that the habit of his nephomaniacal practice stems from the many episodes of drunken stupor during which he found himself forced to cloud-gaze while sprawled out and immobilised on the ground.

But 'The New Noah' recounts a strident hypothetical past wherein the faithful servant turns a faithless deaf ear to the divine telos, and instead builds a consciousness based on altercation and vitriol: 'We are sailing and fear cannot bend us, / And we do not listen to God's word', he whispers into the ears of the land animals aboard his anti-ark.[70] He will conjugate the master plan no longer, beholden neither to principles of extinction nor those of exemption, but rather rows the heavy oars with gaze fastened only on the clouds. He longs for no second beginning among the pebbles of new soil; his wheel swerves to the aerosol patterns of droplets and crystals hanging like

---

70 Adonis, 'The New Noah', in *Victims of a Map*, tr. A. al-Udhari (London: Saqi Books, 2008), 125.

chandeliers above the doomed ark. In this sense, Noah (from the Babylonian-Assyrian *nukhu* meaning 'repose, rest') comes to embrace sheer nephological restlessness and thereby leaves the safe zone of prophetic duty for the counter-epiphanic realm of the saint. And what is the exact difference between prophetic experience and saintly experience? Are they not different rungs on the same ladder of madness or derangement? Do the saint's rabid tears not have something of that swirling luminance and reflectivity found only in clouds? Are they not the perfect image of a consciousness unanchored?

Note: The fictive or apocryphal re-narration of Noah's flood story is an understudied common thread among leaders of twentieth-century literary vanguards. In Iran, the poet Ahmad Shamlu (of our larger configuration here) composes a romantic heresy with the following lines: 'If time and space were under our will / Ten years before Noah's storm, I would have fallen in love with you / and you could have seduced me until endtimes / one hundred years would have passed in praise of your eyes / and thirty thousand years in praise of your body'—thereby freezing our gaze upon a couple who refuse to board the ark and join its trial of suffering, and instead select a corner where they may die in one another's arms as the dark rainclouds gather. This is eros without reproduction, and thus the misanthropic unlearning of all devotion to the rest of humanity (they praise only each other as emblems of wasted time). In Portugal, José Saramago ends his novel *Cain* with the teleportation of the fratricidal, marked one onto the ark, where he systematically murders Noah's entire family before driving Noah himself to jump suicidally overboard into the waters of the deluge. Cain's extinction-mission against Noah is again the stuff of misanthropic dreams for the one known as 'The Wanderer', the smoke of whose earlier sacrificial offerings to God was beaten down from reaching the desired clouds above. Lastly, in Japan, Kobo Abe's *Ark Sakura* sets the militant gesture of Noah in the guise of an obese doomsday prepper named 'The Mole' who has spent years converting a massive underground quarry into a bunker (or ark) for the impending nuclear holocaust. Having stockpiled enough resources to sustain several hundred people, he goes searching the marketplaces for a crew to join his vessel, only to meet an insect-seller of clockbugs (mysterious legless creatures) and two male and female con artists known as *sakura* ('decoys') well-versed in embezzling, pickpocketing, and physical diversion, who steal boarding passes to the ark. Together they enter the distended belly of the ship equipped with weapons and hydraulic pressure machines and security devices, but soon find themselves perpetually besieged by a cult of elderly hegemons known as The Broom Brigade and a gang of utopian juvenile delinquents, leading The Mole to dynamite the cave's connecting passage as he escapes to the surface again and abandons the ark's passengers below. Thus the story of omnicidal destiny ends with yet another misanthropic betrayal of the race of regurgitated ignorance and a renewed desire for the cloud-formations aloft (even if they be the mushroom clouds of atomic despair).

Clouds and the fire necklace; the people; melting; tears

Aviomania (Flight)

> *I realized that I had an ancient partner in sorrow. Was not that ancient painter who hundreds, perhaps thousands, of years ago, had decorated the surface of this jar my partner in sorrow?...Until now I had regarded myself as the most ill-starred of created beings. Now I understood for a space that on those hills, in the houses of that ruined city of massive brick, had once lived men whose bones had long since rotted away and the atoms of whose bodies might now perhaps be living another life in the blue flowers of morning glory; and that among those men there had been one, an unlucky painter, an accursed painter, perhaps an unsuccessful decorator of pen-case covers, who had been a man like me, exactly like me. And now I understood (it was all that I was capable of understanding) that his life had also burned and melted away in the depths of two great, black eyes, just as mine had done.*
>
> SADEQ HEDAYAT[71]

The Aviomaniac demonstrates how mania alone transforms the uncanny into a definitive resource of the will: no longer the logic of strange familiarity and involuntary haunting, here it assists the flagrant expansion of a

---

[71] Hedayat, *The Blind Owl*, 40.

logic of resemblance into supra-identical manifestation ('exactly like me'); no longer the living-doll automaton onto which one projects the dread of losing one's eyes or the repetition-compulsion of retracing one's steps, but rather a manic spinning of concurrence and recurrence to the point where something takes flight. Doubling is thereafter superseded by Levitation—all phenomena fly into one another, across temporal-spatial frontiers, like the whip of the text's skeletal hearse found 'whistling through air' or the vapour from the horses' nostrils seen 'rising from their nostrils like a stream of smoke'. Remember that this is the same author who dedicates his entire book to the shadow looming across four walls, for it is the harbinger of a sinister equator (imaginary line connecting all lands) that renders flight over to perception, sensation, death, violence, omen, passion. Everything is dispatched, gift or communiqué: not inanimate eeriness but hyper-animated coevality, such that it is never a matter of achieving the scientific criterion of actual flight, but only of the acceleration of manic likenesses to the point where they appear as if suspended in mid-air and then thrust into boomerang trajectories (ejecting clues everywhere). Alas, there is always something ecstatic in such conspiratorial implements, like the exultation of wearing a translucent mask of one's own face, which chisels and inculcates the manic subject's countenance into all strata of world in favour of complexity (not monotony): more clearly, it is a suction-pump that transposes the most mismatched appearances into sudden lookalikes; its precipitous rhythm is set to procure new details; it does not shun the complication of the new find, but rather steals it into the cabal's configuration, for mania immediately ratifies the minutiae or peculiarity of otherness as an essential technicality of its own machination (the long-lost piece). Such is the ardour of the spiral. Its conundrum takes all comers ('partners in sorrow'); it forms asteroid constellations out of otherwise estranged fragments; it demands that all hidden objects or forbidden auras join the trapeze-act of the shadow's euphoric malady.

Note: There is an occasional tendency among both manic and schizophrenic authors, when reading others' books, to accuse long-dead writers of having time-travelled (flown in time) to plagiarise them. The gentler variation of this strain is the belief that the former author composed the text as a specific message to the present-day manic reader, somehow anticipating their later arrival and contingent detection of the work, while the more aggressive strain perceives a connivance whereby the former author either somehow stole the internal thoughts or the physical manuscript of the manic subject. This is experienced as thrilling (all novelty is return), as some kind of beautifully evil fellowship, especially since the proof of such aeronautic robbery is simply the absence of those words from their current mind or the absence of pages from their desk. They are now absolutely assured that these products once existed there, buried in a certain drawer: the militant certainty of their suspicion alone is remarkable in itself, replete with fantasies of pirate ships that cross continents or centuries, but those interested in questions of literature, philosophy, or art might also ponder the kind of raw hermeneutic intensity that emanates from this view of all preexisting statements, ideas, and images as satellites in the outworld of one's consciousness.

> *Flight and the ancient partner; decoration; surface; ill-starred being; ruin; atom; exactness; the alike; understanding*

Basimania (Falling)/Trypomania (Holes)

I decided that I must be like someone plunging to the bottom of Niagara Falls who's still captivated by the beauty of the scenery, or like someone falling from the fiftieth floor of a skyscraper who finds himself admiring the flowers on the balconies as he passes by them on his way to death...

GHADA SAMMAN[72]

The Basimaniac unlocks the true secret delirium behind plummeting from heights, something associated with parachuters, base-jumpers, cliff-divers, and hang-gliders: namely, the slowing-down of world. It is not actually about the adrenaline spike associated with pulling the ripcord while plunging rapidly to earth, but rather a horizontal flattening wherein existential reality appears to come to a standstill. The energetic dimension of the freefall wherein consciousness is provided a rare perspective from which it can catalogue each descending layer, thus proving mania's simultaneous capacity for vertigo and extreme focus in sixty seconds, whether dropping from waterfalls or skyscrapers: it is quite literally 'life passing before one's eyes'—not an individual past (as in a traumatic accident) but rather the mental inventory

---

[72] Samman, *Beirut Nightmares*, 20.

of stones, metals, trees, colours, edges, and geometrical shapes that take on an almost stationary museal quality along the slope of descent. An apothecary's cabinet with slots for everything.

Another version of this observational delirium reaped by the falling body is the one who drops themselves subterraneously, as in the following excerpt by another member of our literary configuration, which captures the sensorial features of Trypomania (obsession with holes): 'I fell: the damp ground, barer than an earthworm, more elementary than a bacterium, a real larva, an embryo, a mollusc, my teeth turned to pablum…and I have no power to rectify everything that falls and slips away….'[73] Here the manic author does something far more daring than just identifying with some precedent of human underground experience: for instance, they could have easily inhabited the long hours of those miners who dwell amid dark tunnel shafts, beams, and shining veins of coal or ore, holding pickaxes and helmets, braving dampness and the ever-present risk of explosion, drowning, or black lung disease (and who also consistently note the exceptional slowness associated with going lower). No, instead the author here falls across entire species-states, naming those burrowing creatures who turn perforations across the earth's surface into habitation or refuge, whether to

---

73 Bensmaia, *The Year of Passages*, 53.

store food, sleep, escape predators, bear offspring, or simply to move between spaces. What at first glance appears as self-denigration in fact marks a deep admiration for those who dig themselves unperturbed sites where the world's pace can halt for a short or extended while.

Note: The discourse of falling allows us to inaugurate an equally pivotal philosophy of *following*: for mania drastically redefines how things pursue or supplant one another. Let us enlist three specific examples of the human relation to animality in order to fathom the great contrast between so-called sanity and madness: for if neurosis and human narcissism are conjoined twins, then we can rest assured that mania and inhuman fascination enter into their own unique kinship.

Case 1: Dr. Harry Frederick Harlow was an American psychologist whose studies into maternal bonding among rhesus monkeys took a disgusting turn following the early death of his wife, at which point he constructed an experimental cage called the 'vertical chamber apparatus' (an inverted pyramid which he fondly re-termed the 'pit of despair' or 'well of loneliness') to test whether he could induce depression in monkeys and destroy their species bonds. The ensuing coercive methods and results were those of pure abasement: after prolonged periods of seclusion (up to years), he documented that the 'total isolate' monkeys would remain huddled to one side, barely moving or playing, with some self-starving to death, while also becoming abusive or neglectful toward offspring (including disaffection, cannibalisation, and skull-bashing reactions). Most of his test subjects, however, simply surrendered to the enormity of their sunkenness within the pit's corners, thus rendering the sadistic doctor victorious in replicating an animal paradigm of psychological misery.

Case 2: The ancient cynical philosopher Diogenes of Sinope's association with animality is self-evident in his appellation of 'The Dog'—a name given him for reasons of his shameless aversion to all custom, as he crawled around Athens naked on all fours, eating from trash heaps, indulging bodily functions at will, and consorting with stray creatures. He also reportedly learned the lesson of *askesis* (ascetic discipline) while watching a mouse seek unconventional shelter, informing his own decision to live in an abandoned ceramic tub with no material possessions or official home, and gave instructions to toss his body beyond the city gates after his death so that wild animals could devour it.

Case 3: Arabian falconers have a thousand-year heritage of cultivated training and hunting practices, during which the birds were considered as almost sacred animals for their role in bringing ancient tribes supplemental food for survival. Today the most futuristic societies of the Middle East remain transfixed by the falcon as a competitive luxury item—each individual raptor costing sometimes millions of dollars and requiring specialists' care and being catered to in falcon hospitals, breeding centres, racing grounds, and hotels along the Persian Gulf. Nevertheless, there are accounts claiming that the original falconers of the region, those of gloved fists, were prone to more dire thoughts when taking their birds hunting for long desert stretches: after lifting the bird's leather blinders and awaiting its return with small game, watching it fall through air with razor-like talons, they often reflected on the hypothetical evacuation of the earth, thus bringing mania and omnicidal fantasy full circle again.

These separate cases are encountered by way of three divergent glimpses onto three conceptual folds: (1) each posits a specific theory of following; (2) each skirts the dividing line between human and animal; (3) each links itself to varying experiences of fallenness and holes. In the first instance, we observe a professional psychoanalyst's brutal and perversely narcissistic mission to impose anthropomorphic suffering (to make the animal follow his own human fallenness). In the second instance, we observe a manic alternative when a philosopher's adulation of undomesticated beings leads him to disdain social comfort and resort to instinct (to make the human fall from its false traditions and follow animal nature). In the third instance, we observe yet another manic path in the distant stare of the falconer who recognises their simultaneous inability to chase the free birds and their inability to rejoin the human race, instead allowing idleness to push them into the borderlands of apocalyptic imagination (to make following impossible, and thereafter to allow both human and animal to fall away from all worlds). Only the latter two treatments cited—those of a certain basimaniacal and trypomaniacal urgency—can serve as potential antidotes to the authoritarian measures and death-deserving accursedness of the first condition that we call psyche: for they are the overdue mercy-killing of what never should have arisen to begin with.

Falling and the bottom; captivation; scenery; admiration; the balcony; passage; death

Part 13
Phonomania/Acousticomania
(Sounds, Voices, Noise)
Questiomania/Erotetomania (Questions)
Silentomania (Silence)

Phonomania/Acousticomania (Sounds, Voices, Noise)

> *and at the limits of vision*
> *shining planets spin.*
> *the earth in elevation reaches repetition,*
> *and air wells*
> *changes into tunnels of connection...*
> *...and in the chemical space after sunrise*
> *there is only sound,*
> *sound that will attract the particles of time.*
> *why should I stop?...*
> *...sound, sound, sound,*
> *only sound remains.*
>
> FORUGH FARROKHZAD[74]

The Phonomaniac allows us to ask the question of mania's relation or non-relation to the hearing of voices. Whereas schizophrenia is often diagnostically associated with this condition—susceptibility to auditory hallucinations and sub-vocal speech that grows increasingly loud, aggressive, painful, and persuasive—and also with a defective

---

[74] F. Farrokhzad, 'It Is Only Sound That Remains', in M.C. Hillmann, *Iranian Culture: A Persianist View* (Lanham, MD: University Press of America, 1990), 149.

recognition circuit whereby the mind supposedly fails to identify its own internal voice as such, mania furnishes a slightly different modality based on *invigoration* and *rasping*. More exactly, the poet above, for whom 'only sound remains', devises a philosophy of federation and rancour whereby certain intonations are classified as her own belongings, others as part of those enemy-formations that make their garrisons in the air around her. The sonic forces that play to her delirium she calls 'the sound of falling starlight'; those that acoustically oppose her are part of 'the swamp's spawning ground' and 'the morgue's thoughts'. Thus every incident, stranger, or material object emits/conceals an auditory position that must be detected: she sifts through transmissions as a 'descendant of the house of trees' while others speak in false tongues to aid the 'local government of the blind'. The result: an infinitely parasitic banquet of phonic semblances (cacophony, din). The method: a poetics of rage that carefully curates the galleries of sound so as to determine who speaks for her alliance, and who against it (code, secret language). Never outrage, only rage: for outrage is always reactively dialectical, a negative symptom of resentment, and is predicated on an idealistic humanist belief that we are owed something better, that we have been somehow cheated of our rights and deserve some hypothetical second life. Rage has no such entitlement, scapegoats no particular enemy, and instead proceeds with immanent articulations of fury. It always moves toward the indicators of violence, like one of those curious children in fairy tales who wander after evil sounds; it believes that this single conflict of voices alone is what makes 'shining planets spin' and 'attracts the particles of time' toward the venue of a last stand.

But what if her taxonomical processes fail to catch the impostor's call? Here we unlock the amazing resilience afforded to mania in the face of utter failure: when some dream fails to materialise, it can always be blamed on the sheer aural efflux and interpretive complexity of the many voices speaking at once. It is hard to hear, and to know what one hears: like those doomsday cults whose established end-of-the-world date passes without incident or fanfare, and whose group members undergo no major crisis of faith but rather instantaneously regroup on the basis of the idea that they misdeciphered the correct calendrical timetable or that other detractor voices polluted the listening act. All that remains is to select another numerology; to return to the alert ringing of their impatient and apprehensive ears.

Note: There is telling in pre-Islamic Arabian mythology of a blue-eyed tribal woman named Zarqa' al-Yamama who possessed supernatural powers of sight and intuition. This not only rendered her an effective prognosticator of events, but also gave her an invaluable sixth sense in knowing when enemies were gathering to attack:

specifically, legend states that she was able to envision riders approaching a week beforehand. Nevertheless, her enemies soon became aware of Zarqa's anticipatory gift and therefore disguised their soldiers' movements behind trees; when she reported this strange image of advancing trees to the tribes, the elders dismissed her warnings and accused her of madness. Once the enemy forces arrived to conquer her tribal camp, they slaughtered all the men and ripped out Zarqa's eyes before crucifying her. Nevertheless, what is often ignored except in obscure mythological sources is that her precognitive talents derived not from sight but rather from sound (she would *hear* the enemies' rustling), but that she always lied by falsely attributing her predictions to her eyes in order to protect the true phonomaniacal source of acumen.

Note: There are some correspondences here to the so-called Cassandra Complex wherein futural advice goes unheeded and is met by fatal disbelief, often bringing suffering or persecution to the bearer of ill news, though mania prides itself on its highly persuasive ability (convincing others to hear what is coming; sharing a conscience of being's minor keys).

Sound and limits; elevation; repetition; the well; the tunnel; connection; attraction; particles; time; particles; the remaining

Questiomania/Erotetomania (Questions)

> *After you receive the client's file you cannot ask questions as you could before. You have to submit your questions in writing. All your questions, proposals and written submissions will be documented in your personal file. You absolutely may not write to me about work matters by email or call me on the phone. You will write your questions on a special form which I will provide you with later...I know you now have some questions that are nagging you, but you will gradually discover that the world is built to have more than one level, and it's unrealistic for everyone to reach all the levels and all the basements with ease.*
>
> HASSAN BLASIM[75]

The Erotetomaniac reflects, above all else, mania's positive relation to ambiguity and mystery. The quoted scene, however, depicts this through its opposite: a young candidate sits in a cold room being interviewed by the head of a secret society of 'corpse exhibitionists' who offers infinite freedom to kill, maim, and stylise death itself—but without any right to question anything. This represents the

---

[75] Blasim, *The Madman of Freedom Square*, 45–46.

role of questioning within circles of power (as a gesture of ossification and infirmity) as opposed to its role within madness (as a gesture of cascade and echo). In opposition to the interrogators who pound mind and body into submission, making victims repeat the same answer in order to trip them into revealing inconsistencies, here the question only enhances fascination through a morphine drip of conjectures. The dread of the investigator's corner—for 'the question of humanity can be solved only by constant dread'—is thereby undone by the intoxication of the mad architect's gateway to the oblique, the off-lying, and the dioramic.[76] In the interrogation room, the question intimidates; in the manic imagination, the question astounds. This shows that there exist both disenchanted and enchanted variations on hierarchy, in addition to both oppressive and liberating forms of vagueness. It also underlines the experiential difference between being dominated and being doomed—the condemned of the closed prison versus the condemned of the open labyrinth, library, or cosmos.

In ancient mythologies, gods of curiosity were nearly always presented as minor deities, for this prejudice downplays our fear of their accelerative potential. In capitalist modernity, curiosity devolves into a technics of the search that allows for glances of the bizarre without

---

[76] Ibid., 3.

any actual adventure (virtual insularity). The forces of inquiry are therefore always restrained from attaining manic status: the questioner threatens regimented space (they go farther astray); the questioner threatens regimented time (they lose track of hours and days); the question itself expels language into tics (the flourishing). This is the hilarity of nearing ineffable or untellable things; the query becomes a foaming cataract and thought itself a colosseum of many arches. This is the interim where all life must make provisional arrangements.

Note: The Mondrian Doha is a destination hotel in Qatar, fashioned by Marcel Wanders, which plunges architecture and design into the realms of the questionable (in terms of scale, amount, placement, and functionality). In its central lounge one finds a gargantuan black staircase to nowhere, alongside oversized rippling columns, golden eggshells, and giant hanging bells; down one hallway is a spa with strings of pearl and crystal suspended above rows of floating basket-seats; down another hallway is the room of cloud gardens with white trees of life branching everywhere; a twenty-four-carat gold elevator takes one to the Black Orchid nightclub or to the rooftop pool bombarded by stained-glass windows overhead; beyond this, an assortment of Moroccan lamps, water basins, Arabian horses, and arabesque tiles make up the rest of the hotel's presentation. On the one hand, this is simply an Orientalist fantasy commissioned by

Persian Gulf royalty to produce a self-exoticising simulation. On the other hand, however, the designer's admitted technique takes us into more interesting spheres of manic imagination: he claims that every single detail is derived from one of the stories of the *Arabian Nights*, with those lone images or objects then compulsively multiplied into several undulations across each space. To their credit, this is the exact same methodology of narrative exaggeration attributed to Marco Polo, nicknamed *Il Milione*, 'The Million', for his tendency to see one phenomenon in a faraway land (e.g. an elephant) and then relay that he had observed a million of them, and also because in the mediaeval world his travelogue was said to contain a million lies. Marco Polo is the master of extracting a unique feature, spinning it into an aggregate, and subsequently constructing an entire hyper-fictive civilisation or metropolis around it.[77] Each solitary trait becomes many, one after another, in serial propagations, as one night becomes a thousand and one; everything is larger, heavier, and more profuse than the original perception, taunting us with the incredulous fact that 'the world is built to have more than one level'. With this established, one can then ask whether this is not the very sign of luxury itself—to unnecessarily proliferate; to bring taste

---

[77] This narrative-design technique is rendered brilliantly in Italo Calvino's *Invisible Cities*, as the storyteller Marco Polo responds to a dying emperor's questions with images of embellished and exaggerated worlds.

QUESTIOMANIA/EROTETOMANIA

to questionable levels—and whether mania is therefore not the very sign of being's luxuriation.

Questioning and the file; submission; writing; the proposal; the document; form; nagging; discovery; levels; basements; dis-ease

Silentomania (Silence)

I don't want to return home,
the way the Crusaders returned.
I am all this silence between two fronts:
gods on one side, those who invent their names on the other.

Yet I came down from the Cross, fearing heights, and
keeping silent about the apocalypse.

MAHMOUD DARWISH[78]

The Silentomaniac is a figure whose apparent composure is misleading, for their manic refusal to speak is in fact the simple after-effect of having already seen too much (horror, revelation) or heard too much (dissonance, sonic war) or said too much (imploration, screaming). Something excessive has happened to bind the realm of hyperacusis (rare hearing disorder associated with ear-splitting sensitivity to environmental noise) to that of speechlessness. The self-muting tongue is not an effacement but rather the insignia of one who has travelled to the experiential outlands where crusaders burned down worlds and lived to tell of it (yet choose not to); their inarticulacy is itself the groan of one who has scaled the heights of human

---

78 Darwish, *Unfortunately, It Was Paradise*, 83, 160.

decimation, and who carries a hundred echoes of Golgotha in their head. All frequencies and volumes of sound are therefore indecent to the figure of the survivor: yes, survival is an impressive state of mania in its own right, one that consummates itself in silent endurance while forever haunted by omnicidal shadows (for the others died). This is the quietude of the one who reappears but 'doesn't want to return home'; this is the self-gagged nature of the one who hears ending spells spoken everywhere but 'keeps silent about the apocalypse'. Why? Because they have a taste for lone survival, a manic sulking toward their own inevitable surpassing of the next round amid those whose invented names fall short. This is not the zero-sum game of the witch who drinks beautiful maidens' blood in order to stay young: there is no apparent requirement that the silent one's permanence be purchased at the cost of the obliteration of the rest—and yet they are always hushed, and still they are always left standing atop the historical rubble. In this deepest sense, there is absolutely no reason to speak, only to remain glowering, for it will happen again soon enough (all already over). Not a god, but the one who even God can't kill: such is the mania of the only one who forever walks away.

Note: There are a few rare anthropological works about North African rural peasants who claim to have married a member of the jinn race. In particular, one Moroccan tilemaker in a landlocked town between the

Atlantic Ocean and the Algerian border was visited by an ethnographer who had heard tell of his belief that a camel-footed jinni had stolen into his modest house one evening and bound him into an eternal wedding bond. The illiterate man would go about his daily practices before the anthropologist while his invisible spirit-wife presumably stood in the room: he would sweep the floors beneath her supposed seat; he would set places at the dinner table for them both and prepare their nightly bed with two pillows; he would explain her magical histories and her jealousy; he would talk with her affectionately, call out to her, smile and laugh toward her impalpable form, or plead in her terrifying moments of attack, and never receive an audible response. It was never even clear to the anthropologist how many other fanciful titles she possessed beyond her formal name, 'Aisha Qandisha', though she was known mainly throughout his visitation as 'the Lady'. Other villagers were reportedly tolerant yet avoided long encounters with the man who spoke to sullen air. For what does it mean to experience infatuation with a silent being? This mania that falls in love only with the most subdued.[79]

Silence and return; crusade; the front; the invented name; apocalypse

---

[79] V. Crapanzano, *Tuhami: Portrait of a Moroccan* (Chicago: University of Chicago Press, 2013).

Part 14
Gymnomania (Nakedness)
Ommatomania (Sight, Eyes)
Faciemania (Faces)
Iconomania (Images, Portraits, Icons)
Idolomania (Idols)

Gymnomania (Nakedness)

I see a naked man crushing hurricanes in ecstasy.
Baptized by waterfalls, he drops to his knees
and disappears.

ADONIS[80]

The Gymnomaniac places us before a delicate existential question: Why do those of exceptional power so frequently die young? In Greek mythology, the wisest centaur Chiron, with human torso and horse's hind legs, known for taking both Hercules and Achilles under his private tutelage to train them in archery, gymnastics, and the lyre, and who traded his own immortality for Prometheus's freedom (and was later honoured for this sacrifice, becoming a constellation), often warned that those privileged to receive his instruction would pay the price of an early and violent demise. Note that he himself was a figure of nakedness, both in terms of the physical exposure of his upper and lower body in early mythic images, and later in the cosmic sense of his clarity as an illuminated star formation. Yet it is said that he was most civilised, courteous, and possessed of gentle nobility despite his tremendous skill in the arts of war, thus raising the question: Can shyness also be a manic style?

---

80 Adonis, *The Pages of Day and Night*, 86.

Similarly, in the above passage we encounter one who somehow binds nudity and humble graces in a single action: on the one side, we find him bare-skinned while 'crushing hurricanes in ecstasy' (a testament to heedlessness, blatancy, and unclad will); but this brashness turns to a more reserved pose when he kneels to be 'baptised by waterfalls' (a testament to the demure and the penitent); lastly, in the final line he transitions from both rash and hunched postures to complete disappearance (a testament to mania's special ability to disrobe into pure glare). Is he actually concealed, or has his nakedness achieved a blinding effect? This is how we may potentially reconcile the two sides of the gymnomaniac, a figure of both breakneck strength and soft-spoken virtue, like the civilised centaur who nurtures others, but simultaneously condemns them to die by accelerated, unnatural causes, only to win eternal luminosity in the night skies.

Note: It is only fitting at this juncture to pursue the relation of the master to nakedness: for masters perceive their pupils in their most rudimentary states, devising techniques to undrape and peel back layered potential in order to turn them into something gallant or polished. To that end, a name that deserves incontrovertible recognition in these pages is that of Nima Yushij, sole master of Ahmad Shamlu and founder of Persian new poetry, who took an entire cataclysmic generation under his wing and taught them to become undeniable (another aspect of nakedness). Nima himself (a pen name meaning 'the sun') had been a shepherd in the northern provinces of Iran, and his extended sojourn among animals and elements made him acutely aware of raw forces. He saw both cruelty and subtlety in moons, stones, and herded flocks, and they say he often opened his robes to the light breezes while walking in the deeper chasms of his region. He was himself 'the naked man crushing hurricanes in ecstasy': the few surviving pictures of him capture his thin unassuming frame and baleful eyes; he is either wrapped in heavy black sweaters or dressed in loose white shirts with buttons unfastened; and indeed his poetic voice combined this rare duality of roughness and defencelessness, something like gravel, nowhere more apparent than in his faint omnicidal summoning of 'the shattered and desolate and drunken wind whirling downward' to uproot entire cities.[81] He believed that his honesty (another conceptual aspect of nakedness) had garnered him enough sympathy to call forth natural phenomena—storms, rains, dawns—and even depicts this ability in a poem titled 'Night Rancour' in which unclothed men pace a shoreline, slowly convening the elements to bring about the bane of existence.

Nakedness and crushing; the hurricane; ecstasy; baptism; the waterfall; kneeling; disappearance

---

81 N. Yushij, 'My House Is A Cloud', in *Modern Persian Poetry*, tr. M. Kianush (Ware: Rockingham Press, 1996).

Ommatomania (Sight, Eyes)

In the dim light of the lamp, Cain saw the eyes. Were they whispering the secret of creation? Speaking of the fashioning of the desert, of the universe? Saying something of doomsday? Were they telling how he'd betrayed the gazelle, threatening some reprisal? He exchanged speech with those eyes, and roles too. He vanished in them and they in him, so that none could tell where he was or what he was.

IBRAHIM AL-KONI[82]

The Ommatomaniac is the only conceivable subject that can turn the proverbial or figural expression 'staring death in the face' into the literal belief that they see death itself: still, it is not enough to simply see death (which places one instantaneously in a too-late temporality), yet one must also know what one sees (recognise it as death) in order to earn that split-second opening of an exceptional window of consciousness. This awareness might even allow a sidestepping of the fateful date, since death does not like to lose the upper hand of its surprise: if one dies precisely when death appears (at the mere sight of it) since death follows the vampire's principle

---

82 Al-Koni, *The Bleeding of the Stone*, 128.

of turning everything it encounters into itself, then one unwinds the clock by spying the hour before its intended arrival. Both pure disobedience and pure advantage, this rarest temporality.

Beyond the stereotypical image of the skeletal reaper, many folkloric traditions narrate the appearance of Death in different guises: a visitor to a hotel staying on the eleventh floor; an old woman collecting wares on a side street; a child with green eyes who whistles into the beyond; a wraith playing chess on the beach; a daunting godmother or godfather, or a scraggly beggar; sometimes a fox or wolf that crosses one's path at twilight. In modern literature, death can take the form of a letter-writing vixen who becomes enamoured with a cellist, an accountant making notations on a café's corner bench, a gambler with a stacked deck of cards, or a travelling salesman with the conman's trademark grin. In older myths death can take the form of three fanged, blood-sucking sisters or a bearded man with wings; a wagon-driver with wide-brimmed hat; a ruler of crossroads who stands at each nexus of the world at midnight; a cruel judge, guardian angel, boatman, rider, well-dressed aristocrat, damsel, or dancer. Sometimes these caricatures are accompanied by a held object: broom, rake, skewer, chain, coin, scythe, whip, envelope, cane, lantern, pocket watch, or notebook. Sometimes they are accompanied by psychopompic creatures (owls, stray cats, panthers, deer) or carrion-attracted insects (crickets, flies, maggots, scarab beetles). And on those most brilliant occasions of expert storytelling, death can even assume spatial extension in the shape of an entire town or village, or attain still greater abstraction as a feeling, mood, shade, or chill. Quite simply, then, ommatomania is a matter of observing fatal entities before they wish to be seen—mastering the velocity of mortal foresight and thus perfecting a trickery of the highest degree (to falsify the almanac's tables).

If our last section dealt with the accrual of early deaths, this section is dedicated to the opposing breed of late deaths. As already noted, such feats are achieved by somehow ransacking the thicket of death's own vision in order to steal ahead of the event and meet it before the conclusive hour of rendezvous, which is precisely what happens in the above passage: the protagonist Cain, named after the mal-archetype of all human tirades, stares into the eyes of a sacred gazelle in order to 'vanish in them and they in him'. This hunted being (itself always one step ahead of the rifle) knows the entire destiny of things from start to finish, and somehow passes on to its would-be killer the very secret of cunning: to walk the earth as a hidden one: 'none could tell where he was or what he was'. Indeed, this is the essence of death's own power, available to mania alone: to be overlooked and therefore always in the lead. This is perhaps what our tribal North African author meant two decades ago when he wrote: 'In the unseen we live; in the seen we die.'[83] And perhaps what the Danish philosopher meant two centuries ago when he wrote: 'I die death itself.'

Note: The famous Mesopotamian fable known as 'Appointment in Samarra', or later 'Death in Samarkand', tells of a rich merchant whose servant, one day while shopping in the bazaars of Baghdad, sees a woman that he is certain embodies Death itself. She signals toward him abruptly, and in a panic he rushes home to tell his master who then procures him the fastest horse upon which to race away to the city of Samarra. The next day the merchant himself goes to the bazaar and finds this feminine personification of Death, asking her why she startled his servant with such an ominous gesture, to which she replies that she was not threatening him but rather was surprised to see him there, since they had an appointment that same night in Samarra. But this cautionary tale speaks only to the normal human scheme of things: conversely, the mad-sighted can spot the sneaking and the evil-intentioned from miles away. A visionary who beats finitude to every juncture, he would always already be four towns ahead of death's caravan. Let it be known, then: mania alone can outrun determinism—even the ultimate determinism of death herself.

> *Sight and dimness; the lamp; the eyes; secret creation; betrayal; reprisal; speech; roles; vanishing*

---

83 Al-Koni, *A Sleepless Eye*, 5.

Faciemania (Faces)

> *I think they've raked our faces over, that they take our good Algerian faces for granted...I see pullulating and prospering all these photomats that take the pictures of our slobby faces pasted in our algae-scum-colored passports! In black and white it's all the same mug of an old dried-up mummy. With or without colors it's all the same look of men wanted dead or alive!*
>
> RÉDA BENSMAIA[84]

The Faciemaniac provides us a point of departure from which to evaluate delirium's ability to nullify the technological disenchantment of appearances, should we require a counteractant or antiserum for the depreciative effects of modern surveillance, telecommunications, computation, information networks, digital post-human war, and remote cybernetic control. If the epochal schema is seemingly one of robbing the face of its wondrous mayhem by subjecting it to so-called dehumanising (but perhaps all-too-human) practices at every border and port of entry, filtering the visages of the foreigner, the outsider, the intruder, the immigrant, and the enemy through the new gauntlets of empire (those of pre-emptive

---

84 Bensmaia, *The Year of Passages*, 15.

criminalisation and paranoiac feedback loops), then mania must be called upon to elevate the facial image from this medialogical deflation. The scientific reduction to 'black and white mummification' in the passport or inspection screen is, as the above author suggests, just another pretence employed as part of the colonial plot to tarnish the look of alterity.

Question 1: Can mania overturn modernity's practice of negating the enemy, in favour of the ancient exaltation of the enemy's face? Without wishing to underestimate or idealise the brutalities of ancient conquest, it is the case that older tribes and civilisations often engaged in highly elaborate storytelling regarding those groups with whom they entered into conflict: supernatural strength was ascribed to the adversary; they scaled cliffs with their bare hands, they were supposedly fearless or possessed miraculous powers of endurance. This narrative ritual of over-projection obeyed a clearly vitalist ethos: one would only want to perish fighting or prove victorious over the best conceivable requiter (ultimate war). Hence the enemy's face, too, was endowed with resplendent qualities—never the gross sameness of the modern identity card whose printout captures only debasement, humiliation, and biopolitical subjugation (the offender *in potentia*). In past millennia the face instead played its part in a culture of violent intimacy and respect—the skulls of slain opponents were even later worn as helmets or used as decorative bowls proudly displayed in the houses of the victors.

Question 2: Is the maniac susceptible to the same debilitating contrast between their self-image and 'objective reality' that is so rampant in standard human psychology? If most individuals detest recordings of their own voice or dislike unedited photographs of themselves because these representations deviate from their own sensory experience of hearing/seeing themselves, would it be an equally effective anti-quixotic strategy to place a dirty mirror or bad mugshot before a maniac and thereby disabuse them of their delusions of grandeur? Would the supposedly impartial, 'raked' close-up succeed in blotting out the regal features they entertain in their madness?

Answer: The *Wanted* poster. The great twist here would be to somehow experience not disillusionment but enhancement via defacement and discrepancy, like the Western outlaw who revels in the increased degeneration of their likeness on the sheriff's notices. In true manic form, and against the enforcers' perceptual efforts, these gunslingers would crave to see the arrest warrant take on progressively more gaunt and sinister exaggerations (alongside the escalating bounty). *Wanted Dead or Alive*: the crucial term being 'wanted'—like a beacon of universal desire with all the fringe benefits of hype and overestimation that accrue only to the most notorious. This would require the full inhabitation of power's visual mistreatment, if only so as to apotropaically reciprocate its telescopic spell: to enjoy those processing-systems and artificial intelligences that bend one toward greater ugliness and the unsightly; to become precisely the mummy that sends quantitative functionaries scampering for shelter; to become the face that haunts the surveillant's dreams.

Face and raking; pullulation; the photomat; black-and-white;
dryness; the mummy; the wanted

Iconomania (Images, Portraits, Icons)

> *You draw the lines of resemblance:*
> *the sigh and iron and unslaked lime*
> *smoke and lie and pain. —*
> *For oblivion is not*
> *our virtue.*
> *Draw the image of my age*
> *in the curvature of the lash amidst an incision-streak of*
> *hurt;*
> *and my neighbor*
> *alien to hope and God;*
> *and our respect*
> *which was converted into coins and sold away.*
>
> AHMAD SHAMLU[85]

The Iconomaniac takes us straight back into the atmosphere of the guild and its proficiency in circulating mania through the arteries of collective action: for here the poetic author assumes the voice of the master whose commanding challenge to the disciples before him—'You draw the lines of resemblance'—reflects mania's capacity to take an ensemble form. No bargaining is allowed; all that matters is the forging of the icon together. Nor is

---

[85] Shamlu, *Born Upon the Dark Spear*, 90.

this a construction of community or intersubjectivity via idealised definition: like the vampire or wolf, both of which maintain a code of both radical solitude (conscious that they belong to a larger race but minding their own secluded business) and radical alliance (knowing when to occasionally synchronise for the sake of hunting or overpowering threats), the guild loses itself in the centrifugal and centripetal force of its agenda, which demands both extreme individuality (style, originality, improvisation) and extreme collaborative awareness (synergism, rivalry, the throng). This is how the consuls train the members' ultra-productive potential, as an inconsolable consortium of arms.

But what is the criterion of the guild's manic concert? The master here has commissioned a harrowing exercise in imagination and craft—'Draw the image of my age'— which gives us our first indicative clue: that the illustration must be a kind of epochal summation. But for whom? Certainly not for the living witnesses of the era itself, for that would simply play to myopic attestations of narcissistic investment. Nor for posterity or some notion of historical succession, for that would assume a linear relation to the oncoming generations which would take the self-conscious shape of a communicative explanation. No, this creative exploit is aimed only at an irrelevant temporality (another time) and spatiality (another world); it presumes an alien watcher, for the guild treats its work as a largely exogenous deed. To make merchandise for such an extrinsic viewer, however, means that one must supply images of the momentous without even the slightest reliance on context, familiarity, understanding, or shared epistemological parameters. The aesthetic must abdicate even conceptions of universal signification and avoid humanist or naturalist archetypes of any sort, since they are liable to fall on deaf ears when received by something partitioned from all acquaintance—'Alien to hope and God', which conceptually implies the total loss of futurity and universality.

We can picture the young acolytes standing beneath torches in the guild's main hall listening to their master's unsparing rallying cry: he teaches them that the true secret of the guild is not tradition, but rather the realisation that all traditions are caught in the sands of an omnicidal hourglass. Only the icon lasts, for 'oblivion is not our virtue', though this is not meant to promote cultural-artistic preservation: here mania throws vision toward the outer rims of possibility, beyond the immediately proximate, beyond the death of inherited ages or neighbouring worlds, dreaming only of the work's discovery aeons later by some absolute stranger. But even if we can fathom the intended audience as a nameless and faceless anti-scion, what should the image itself look like? The second clue arises in the second line, which breaks general symbolic orders of 'resemblance' into a flurry of expressionistic molecular phenomena ('the sigh and iron and unslaked lime'), although these details are linked to a careful conceptual arithmetic ('smoke and lie and pain'). For what do we want the guild's iconomaniacal item to convey about their disappeared sect and its irretrievable rise and fall? 'Smoke' (that they were ephemeral, despite the immense will of their legion); 'Lie' (that they were inauthentic, despite ushering in demiurgic accomplishments); 'Pain' (that they suffered greatly, despite the beguiling nature of their deeds). Moreover, they want the figure of this after-limits archaeology to know that their 'respect was converted into coins', meaning that they went unpaid, underappreciated, were bought and sold, subjected to constant indignity. And lastly, what is the desired effect of the icon? The dual phrases 'curvature of the lash' and 'incision-streak of hurt' answer this question: to inflict agony even upon the one with zero affiliation or broader knowledge of the story; to rip wounds in the perception of the outcomer. To stamp a double-dealing manic image that would induce repercussive drumfire even in the mind-body of the farthest interloper (to wince and thresh upon contact).

Note: The guild's concentration of mania into a traded icon resolves the long-debated divide between speculation and experience that still troubles philosophy. On the one side, there are entire affective leagues that are not conducive to easy cognitive translation, nor does the latter account well for the waves of aesthetic inspiration; on the other side, there are certain topics (e.g. extinction) that obviously extend beyond any immediate sensory or material saliency, thereby requiring the mind to journey into abstraction. But this apparent impasse can be surpassed in one concrete way: the renunciation of hierarchical authenticity altogether in favour of the conspiracy of manic imagination (where thought and feeling partner together to serve varying methodological functions for the stratagem of dark wonderment). Madness, then, is like the nightmare that fills in mental and affective blanks through creative unreality, allowing unexampled speculative images to streak across consciousness while also running the machinery of mood, sensation, and bodily engagement (panting, sweating, racing heart). This is how one both contemplates and touches upon the intense, the impossible, the delirious, the no man's land. But with one further substantial qualification: that the mechanism that so joins speculation and experience no longer be the self, but rather the icon. For while the post-doomsday guild reaches into an alternative time-space indifferent to its own, the full mental, aesthetic, and affective energies of its subjects are all reconcentrated into a single constructive thing (not a given object, but rather a willed object): the icon is at once radar, receptor, and host of as yet unbuilt thought/experience; the icon is its own pragmatic absurdism, bringing hammer and nail to the exploratory; the icon makes remoteness a matter of empirical masonry; the icon is what forms the lash extending into oblivion.

Icon and the drawn line; resemblance; smoke; lie; pain; oblivion; the image; the age; curvature; lash; the neighbour; conversion; coin; the sold-away

Idolomania (Idols)

> *One of them said: 'This mannequin would make a good decoy for catching snipers. We'll make her into a battlefield scarecrow that can dupe the "fire birds." Come on now— let's try out this novel idea'...Hardly had the platform carried her to the middle of the street before someone fired a shot that struck her right in the head. She didn't feel any pain and of course she didn't bleed...Even when she discovered that she caught fire, she didn't grieve over what had become of her once-spectacular body.*
>
> GHADA SAMMAN[86]

The Idolomaniac laments today's perceptual insensitivity toward the graven image that once brought down the jealousy, envy, and destructive anger of monotheistic gods. The mannequin, the scarecrow, the decoy, the sculpted deity—these paragons were the original vanguard of fortune and possibility, while even more importantly upholding the essential commerce of the substitute: to take the turn of finality, to withstand the outside's chaotic impact and become the payer of prices on behalf of its reverent subject. They therefore absorbed and conducted the hailstorms of an otherwise relentless

---

86 Samman, *Beirut Nightmares*, 275–76.

existence—subsuming the exorbitance of pain, blood, and loss—as the incrementally-deepening chips in their stone facades, the weathering of their small shoulders, showed proof of their role as great surrogates. And now, some egotistical human sniper shoots a bullet straight into the idol's forehead: he is an interchangeable ideological cliché; she is a rarefied object of the inconceivable; his garish fatigues are adorned in gaudy symbols; her rags and exposed stomach embody the power of sheer simplicity; his mouth robotically chants the slogans of his leaders; she remains in magisterial silence, answering to no one; he is fixated on controlling the here and now; she plays the patient long game, like the mystic who, when asked his birth date, responded 'ten years from now', and when asked when he would die responded 'a long time ago'. Their squadrons then set her alight; she does not flinch or cry out, and as the consuming flames grow higher we are told that she 'didn't even grieve over what had become of her once-spectacular body'. Yes, we are far distant from those days when believers would swear they saw tears of blood dripping from the corneas or irises of their statues; there is now a vacuum where once there was intimate investment in the idol's tiny squinting eyes (and what happens when forces of radical negativity are denied their blackmail?). Only the maniac realises the error involved in not giving the idol the status of a martyred entity; she is rueful of the modern human subject's neglect of the ancient logic of human sacrifice, which always demanded exaltation of the cannibalised tribute: after all, the sacrifice was showered with the best tents, jewels, and foods for perhaps a year before being carried aloft in the people's hands to be made into radiant offering.

Note: The regulatory effect of the idol is something best understood as a longstanding anthropological calculation, for it presumably brokered the balance between life and catastrophic will. Its worship was therefore a miniature violence necessary to honour/allay the full-scale omnicidal prospects of the world, whereas modernity's blind drive to utopia has precisely realised those dystopian outcomes (ecological, technological, ideological). But manic outbursts always return. For example, in the southern Bosnian city of Medjugorje there lies a Christian pilgrimage site where, in 1981, six village children claimed to have received visions from the Virgin Mary, who to this day supposedly sends enigmatic reports to three of the now-adult vessels at certain times of the month in the shape of fractal images or messages. These 'nine secrets' are believed to be her final attendances upon earth before the apocalypse, and many visitors to this destination also claim to have experienced supernatural optical signs such as the sun careening through the sky or shadow-crosses appearing in their palms. Psychoanalytic explanations of Medjugorje have ranged from theories of the children suffering Oedipal ordeals to auto-hypnosis or auto-apparitional syndromes, and the child-seers have even been subjected to multiple electro-oculogram readings to ascertain the cause of their prolonged, collective psychokinesis (influence on physical subjects and objects without physical energy).[87] But what consistently baffles such subject-centred investigations time and again is the degree of synchronism across these visionary instances (near-identical frequencies of reaction time, speed, motion, facial expression, eye blinking patterns, and bodily tremor), for what psychoanalysis inevitably misses is the manic influence wielded by the idol itself, and how statues of the Virgin throughout the village spread a net of idolatrous immanence over those who flock beneath her flowing dress. As another in our literary configuration writes tellingly: 'In his house there's an Idol that doesn't speak. An Idol cheered and worshipped. The quieter he becomes, the more the wisdom of his silence stirs up a storm of applause.'[88] So it is that the children once had an idol upon the hill, and now themselves have become idols in their own right; so it is that for decades these favoured six thaw out omnicidal directives in a parish between the mountains.

> *Idol and the decoy; the battlefield; duping; novelty; the platform; pain; blood; grieving; the spectacular body*

---

[87] J.P. Pandarakalam. 'Are the Apparitions of Medjugorje Real?', *Journal of Scientific Exploration* 15:2, 229–39.

[88] Darwish, *Memories for Forgetfulness*, 156.

Interlude: Book of the Opium Den (Philosophy of Smoke)

We must enter the *faramoosh-khaneh* (Persian for 'house of forgetting', an alternative name for the *tariak-khaneh* or *shirekesh-khaneh*, meaning 'opium den'), we must rest horizontally across its smooth planks and breathe deeply of its dust, to contemplate a philosophy of willed oblivion. For opium is not a simple business of annihilation, but rather involves processes of temporary transmutation; it conducts a paradox of physical ethereality whereby one learns to become at once smoke, drug, and poison. There is an elegant ritual in play here: the reclined body, the slanted head, the lit pipe and charcoal grills, the careful assortment of objects and implements, the choreography of postures and the channelling of consumptive fumes. All of these make possible the delicate exercise of inhalation and exhalation that allows us to begin devising an 'atmospheric methodology' (or perhaps a 'phenomenology of mood').

OMNICIDE II

FUMIMANIA (OBSESSION WITH SMOKE)

Principle 1. Vanishing (Becoming-Subtle)

> *I was sitting beside my opium brazier. All my dark thoughts had dissolved and vanished in the subtle heavenly smoke.*
> SADEQ HEDAYAT[89]

To enter the opium realm, we must become servants of this small corner of experience that synchronises mouth, throat, and lungs in a near-lethal rhythm of fumimania (captivation by smoke traces). Nevertheless, the smoky half-sleep that arises here is to be radically differentiated from the realm of the unconscious: indeed, the opium daze is more an art of gradual disappearance (outward, skyward) than a plunge into psychological depth (inward, downward). And the key to such an aptitude for flight and evanescence? The elevation of a single object (the brazier) over any centrality of the knowing subject (the 'I'). The apparatus of resins and charred seeds, the micro-oven of shaved poppies, its juxtaposition of burners, apertures, and bowls, the seamless conversion between sticky wax and crushed powder: all of this is rendered viable by the subordination of consciousness (in a non-sacred ceremonial offering) to the all-encompassing brazier.

---

89 Hedayat, *The Blind Owl*, 104.

INTERLUDE: BOOK OF THE OPIUM DEN

It assumes the function of a magnetic pole, or a reed instrument through which 'dark thoughts' undergo a subtilisation ('dissolution', 'vanishing'). He blows himself through the wooded mouthpiece, and thereby approximates the narrowness within: never transcendence, just dispersal (via the article). 'Heavenly' means something altogether different here, under the vial's dominion: a plane of existential thinning, evaporation, and fineness.

Opium and the brazier; dark thoughts; dissolution; vanishing; subtlety; heaven

Principle 2. Immolation (Becoming-Merciless)

> *Writers, a call to cigarettes! Literature considered as opium smoke!…Literature as a physical test of intellectual suffocation! Literature and smoke, literature up in smoke.*
>
> *The city is giving birth to my cerebral death, I feel my head airing out its atoms of the great state, I feel my head airing out its atoms of literary opium, and I expose my bare skull to the healing rain…*
>
> RÉDA BENSMAIA[90]

The opium smoker must not simply lose himself in the complex staging of accessories: the dangling of glowing

---

90 Bensmaia, *The Year of Passages*, 39/106.7.

oil lamps, the positioning of ceramic trays and metallic paraphernalia, the scraping or whisking motions of what were once called 'dream sticks'. There is also a severe 'test' at stake in the first excerpt above (manifesto of disintegration), an insurgent imperative of the rebel, dissident, or saboteur that turns the opium den into a headquarters and stronghold of miasmic plots. It is in this sense that opium's reactivity fulfils both a perfect philosophy of distraction and a perfect philosophy of focus: the grey-white mist forms an exclusive perimeter around the execution of an urgent gesture; its haze is a barricade against awareness of any outer reality (revolutionary indifference), concentrating the gaze instead on the circulation of an emergent, all-important design (revolutionary passion). Sensation thereby becomes a call to arms, the thick air emulating that of the tear gas inhaled during street riots, or even the crazed fog of war, and with it, all aesthetic actions in this domain are equally consigned to a literal trial by fire (martyrological 'suffocation').

What outer threshold of creative fanaticism requires the burning of one's work? What outer threshold of creative conviction requires the burning of oneself? We have certainly seen avant-garde movements put their own artistic products to the flame, setting alight their canvases and sculptures according to suicidal-masochistic creeds or proclamations of euphoric purging, and we even know of avant-garde performers inflicting perceptible

INTERLUDE: BOOK OF THE OPIUM DEN

damage upon themselves in a sort of subject-object exchange whereby they become yet another dispensable stage property, but in the *faramoosh-khaneh* we find ourselves speaking of another register of violation. No mere symbolic theatres of operation; all representational orders have been overtaken by the borderline materiality-immateriality of ash and ember.

What exactly is being choked (to death) in this time-space contraction around a single smoke-ring, and what are the exact terms of this immolation reflex whereby all language or thought goes 'up in smoke'? On whose undressed bodies are this era's writers suddenly commanded to put out their still-crackling cigarettes (whose pleasure is being purchased by this pain)? Why must they seek the exposure of 'bare skulls' beneath the oppressive city's rain, all the while enduring conflagration with the ferocious look of armed devotees? Headless authors, marching in succession, their cerebra enkindled in service of the 'atoms of the great state'.... Is this something like the calculated act of brush-clearing in forest lands, or more the naturally spontaneous effect of the wildfire? Either way, it is intended to evacuate an otherwise saturated horizon of the event, to restore the zero degree and thereby prepare infinite conceivable room for who knows what inflections of chance, destiny, potentiality. The pipe is an epochal knife (sharpened against history); the pipe infuses unstoppable momentum; the pipe teaches its smoker to proceed mercilessly. Rage, storm, and the veritable transubstantiation of the exhausted subject into pure exhaust: such is the militancy of the opium den's inscription.

Opium and writing; testing; suffocation; cerebral death; atoms; exposure; bareness; healing

NARCOMANIA (OBSESSION WITH DRUGS)

Principle 3. Solitude (Becoming-Innocent)

> *In caves of loneliness*
> *futility was born,*
> *blood smelled of bhang and opium,*
> *pregnant women*
> *gave birth to headless infants,*
> *and cradles out of shame*
> *took refuge in graves.*

FORUGH FARROKHZAD[91]

Opium's storytellers have fashioned several narrative genres to attempt to capture the elusive touch of the drug, although none have come closer than the fairy tale (and by extension the poetic imagination of the child). For despite the fairy tale's chaotic shapes and intimations, all of which grant it autonomy from psychological

---

91 Farrokhzad, *A Lonely Woman*, 49.

INTERLUDE: BOOK OF THE OPIUM DEN

substructures and mythic archetypes, there are certain recognisable conceptual paths that enable trespass into unrecognisable places. The first aspects, scrawled in large letters like signposts before the open mouth of the jungle, island, labyrinth, or rabbit-hole: 'Loneliness'; 'Futility'. Radical solitude and absurd perception are thus the initial points of departure for the procedural wresting of reality into unreality—and could we think of a better agent than opium to confer upon us this wisdom of the loneliness and futility of things?

Still, these thematic strands forge only a nihilistic springboard, and never a nihilistic destination, which effectively isolates the child's wonder ('in caves') and resurrects their ever-threatened innocence ('was born') so as to unleash experiences of wildness, curiosity, adventure, and formless temptation. Uncorrupted narcomania (as encountered exception) is thus diametrically opposed to addiction (as neurotic repetition-compulsion), for it never aspires to an identical trip but rather always to an untold dimension (by traversing the hollow spot). Opium: Surrealism five thousand years before Surrealism; Pataphysics five thousand years before Pataphysics (the study of imaginary phenomena and imaginary solutions).

So why such drastic distance from the human species (fatigued by one's race), and why this kinship with trivial perspectives on being? Because this is what allows a conspiracy of boredom, derangement, and desire to fill the void with innumerable prototypes—animality, monstrosity, machines, ghosts, celestial or vegetal visitants, abnormally animated or talking things. Note that she is not alone in her aloneness: she quickly speaks of 'pregnant women' and 'headless infants' who clamour and flood the otherwise empty forum of the cave (itself a lesson in the relation between wish and will). For if Hell is brought about by static otherness, then paradise is not the retreat into absent seclusion but rather the invention, projection, and accompaniment of a phantom-carnival whose participants blur all lines between the precious and the unclean, the lyrical and the vulgar, the moral and immoral creature. The drug's latex residue thereby serves as both enclosure (it banishes the ideal body) and portal (it invokes physiological strangeness).

The *faramoosh-khaneh* (in its highest orchestration) follows this same logic of the festival, masquerade, or playground where mad indulgence reigns above limitation, expectation, or need. First she locates the cavern; then she summons those of diluted-smelling blood to dance across its stone walls: an invitation to those who might smoke freely in her 'refuge', unearthing a new entourage (the unspeakable gathering), those who master the minor techniques of pretending and shadow-puppetry behind all visions of remoteness.

> *Opium and the cave; loneliness; futility; pregnancy; infancy; headlessness; the cradle; the grave; refuge; shame*

INTERLUDE: BOOK OF THE OPIUM DEN

Principle 4. Secrecy (Becoming-Entranced)

> *He sprinkled a secret drug onto the water. The suspect particles flashed in the light as they fell and then scattered over the water's surface. He watched them quickly spread—zealously, like entranced mystics—to contaminate the entire pool.*
>
> IBRAHIM AL-KONI[92]

We should perhaps overlook the *faramoosh-khaneh*'s centuries-long intersection with actual mystical circles in favour of the more insidiously fascinating relation between narcomaniacal zones and mysticism. Temporally, they are connected by their shared preferences for nocturnality, untimeliness, stillness, and eternity. Spatially, they are connected by their congregation in outskirts, undergrounds, and confined quarters. Epistemologically, they are connected by their predilections for obscurity, perplexity, circularity, and imaginative excess. Sensorially, they are connected by the throes of ecstasy, serenity, and vertigo. Metaphysically, they are connected by their varying quests to devour godliness (through immanent contamination, never purity) by compartmentalising the universal into the particular (a single swallow, puff, or drag), and by the conceptualisation of otherworldliness

---

92 Al-Koni, *The Seven Veils of Seth*, 20.

as a nearby surface (albeit one stretched endlessly across a lone layer).

Principally, though, it is a profane adoration of lightness that binds the territories of opium to those of mystical worship. Notice the terminology of the above passage—'sprinkled', 'particles', 'flashed', 'quickly spread'—clear evidence of how the mystic or opium dealer aligns and orients their followers toward the insubstantial. Priests, sorcerers, and shamans of both pagan civilisations and nomadic tribes understood this collusion (against gravity) in their earliest trances, their populations forever oscillating between drought and opulence, strung out across the desert's infernal dawns and freezing cold nights, its blinding suns and luminous stars, all testament to the frailty of creation's spiral. Opium: Revocation of any unifying theory of the ground (dwelling, habitation); rather, there is only manipulation of the drift (abandonment, hovering, pneumatic trajectography). This is the philosophy of secrecy and trance flowing across the watery pool and through the inner chambers of the drug den: 'they fell and then scattered' (epithet of existence, condemned to lightness).

Opium and sprinkling; secret; water; suspicion; the particle; light; scattering; surface; spreading; zeal; the mystic; the trance; contamination

INTERLUDE: BOOK OF THE OPIUM DEN

Principle 5. Horror (Becoming-Caged)

> *Here they recommend the leeching of healthy hearts*
> *so that somewhat high and delirious like an intoxicated canary*
> *you give yourself over to the tune of the sweetest melody*
> *of your existence up until death's threshold*
> *for you know that*
> *tranquility*
> *is roasted corn in the stomach's reed-tripe*
> *which fulfills its destiny in a cage,*
> *as the security officer places the paper slip of relief in your palm*
> *and the pill-bottle of codeine in the pocket of your gown*
> *—one in the morning, one at night, with love!*
>
> AHMAD SHAMLU[93]

What rare typologies of fear arise when the otherwise illicit tonics and ingredients of the *faramoosh-khaneh* are thieved by regimes of biopolitical power? What fresh paranoia now accompanies those once-savoured narcotic clouds when they are displaced from their badlands and assimilated into pale regimented institutions? When its beautiful malevolence filters through mechanisms of sadistic control? The name of this stolenness is the

---

93 Shamlu, *Born Upon the Dark Spear*, 118.

Hospital, where opium is deprived its wayward qualities and made to 'fulfill its destiny in a cage', its tropospheric veils now condensed into the foreign compositions of the pill and the syringe.

A new definition of horror accompanies the Hospital, though it may be funnelled through a false high or perverse delirium that facilitates 'the leeching of healthy hearts'. It is the pseudo-intoxication of the stupor as opposed to the drug slumber of older periods: behind the mask of alleviation, it imports the awful logic of nightmare, suspicion, and anonymous threats. The poppy's carelessness morphs into a totalitarian prescription of care, its prior capacities for hypnosis and pacification now imitated by analgesic regulation. For where opium is misanthropically transformative (one sheds one's human scales), the opioid is anthropocentrically binding (seeking a cruel utopian sameness). Opium bestows a certain arche-intelligence; the opioid leaves patients strolling courtyards with half-comatose stares. Opium endows one with hyper-sensitivity (through ventilation); the opioid breeds numbness (through domination). The broker of the unbound somehow becomes the broker of containment, its former subcultural hiddenness wrenched into mass epidemic waves: a sedative to promise countless slaves.

Thus we return to the poetic passage above and its careful sketch of a horror-show based not in pain but in

INTERLUDE: BOOK OF THE OPIUM DEN

the painkiller. In the opium den we found attendants graced with indistinct presence and refined passivity, quietly entering and exiting each corner with an almost phantasmal aspect; in the opioid hospital we hear the loud interventionist footsteps and feel the authoritarian looming of the staff (systemic minions). No, the gentle narcomaniacal overseer, caretaker, or curator is not the same as the warden, superintendent, or administrator of synthetic compounds. In the opium den, we set an elaborate backdrop for sentiments of micro-exaltation, micro-apotheosis, and insignificant invincibility; in the opioid hospital, we sustain states of impoverishment, disadvantage, and subsistence-level perception (kept barely alive). In the opium den, we prolong the true aim of the eternal return (recurrence of the most perfect hour, or 'the drunken happiness of dying at midnight');[94] in the opioid hospital, we are obligated to play out the most wretched conditions of weakness (inexorability of the worst possible moment). This is how horror becomes routinised into dread—official, codified, trading short-lived desertions for long-term dependencies—as 'death's threshold' finds itself resewn each day into the 'pocket of your gown' (gift of the watchkeeper).

Opium and leeching; delirium; intoxication; sweetness; threshold; tranquility; destiny; the stomach; the cage; the bottle; the pocket; relief

---

[94] F. Nietzsche, 'The Drunken Song', in *'Thus Spoke Zarathustra', The Portable Nietzsche*, tr. W. Kaufmann (New York: Penguin, 1954), Verse 6.

OMNICIDE II

IOMANIA (OBSESSION WITH POISON)

Principle 6. Distillation (Becoming-Sunken)

> *I sink into your hell and I scream out:*
> *I distill a poisonous elixir for you*
> *and I give you life*
>
> ADONIS[95]

In the hands of the incompetent or malevolent supplier, opium's milky liquid transitions almost unnoticeably from tranquilising agent to venomising agent. 'I distill a poisonous elixir for you, and I give you life', he rasps, like someone with elite knowledge of the balancing-point between vitality and terminality, transience and permanence, momentary calm and irrecoverable sunkenness. For just as Sleep and Death were deities often personified as brothers, lovers, or close allies in mythological descriptions of the first civilisations, so does the opium den's trade tiptoe across this fine iomaniacal line between two untrustworthy gods.

Modern thought should study those ancient and mediaeval orders (of physicians, astronomers, alchemists) that diagrammed toxicological classifications of salves and ointments extracted from dangerous plant

---

95 Adonis, *A Time Between Ashes and Roses*, 135.

species: deadly nightshade (*Atropa belladonna*), black henbane (*Hyoscyamus niger*), and mandrake (*Mandragora officinarum*), each with their unique alkaloid mixtures of atropine, scopolamine, and hyoscyamine. Moreover, they were among the earliest to employ the opium fields for medicinal purposes of anaesthesia (soaking sponges during surgical operations) and even euthanasia (mixing it with hemlock), again walking the nameless tightrope between salvation and demise. So it is that the grand libraries and palace laboratories of Baghdad, North Africa, and Persia became accomplices to the forbidden lounges of the *faramoosh-khaneh* and its customs of sublime impairment.

Such early scientific visionaries initiate us in a great philosophy of concoction. They developed intricate methodologies of delivery (ingestion, inhalation, skin absorption) and of brewing (fermentation, acidification, frothing) in order to experiment with the internalisation of semi-fatal substances—an expert practice of measuring proper degrees, weights, and dosages of the inconsumable that would bring their willing disciples to the fragile limits of poison time and time again. The heart stops beating, a slight excision or antidote is administered to wrench them back among the living, and an acute notation scribbled in the tables of some esoteric pharmacopoeia (to warn future generations of what goes too far).

Opium and sinking; hell; scream; distillation; elixir; gift; life

OMNICIDE II

Principle 7. Beastliness (Becoming-Massacred)

> *While I wait for the poison to work*
> *The blood of a demon bile spit out*
> *Spit out by beasts all massacred.*
>
> JOYCE MANSOUR[96]

Is there a modicum of evil borne by the opium experience, and does the opium den situate itself amid base materialist dregs? For she speaks of an iomaniacal demon, of the diabolical patience required to 'wait' for poison's symptoms to take hold, and of the viscous pouring forth of blood, bile, and spit in a single line.

Let us picture the actual tactile setting of the *faramoosh-khaneh*—its part-ruined edifices and paint-chipped walls, its poor velvet couches and linen beds lain close to the floor, its dim-lit lanterns and candles—as a site in which luxury and dilapidation coalesce, restoring the paradoxical aesthetics of decadence (in the best artistic sense of the term). Like all concepts of waste, it bears both lavish and crude temperaments; it is built for an inverted aristocracy (that of superior outcasts) for which one must be simultaneously cultivated, discriminating, and tasteful while also negligent, contemptible, and self-destructive. Supreme stylisation of the dishonourable.

---

96 Mansour, *Essential Poems and Writings*, 73.

INTERLUDE: BOOK OF THE OPIUM DEN

Note: Nearly a hundred years ago, in the salt desert provinces of central Iran, a distant relative was known to withdraw each evening into a private room and smoke opium. However, it was also common knowledge that a long white snake lived between the walls of the house and would emerge each night from a hole in the upper right-hand corner of the ceiling to partake alongside the elder man. It had become equally accustomed to the nocturnal ritual and to the drug's alluring potency, and upon detecting the first scent would slither forth slowly to join its familiar human counterpart for several lost hours, resting at the foot of the opium brazier and flicking its tongue in satisfaction. We might speculate as to whether serpents, too, hallucinate.

Animality is a natural inheritance, whereas Beastliness signals another (lower) primordialism: defective, anomalous, cryptogenic. A poison derived from 'beasts all massacred', she tells us above, such that this entire discourse brings us to the doorstep of the *faramoosh-khaneh* as a kind of bestiary geared toward the encapsulation of fantastical traits. Indeed, the den's own funhouse architectural arrangement reminds one of the illuminated manuscripts of bestiaries and *aja'ib* literature (compendia of 'strangeness') from the Middle Ages—e.g., Zakariya al-Qazvini's *'Aja'ib al-Makhluqat wa Ghara'ib al-Mawjudat* (*Marvels of Things Created and Miraculous Aspects of Things Existing*) or Abd al-Hasan Al-Isfahani's *Kitab al-Bulhan*

(*Book of Wonders*)—which combined calligraphic text with illustrations of exotic, rumoured, or supernatural entities. It is no mere coincidence that for decades now, opium has found itself fastened to the expression 'chasing the dragon': for beasts (like opium) are extravagant, ornate forces beheld with both attraction and repulsion; they also share remarkable capacities for adaptation and doublespeak. But above all else, they sweeten the prospect of non-being (for both predator and prey), for beastliness alleviates any negative concern with death's finitude by charging it with the seductive purpose of dying-on-the-run. It seals the original philosophical task of learning to die well (*ars moriendi*) with the ultra-violent timing of massacre (i.e. at the nebulous climax of ability, energy, hunger).

Opium and waiting; blood; bile; spit; the demon; the beast; massacre

Principle 8. Ephemerality (Becoming-Dream)

He knew that we all, like human rags, imagine and say to ourselves day and night things that are degenerate, even alarming. The important thing is that the hallucination should continue, that the viper of time should bite the ephemeral people who visit the field, that in all our life we should write one story or poem: 'This market is my world,

INTERLUDE: BOOK OF THE OPIUM DEN

my grave and my wings. I am the house of worms that is troubled by a number in a dream'.

HASSAN BLASIM[97]

Opium's epilogue should be composed precisely by sloping or leaning silhouettes, those 'troubled by a number in a dream' (i.e. under its fleeting spell awhile). For this *faramoosh-khaneh*, house of forgetting, house of oblivion, shelter of transient degeneration and degenerate transience, is somewhere we must leave in the end. Thought becomes an emulsion to identity, a banned flower in the garden, contrasting past selves with rising chimeras. But it does not last forever (all are but visitors). In this respect, opium embodies reversibility at its finest juncture: that split second when the idle ones rule the world, and then come undone again. We should beware events that are irreversible; we should also beware events that are reversible: for those who master ephemerality are likewise masters of the return ('that the hallucination should continue'). They will find their way back to the faintness; they will reawaken the 'viper of time', wear their best silken rags, and draw strong influenced breath once more. Everything that is elsewhere and suspended in air belongs to them.

Opium and rags; degeneracy; alarm; hallucination; continuation; the time viper; ephemerality; visitation; trouble; the dream number

---

97 Blasim, *The Madman of Freedom Square*, 58.

Part 15
Praecidomania (Mutilation)
Tomomania (Surgical Operations)
Stauromania (Crucifixion)
Xyromania (Razors, Knives)
Trypanomania (Needles)
Cicatromania (Scars)

Praecidomania (Mutilation)

I love to extract the strongest organs of a genius
To spread them out in the middle of the day

JOYCE MANSOUR[98]

The Praecidomaniac is never the sadistic serial killer who corrals weaker victims into dank basements or private corners only to commence slicing in neurotic, shame-ridden motions (transitioning open bodies into repressive enclosures): no, she is a figure of passionate exhibitionism who seeks only the splaying of peerless internal forms ('organs of a genius') into free, unguarded space. She stacks them into tapering piles in broad daylight to simulate the glory of ancient pyramidal monuments, if only to extol the 'strongest' among us. She places a spotlight upon the inner workings of the genius so that all may behold the pancreas, kidneys, and diaphragms that sit like gears of a deconstructed grandfather clock; her mania craves insight into the pendulums, keyholes, and anchor escapements that make it turn in its perfect circles. Elsewhere she demands that we 'disembowel the actors' and 'uproot the dead' in order to form similar parades and convoys.[99]

---

98 Mansour, *Essential Poems and Writings*, 329.
99 Ibid., 279.

Thus the paradox of using mutilation (wild technique) to understand precision, enlisting the most unsophisticated hacking instruments (hatchet, machete) to penetrate the secrets of prowess or complexity.

Note: Recent reports indicate the rise of several university-funded labs whose research teams have set the hacking of dreams as their main purpose. Through the psyche-mining sensors of newly-designed wearable devices, these Dream Labs aim to trail the imagistic paths of the dream in order to experiment with the possibility of an interactive technology that would assist with memory consolidation, knowledge and creativity augmentation, sensory cultivation, and mood regulation during sleeping hours. Moreover, by using muscle tracking, electrodermal activity, brain waves, and heart rate monitoring to identify those sleep stages most predisposed to influence, the Dream Lab is able to insert images or phenomenal content into the dreamscape via repeated audio recordings of a single word or the releasing of specific scents. This having been successfully achieved, researchers assert that the key reasons to pursue the refining of such dream incubation processes are to glean the alternative intelligence/meaning of the unconscious, and to facilitate or even master lucid dreaming. And yet, at what level is this a mere mechanical reproduction of that same praecidomania described above, which seeks to access and loosen formerly bounded worlds? To what extent is dream engineering not itself an art of mutilation, as etymologically betrayed by the use in both contexts of the term 'hacking', with its insistence upon carving articles of imaginative genius into pure transparency?

Mutilation and love; extraction; the strongest; the organs; genius; spreading

Tomomania (Surgical Operations)

> *At the entry of the dead end, the so-called secluded area of our dreams, Yackoff, the refugee surgeon...Yackoff continues, I can transplant any given organ of one sex onto the body of another sex, without any major technical obstacle.*
>
> RÉDA BENSMAIA[100]

The Tomomaniac is never the messy slasher who rips forms apart and scours within bodily cavities as if following convulsive drives: no, Tomomaniacs are the surgical ones who pride themselves on exceptional training, practice, and expertise in the application of straight, compact incisions. They are enemies of the uncontrolled gash, those whose hands are often reported to move even in their sleep, as if maintaining their suppleness and agility at all times. And yet there is a twist in the above passage: for some disgraced or opportunistic surgeons, or those whose curiosity draws them into more radical adventurism, find themselves selling their skills on the black-market undergrounds of the world. Such is the figure in the opening excerpt, who appears consumed by the mania of transplantation, one of those who would deploy meticulous artifice to traverse the aporias or 'dead-ends' of

---

[100] Bensmaia, *The Year of Passages*, 82.3.

natural compatibility, and whose scalpel therefore makes its nice cuts in service of the less acceptable assignment of harvesting or swapping organs for illicit clients. Which raises the ethical-speculative question of whether all that *can* be done *should* be done. For all the philosophical interest in the inhuman, posthuman, or transhuman form, we rarely ever contemplate the actual doctors who must carry such projects forward 'without any major technical obstacle' in the interests of superseding our inborn rejective tendencies. What happens to the one tasked with such wizardries of reconstructive lifting, tucking, abrasion, and implantation? What befalls them in the reallocative middle ground between donor and recipient, the 'so-called secluded area of their dreams' where the slight existential tolls that accompany this work of abscission, resection, and enucleation are taken, without our paying any heed? Does the consciousness of these surgeons not begin to resemble something like the very prosthetics they attach and implant? And what would it mean for us to apply to consciousness these paradigms of the autograft, allograft, isograft, and xenograft? Would our own inner thoughts not slowly metamorphose into something resembling a foreigner's entrails?

Note: Advertisements have recently gone out announcing the upcoming auction of a near-flawless sapphire ring thought to have been worn by Caligula himself, the young third Roman emperor who ruled for only four years

(37–41 AD) before being killed by the many daggers of his own guardsmen. The intaglio piece is comprised of a gold band inside a sky-blue and light purple hololith with the engraved profile of a woman believed to be his fourth wife Caesonia (who presented her own neck willingly for execution after her husband's slaying, and died accordingly). The ring was held in the private collections of various dukes and other nobility for several centuries, and now goes for open bidding at an estimated value of a million dollars. With that in mind, let us recall some alleged acts of the emperor who became synonymous with cruelty, perversion, and insane decadence: that he dressed publicly as various gods and declared himself a living solar divinity, that he often spoke to the moon, walked on gold coins, drank precious pearls melted in vinegar, appointed his stallion a priest, wasted fortunes on a useless floating bridge, committed incest with his three sisters, killed randomly for personal entertainment, was terrified of lightning, and even inspired the later ruler Nero to demand Christians be hanged burning as human lanterns above the courtyards of his grand banquets to provide light as he feasted. Consequently, whether the ring proves authentic or not, the question poses itself: What exactly is being transferred here by the personal, intimate possession of a mad sovereign from two thousand years ago? Beyond those who hide behind some posture of antiquarian interest (the historical collector), what actual hope accompanies the acquisition of this small treasure? What are the sought-after, signature properties of this assassinated ruler that might be miraculously re-delegated to the purchaser of the sapphire gem? What particular elements of Caligula's story or character are desired by the present buyer? His familicidal urges, his love of surprise executions and sacrifice of exotic creatures in his honour, his toxic dietary habits or neo-godly fashion, or the destiny of a chest stabbed thirty times by Praetorian officers, a body flung into a shallow grave in the *cryptoporticus* (underground corridor) of the palace? Above all else, the mere commodification of the ring bears something of a tomomaniacal temptation: for it plays upon a logic of quasi-surgical transplant from one wearer's finger to another, sneaking in its own tacit reincarnation theorem, as if mere touch were enough to infuse the former's caesarean lustre across time, space, and body.

Surgical operation and the dead end; the secluded area; the dream; transplantation; the technical obstacle

Stauromania (Crucifixion)

> *He said that whenever the terrorists approached Jaafar, the swords they were holding disappeared, and tears were streaming from his eyes. The terrorists didn't have a single sword or knife left. They were terrified of Jaafar and said he was a devil. They stripped him naked in front of us and crucified him against the wall. They hammered nails into the palms of his hands, and he started writhing in pain, naked, with no legs. They decided to amputate his arms with bullets. Two men stood in front of him and sprayed bullets into his arms. One of the bullets hit his heart, and he died instantly. They dragged his body to the river, collected some dry branches, and poured some gas on him.*
>
> HASSAN BLASIM[101]

The Stauromaniac perceives everything in a state of exigent suspension (hanging from a ledge) while also elevating the will to action in states of extreme complexity and anomaly. The plot of the short story quoted above, entitled 'The Thousand and One Knives', will prove consequential to understanding this assertion: A kind and well-liked neighbourhood man named Jaafar sits in a wheelchair (his legs having been amputated as a

---

101 Blasim, *The Corpse Exhibition*, 112.

soldier during the Iraq-Kuwait war), refereeing the soccer matches of local children through his binoculars. The same day, he returns home to hold a secret meeting with three other individuals with whom he shares a miraculous ability: to make knives disappear. He has convened this group regularly for several years to discuss the nature of their mysterious connection. One of them is a butcher, the second a street-kid who performs for money, and the other a scholar who has been tasked by the rest with reading voraciously through literary, philosophical, theological, and astronomical works in search of an understanding of their strange talent. In addition, the sister of Jaafar is the one and only person they know that is capable of making the knives reappear at will, bringing them back each day for their owners by means of the same method they all use, a concentrated staring at the point where tears gather in their eyes. After several intricate developments over the following pages, although they never reach a broader explanation of any kind for their gift, Jaafar is one day captured by extremists who decide to make an example of him and subject him to crucifixion in front of the other hostages. His last effort consists in making the swords of his approaching executioners vanish, one after another, until they unleash machine-gun fire on his naked arms and body. This stauromaniacal image is recounted above by an author who terms his genre 'nightmare realism' (as opposed to magical realism), related in its stark and full ghastliness precisely so as to counter any simplistic accusation that this project romanticises or fetishises madness. In fact, one of our omnicidal study's underlying contentions is that perpetual loyalty to so-called everyday reality is itself just an ideological romanticism and fetishism of a certain lunacy which calls itself normality. No, the serious existential claim here is that certain vital instinctual processes are better exercised by madness (or more particularly by mania) than by the stereotypical orders of sanity.

An important subgenre in psychology literature is that of human response to emergency and the instantaneous formulation, accessing, and hierarchisation of concepts that takes place in desperate situations. The leading researchers in such discourses have discussed the remarkable aptitude for the creation of impromptu categories to accommodate the motivations, goals, obstacles, and significances that arise when under extreme immediate pressure. In opposition to the classic image of the stampeding crowd in a crumbling theatre who trample one another while fleeing mindlessly toward the doors, these studies describe a refined 'orienting reflex' that detects incongruity (the sudden manifestation of what should not have happened, like finding a jaguar has climbed through one's bedroom window) and quickly constructs a new interpretive model of provisional factors: for example, the person who must decide what objects to take while escaping a burning house and instantly negotiates a prioritisation of living things (the child, the pet), valuable things (jewellery, documents), sentimental things (photographs), or irreplaceable things (inherited objects) while also calculating their portability (immovable versus lightweight objects) and location (object proximity versus distance from fire).[102] The striking clarity and accuracy exhibited by the majority of people in such crises demystifies the myth of panic, to the extent that it almost invites us to declare the obsolescence of rational thought (Do we really need time to figure things out?). But let us take this to a more startling level by reconnecting it to the stauromaniacal experience of genocide in our short story of the knife-disappearing band of friends, for the madness of permanent war has made each of them an expert in navigating anomaly, complexity, and the cross-classification of categories: their nation is burning always; their autonomic nervous systems are as well-tuned as androids to outer stimuli; their micro-sorcery is a mere mirror-image of their perfection of situational embodiment; reality itself is the unexpected and the world-altering, and so it is that the wheelchair becomes

---

[102] In this field of orienting reflexes and conceptual processing in states of anomaly, see the respective works of neuroscientist Evgeny Sokolov and cognitive psychologist Lawrence Barsalou. E.N. Sokolov, 'Higher Nervous Functions: The Orienting Reflex', *Annual Review of Physiology* 25 (1963): 545–80; L.W. Barsalou, 'Ad Hoc Categories', *Memory & Cognition* 11 (1983): 211–27. Interestingly, the latter also studies the categories of pressured action that emerge when trying to avoid being killed by a mob.

an escape vehicle or a battering ram or a smuggling vessel or metal scrap to be sold for food. Indeed, it is in the mania of this ambient violence that everything becomes fatally relevant—all a question of preparatory movements of encoding or eliding—as consciousness forsakes both the arbitrary and the prototypical in order to endure being perennially slung up on the cross.

Crucifixion and the whenever; swords; disappearance; tears; devil; stripping; wall; nails; palms; writhing; the instant

Xyromania (Razors, Knives)

> *The offspring of the desert would never flourish until they exterminated both with this magical knife...Here the evil fellow lay at his feet. Here the ruse master was stretched out limply beside him, lost in his frightening dreams, plotting new snares even as he slept...But this magical knife will put an end to his work, his dreams, his snares, and his evil. Slaying him will save the desert.*
>
> IBRAHIM AL-KONI[103]

The Xyromaniac places us before two different narrative-philosophical crossroads with respect to mania's relation to the prized object of desire (here, knives): First, does the maniac desire all knives in existence (the infinite collector), such that we find them rummaging through the drawers of every house or frequenting every knife store in all the cities of the world? Or does the maniac desire only the greatest knife (the one true thing), embarking on the furthermost journeys in search of the finest capstone example of its kind? Second, is the maniacal searcher someone destined or elected for possession of the object, demonstrating special abilities at a young age or in times of crisis, or do they stumble upon the

---

103 Al-Koni, *The Seven Veils of Seth*, 268.

exceptional item without boasting any intrinsic special qualities of their own? In the passage above, wherein a blade-wielding slave stands hovering above the resting body of his cruel 'ruse master', the second answer clearly applies in both cases: he seeks only 'this magical knife', and apparently just about anyone could have chanced across its exceptional power. But the encounter with manic knives and razors always brings with it further complexities, such that we may begin with this further breakdown of conceptual elements:

(1) The intended (disquisition)
(2) The glint (elucidation)
(3) The grain (aversion)
(4) The twist (violation)
(5) The autopsy (automaticity)

With the first principle, we realise the need for a xyromaniacal consciousness in order to isolate a specific target worthy of the specificity of the magical knife, thereby leading us into long disquisitions on the arch-opponent for whom the weapon is intended (languages of invective and screed). Thus the author writes on the next page: 'The blade was coated with poison like the venom of a viper, because the strategist was a viper.'[104] The second

---

104 Ibid., 269.

principle tells us that there must be sensory indicators of the blade's greatness, a glint or shining predication (like an aura or halo) that confirm its capacities as an avenging and vindicating instrument like no other: 'Its tongue gleamed in the sinister light.' According to the third principle, the xyromaniacal object demands that its holder attempt an arduous, counterintuitive action: they must travel into low-lying areas and go against the grain of everything they know or believe in order to satiate the one-track desire of the implement, risking ostracism, onus, or fatality itself: 'Its tongue was as ravenous as a viper's tongue.' With the fourth principle, we arrive at the apex moment of the twist whereupon the xyromaniacal object begs for a violent flick of the wrist, a blow or transfixion that will pierce body and space in order to widen wounds (the turning point of irreversible will). Thus he stares with gritty determination at the knife 'in his palm; its hilt in his hand' in full awareness of the forthcoming twinge. Finally, with the fifth principle, the xyromaniacal subject itself becomes increasingly knife-like in its expression—note the metallic automaticity of the tone that states 'Slaying him will save the desert'—for this is the exact pinpoint second when the narrator abandons their own text, leaving the voice to a radical coldness like that of the telephone operator, and treating all phenomena as if spread out on an autopsy table. No longer the informant; this is now the sound of the invariable.

Note: One may hypothesise as to whether the quantitative infinity of obsessive-compulsive disorders (the need to touch every razor) could be productively redirected by fostering the illusion of a qualitative infinity of obtaining the supreme version (the quest for the ultimate razor), thereby manically reorienting the very idea/feeling of presence.

Note: One can always raise the stakes of a theoretical matrix, as in the pre-Islamic Arabian tale of Shanfara, an outlaw and anti-heroic poet who was allegedly kidnapped and raised by an enemy tribe from childhood. Many years later, upon discovering the truth of his origin and abduction, Shanfara swears vengeance on his false-host tribe and vows to murder one hundred of their number. He writes wild diatribes against them and becomes increasingly adroit, deft, and savvy in the bitter accumulation of their bodies, having slaughtered ninety-eight of them by the time several warriors of the Banu Salaman ambush and surround him to put an end his killing spree. He fights with extreme valiancy despite the odds, and at one point in the ensuing struggle when his arm is cut off by a sword, picks up the severed limb and thrusts it so forcefully into the face of an opponent that it caves in the latter's head, thereby giving Shanfara his ninety-ninth victim. Nevertheless, Shanfara is subsequently overwhelmed by attackers and dies in rage-filled despair, his bloody corpse left to rot in the desert sun for all eternity.

Time passes, and several years later a wandering member of the Banu Salaman tribe just happens upon that same desert tract, and upon spotting Shanfara's gleaming skull decides to kick it carelessly across the sand, whereupon a bone splinters from the skull and lodges itself in his foot, causing gangrenous infection and death. So it is that Shanfara finally fulfils his promise to take one hundred down with him. We can surmise the purest xyromaniacal strategy conceivable at work here: to turn one's own arm and skull bone into the magical weapon; to enshrine one's own physiological fragments as the rattling sabres of some desert-saving destiny; to *become* the razor or the knife's edge.

Razor/knife and the offspring; flourishing; extermination; magicality; the evil fellow; ruse; stretching; the snare; the end; work; dream; evil; slaying; the saved desert

Trypanomania (Needles)

> *We have not yet come to the land of our distant star.*
> *The poem threads us through the needle's eye*
> *To weave the aba [robe] of a new horizon.*
>
> *I see what I want of prison...*
> *Spacious is the land, beautiful through the needle's eye.*
>
> MAHMOUD DARWISH[105]

The Trypanomaniac takes advantage of the needle as a force of mismatched proportionality (disparity between size and effect), converging with those master acupuncturists who study the assorted placements and consequences of the pinprick. As such, the needle's seemingly meagre cylindrical form serves many purposes in matters of life and death, including those of:

(1) poetic passage
(2) horizon-weaving
(3) ominous perspective
(4) pleasure prolongation

---

105 Darwish, *Unfortunately, It Was Paradise*, 31; Darwish, *If I Were Another*, 6.

With the first principle, the poet connects the needle's eye to ideas of exodus, and by extension to the figures of the migrant or the fugitive: it is that crucial lane through which a people of the 'distant star' walk toward other lands, thus connecting it to those who squeeze through the most unsuitable passages and travel across the narrowest gangplanks (bypaths more likely to kill than to afford transit). But the needle is not merely a test for the intrepid, for the second principle extends it as a methodological instrument in the entwining of breakaway horizons: such is the significance of the *aba*, which originated as a loose-fitting garment of the desert nomads whose gaze forever prowls in search of new locales of pasture or oasis (thus stitching together the destinies of the itinerant). For the third principle, we need to summon another work from the same poet in which we find a key trypanomaniacal line 'O sleepers upon memory needles, don't you sense the sound of earthquakes in the doe's hoof? I said: Do you have a fever?'—thereby linking the little piercing tool of polished steel to a grand omnicidal turn (a minimalist sensitivity to portents).[106] Nevertheless, this conceptual knitting of the needle-as-observatory, when extrapolated infinitely, leads one to an awful resolution of all things, for it renders existence an aesthetic matter (rather than some heavier ontology or metaphysics), therefore free of

---

106 Darwish, *If I Were Another*, 196.

ethical dilemma even in the face of chronic anguish—as if destruction were just a tragicomic performance for whatever voyeuristic gods might be watching us through their own needle's eye (all for show).

And finally, the fourth principle introduces us to a paradoxical sequence: for the needle's eye is what allows the imprisoned to perceive spaciousness. Indeed, the fourth uncited line of the first stanza above conveys a similar lesson—'We are captives'—which compels us to reach the intriguing conclusion that captivity is best countered by captivation (like those who dare fake their own deaths). Hence the needle's eye is a wondrous inversion-point, much like the poke to the index finger that sends fairy tale heroines into untroubled sleep: it approximates the sweet trypanomaniacal moment of another in our literary configuration who writes 'I'll sting your tragic torso with thin needles dipped in honey / And you'll smile safe from the night the thorns of all your mouth.'[107] Yes, this smile holds the secret of the reversal of the *death by a thousand cuts* (from the tenth-century Chinese *lingchi*, signifying a drawn-out process of lingering death by incremental acts of flaying), now no longer a torture strategy but rather a specialised use of the needle to implement pleasure by a thousand cuts, enchantment by a thousand stings, mad

---

[107] Mansour, *Essential Poems and Writings*, 239.

secession from the one-dimensionality of the real through a thousand miniature holes.

> *Needle and the distant; thread; the eye; weaving; robe;*
> *the new horizon; spaciousness; beauty*

Cicatromania (Scars)

> *To anyone who saw him for the first time, his face was repulsive. But if you were to sit and listen to his conversation, or to hear his stories about his life, you felt his fascination. If you were to look at his face and pretend the criss-cross of knife scars was not there...Only the scars had spoiled his features, sword scars on his cheeks and forehead, ill-healed scars whose red flesh sparkled from between the furrows on his face. Worse than all of the rest was the scar which descended from the corner of his left eye.*
> SADEQ HEDAYAT[108]

The Cicatromaniac is not merely one obsessed with scars, but also the one who can make others obsessed with their scars ('you felt his fascination'). The above figure is a long-lost fixture of Persian society known as a *luti*, signifying a local urban strongman who adhered to the chivalrous code of *javanmardi* (privileging bravery and justice above all else) and who often kept the peace by force. Some *luti* strayed into banditry and forbidden trades, like the modern mafia, and were consequently given the nickname *jahel* (ignorant), while others commanded immense respect as scimitar-brandishing purveyors of nobility, their names

---

[108] Hedayat, *Sadeq Hedayat: An Anthology*, 45.

being spoken in almost legendary tones, and these were given the nickname *dash* (brother). In the story above we are brought before the scarred face of Dash Akol, an aged fighter of inestimable gravity who watches over the city of Shiraz each night to ward off marauders, often not even needing to unsheathe the sharp cutlass on his belt in order to send rival thugs fleeing into the dark (the mania of the glare). He is the ideal type of generosity, modesty, and lethal courage. Nevertheless, when his honour code is threatened suddenly by his love for a young orphan girl under his care, who he assumes will hate his awkward spots and maculation, he finds himself haunting the wine taverns in despair, repeatedly singing the same line of an old song until falling into a drunken sleep: 'There is no cure for a madman except a chain.' He dies soon thereafter, stabbed in the back by his nemesis, a gang leader who represents the exact opposite trajectory of the *luti* code (abusive, cowardly, and treacherous), the final scar being a fresh tear that reaches deep into his loins. What we learn only too late, however, is that the young woman might in fact have been charmed by Dash Akol's facial tracks, perceiving the many scores on his 'cheeks and forehead' as inviting, fair striations. The author hints at her raptness before these imperfections, and even tempts the reader to become cicatromaniacally lost in these craters whose 'red flesh sparkled' beneath the moonlight of Shiraz.

CICATROMANIA

Note: It is a hardly-observed commonality across clinical studies that manic subjects tend to have more scars on their body than average, this owing obviously to their accelerated speed, non-linear movements, and high risk-taking propensities. But delusions of grandeur are interesting things: for these subjects are rarely ashamed of or eager to conceal these patches of scratched tissue, but rather flaunt them openly, with implicit confidence in mania's keen ability to resignify all physiognomic traits as ravishing beyond belief.

Note: This brings us to another rarely-asked question with regard to those few conquerors throughout history who rode constantly at the front lines of their armies (Alexander the Great, Genghis Khan, Nader Shah, and Napoleon, who reportedly was thrown off his horse thirty-seven times in battle). We must wonder, for the sake of manic analysis: Does the shared assumption of invincibility held by these four conquerors somehow raise the likelihood of their survival? Should they not statistically have perished ten times over? Does their maniacal outlook elevate their chances on the field? Absolutely. To connect back to our above thematic, it should be noted that almost all of the aforementioned figures eventually died from their wounds, their bodies covered with gashes from their many years in many lands (incarnated hymns to the cicatrix).

Note: All of these storied examples, each straddling sympathy and disgust, conviction and vulnerability, flaw and quintessence, reveal the scar as a site of exceptional reversal. Indeed, we did not need to wait for psychoanalysis to coin the term 'enantiodromia' to arrive at the idea that things at their extreme limits sometimes change into their opposites: Sufi mystics long ago understood that 'the universe turns differently when fire loves water'. Besides, the more intriguing consideration is to ask how exactly one might deliberately push phenomena to the point of their enantiodromiacal flip (Have we unlocked yet another hidden talent of mania?), for that willed vicissitude would surely be a perfect game for madness's playground. The scar, then, is precisely that harbour-master who takes the flesh like a gliding boat from smoothness to disruption and back again: it negotiates the pirouette from apparent innocence to hideousness and leaves behind a hybrid remainder of the inversion that has taken place. Like the ghost, mummy, zombie, or vampire (agents of contusion) who die so intensely that they gain eternal life, or those death-seeking conquerors who charged so excitedly toward mortal threat that they somersaulted themselves into temporary invincibility (and then narrative immortality), or the elder kind-hearted vigilante who defended the streets of the city until the evening of his own pure defencelessness, we see how a lone slit marks the outer experiential ridge of the turnaround or

CICATROMANIA

the upside-down. Stated otherwise, the scar is nothing short of disaster washed in the blood of the lamb.

> *Scar and repulsion; fascination; pretending; the crisscross; the spoiled;*
> *the ill-healing; sparkling flesh; the furrow; the worst*

Part 16
Agromania (Open Spaces, Holes, Abysses)

Clithromania (Confined Spaces, Caves) /Claustromania (Enclosure)

Anginomania (Extreme Tightness)

Agromania
(Open Spaces, Holes, Abysses)

> *Do not all these winding roads*
> *reach this injunction and then end*
> *in that cold and sucking mouth?*
> *What did you give me, O words beguiling the naïve,*
> *And O mortification of bodies and desires?...*
> *...Give me shelter, O simple perfect women*
> *whose fine and delicate fingertips*
> *trace rapturous embryonic movements*
> *beneath the skin*
>
> FORUGH FARROKHZAD[109]

The Agromaniac posits duelling forces of openness—sinister gnawing cavities versus freeing emergent forms, the 'sucking mouth' versus 'embryonic movements'—as she goes from corner to corner, room to room, inner space to outer space, to differentiate these interstices of her multi-cocooned world. Indeed, the above stanza is excerpted from a poetic work titled 'Green Illusion', whose abstruse layers of conspiracy confound the reader,

---

[109] F. Farrokhzad, *Another Birth and Other Poems*, tr. H. Javadi and S. Sallee (Washington, D.C.: Mage, 2010), 85.

crevasse upon crevasse, until reaching some kind of a half-crux. On the one side, she must betray all the sources of false-dealing openness that prey upon the gullible (the too-open) and which have caused her to weep for ages: the mirror was a lie of the open; the window was a lie of the open; the street is a lie of the open; the trees and the winds are lies of the open; even her own eyeballs are renounced as deceitful servants of an openness tied to 'magical water and drops of fresh blood'.[110] This is the openness of fatal ironies that leave her 'forsaken like a corpse on water, floating toward the most terrifying rocks, toward the deepest sea caves'. On the other side, however, is a contrary conception of the open tied to gestation and progeny: to await the child who will fight the universe, the true uncompensated force of the breakout. This infant presents itself as an omnicidal challenger to the oral sorcery behind things (the newcomer versus the immemorial). Thus the pregnant women's stomachs form temporary shelters around the coming perforator of vacuous worlds; the women's fingertips take on an almost nanotechnological ability to track foetal motions of what promises to breach the abyss once and for all: mania of the counter-universal rift (the outlet within the void).

---

[110] For these particular lines, we cite an alternative translation of the poem by Michael Hillmann: Farrokhzad, 'Green Delusion', in Hillmann, *Iranian Culture: A Persianist View*, 162.

Note: If one accelerationist principle states that events are increasingly happening too quickly for thought to catch up to them, approaching a singularity whereby human consciousness will always find itself too late, then our author clarifies that this seemingly runaway process of deterritorialised flows is just part of the overall unseen territoriality of the mouth that swallows being whole.

Note: The ancient Greek term *stoma* (from the Iranian Avestan *staman*, meaning 'dog's mouth') has a number of definitions dispersed across vegetal, zoological, and surgical axes, referring simultaneously to the small pores of a leaf, the ingestive opening of a lower animal, or an incisional cut made into hollow organs of the abdominal wall or trachea—as if both the real and the artificial were reducible to a series of ever-chewing mandibles. Manic openness, then, contests the bio-psychic hold of this universal stomaticism (as third innocence).

Note: Few reading this might know that the cited piece corresponds to the biographical fact of the poet's own awful choice: having to leave behind her firstborn son, her only child, in order to gain her independence and pursue writing, the boy being taken away by her former husband's family and she denied custody rights until her early death (thrown through her car's windshield at the age of thirty-two when she allegedly swerved to avoid crashing into a bus full of schoolchildren). This is the final agromaniacal stage—that of *the ultimatum* which is itself both an opening and a desolation: damned if one does, damned if one doesn't.

Openness and the winding; the injunction; the mouth; guile; naivety; mortification; shelter; the fingertips; embryonic movement; the skin

Clithromania (Confined Spaces, Caves) /Claustromania (Enclosure)

> *He settled in this neighborhood, in the basement of a cement tower...*
> *He spread a bed for dreams that evaporated in the steam of bathhouses he'd read about.*
>   *Musk Bathhouse Rose Bathhouse Bathhouse of the Beautiful*
>   *Chain Bathhouse Eyebrow Bathhouse Waterpipe Bathhouse*
>   *Qaishani Bathhouse Queen Bathhouse*
>
> ADONIS[111]

The Clithromaniac takes us into the shallow steam-filled pools of the bathhouse, the ideal space in which to ask another implausible question: Can mania be contemplative? For this, the special architectonics of the bathhouse itself—low-end brutalism, like the house of the Minotaur whose greystone maze has no furniture or ornamentation—appears to bring meditative emptiness into the service of delirium ('a bed for dreams'). The Middle Eastern

---

[111] Adonis, *Selected Poems*, 284.

and North African *hammam*, whose concrete-slab cellars have always been haunted by rumours of immoral behaviour and subversive activity, is actually most threatening to world-orders for its logic of atmospheric emanation (linking calmness to contraband reflection). Its confined spatiality, its strange textural mixture of rock, water, vapour, and cement, proves conducive to a pondering that goes beyond even the radical implications of the daydream; for while reveries are born of generalised boredom in respect to the real, the subcultural haven of the bathhouse is born of the sneaking suspicion that this below-surface pit looks precisely like the dreams/minds of those peoples who lived before the very concept of the real. A becoming-elemental in which consciousness itself starts to follow the basic conditions of filtration, drainage, trickling, rivulet, effluvium, and flotation. Furthermore, there are many houses that go by many names—musk, queen, chain, waterpipe—each promising its own convincing chamber of vision and its own separate carousel of tactility.

Note: While the neurochemistry of delirium is still not well charted, there are two known details of relevance for our understanding of its altered states: that delirium often stems from hypoxia (oxygen starvation to the brain), and that sedatives often enhance delirious mental activity. It is worth recognising, then, that the old bathhouses were known both for their limited air supply underground

CLITHROMANIA/CLAUSTROMANIA

and also for the ataractic powders often mixed into the bathing pools.

And yet, specifically what kind of delirious thoughts are exclusive to such confinement? Does not a certain wariness slip along the bath's supposed state of unwariness? Beneath the functional ritual of soaps, sponges, and washcloths does there not rest some insight into the non-pristine nature of things? For this, we turn to the partner concept of claustromania (obsession with enclosure) to gain our first directions:

> He, the defiant one, will chart the lower layers of creation,
> empowered with water that carries desire
> in an essence half lead and half myth,
> in the avalanche of limbs
> where the elements are shot and matter is shattered.[112]

The passage tells us everything, for it connects a sort of pacified delirium to the lurking secret of the elements themselves: that they defy the earth, and want out of its enclosure. We follow the details of the poet's language: that the watery body of the bathhouse-goer soaks in the power, desire, and avalanche of these forces kept below, straying between heavy metals and long-forgotten

---

112 Adonis, *Selected Poems*, 303.

stories, as meanwhile its cement walls betray the fact that the elements cling to the possibility of shattering their own terrestrial margins (domicide: the killing of one's home). The antecedents repudiate such false totality. The thoughts of the 'lower layers of creation' are therefore consumed by the fact that worldliness and elementality are no allies whatsoever, but are rather locked in the antipathy of a claustromaniacal struggle: to contain or burst at will (and where does this leave the human form, composed as it is of these same elements?).

Confinement and settling; the basement; cement; the tower; the bed of dreams; evaporation; steam; the bathhouse; defiance; the lower layers; lead; myth; avalanche; shattering

Anginomania (Extreme Tightness)

> *What but sheer madness was thrusting him on now, to aim this noose toward the horns of the mighty waddan? What secret power was leading him to entangle the great beast's head, and so bind their fates together? Had this too been long since written on the tablet of destiny, written before he was ever formed in his mother's belly and born into this harsh world? What was this ecstasy? Was it the fervor spurred on by songs and music and the beating of Sufi drums in the oases, of which his father had told him?*
>
> IBRAHIM AL-KONI[113]

The Anginomaniac flexes the imagination against multiple constrictions: the noose, the horns, fate, the womb, and the drum—and all of this simply in order to tie themselves (by close-fitting force) to the destiny of the supreme class. Whereas the neurotic's approach to greatness resembles the assassination of a celebrity by the fawning social misfit seeking attention at all costs, the manic version stems from a paradoxical belief that they themselves are the best practitioner to ever walk the earth (and their consequent desire to test themselves against all present and prior greatness). This is not the competitive paranoia

---

[113] Al-Koni, *The Bleeding of the Stone*, 47.

of the ego, but rather what the simultaneously strictest and most free-moving philosopher called the generosity of the 'best enemy': to proceed from the image of being the finest to cross this existence—the thinker must perform themselves as the lone oracle, the poet must call themselves the cardinal owner of the last word, the artist must announce themselves as the arch-shapemaker of all ages—in order to survive the tightrope walk (another anginomaniacal image). Again, this has nothing to do with a contemptible narcissistic pride: if one collects those philosophical, literary, and aesthetic figures over the centuries who enunciated their superiority to all others, one would note a shared stance of humility among them, for anything less than primacy would be to waste time and to insult craft. One must conceive oneself as the most dangerous rendering to arise since the very prelude of one's medium: otherwise, why bother to knowingly produce inferior samples? Manic elocution is to cry out 'No other can touch me' as a testament to modesty: for all else is offensive self-indulgence.

And how does this connect back to the compulsion toward extreme tightness? The only surefire way to validate singularity, distance, or dominance is by banding oneself and breaking oneself against the luminaries of the game. This battling protocol is found prevalently in most movements of street poetry and street art throughout history, as the newbloods try their teeth out on the leathery skin of old veterans; or, to borrow a page from the maniac's playbook, it can even involve calling oneself the second coming or improved reincarnation of long-gone personalities of lionised status.[114] No doubt, such is the amazing balletic contrivance and zealotry of a recursive temporality whereby great forerunners supposedly existed only so as to dare or challenge the present manic figure (the precursors taunt, snarl, and rile from afar). This knots them together in an inspiring tension, a cross-epochal vice through which names grow polysemous and their prestige is re-peddled as another's pendants: in this way, past formations are spattered, unspooled, and compacted into new subsets. In opposition to those stories of sycophants who followed every footstep or memorised every line of their favourite author, made extraordinary efforts to live in the same city, cultivated the same habits, enacted the same methods, and yet still stopped impossibly short of grasping the other's creative spark, the anginomaniac seeks an alternative tableau of tightness along the lines of the Parthian Shot (famed technique of ancient Persian Empire horsemen who could shoot arrows while riding away from their enemies, firing over their shoulders at onrushing foes).

---

[114] This manic technicality is shared by that messianic logic whereby the latest arrival in the sacred line is simultaneously the accumulation and supersession of all prior prophets.

And what is the final concern of this tightness that strikes its charging target through withdrawal? It is that here, mania shows us a paradigm of intimacy alongside complete anti-modularity: that no pieces should be interchangeable within a tradition; in fact, when such flexibility of components occurs, the tradition should be destroyed and put out of its misery. Nothing is isomorphic, leading to styles that are inimitable even when taught (a densification process that allows neither forebears nor followers).

Note: My grandfather often told the story of an old wrestler who had taken a young protégé under his wing, training him in every iota of his own athletic wisdom over several years, until the day the youth arrived and arrogantly called out his elder teacher to a contest. The younger fighter was convinced of his superior fitness and strength and was nearly victorious, until the old master flipped him with an unforeseen move that pinned him to the ground. Furious in defeat, the young wrestler jumped to his feet and angrily accused the old wrestler of never having taught him this single tactic, to which the elder replied: 'Yes, I saved it precisely for this day.' The lesson is evident: that maniacal experts always sponsor this undisclosed modicum of difference that allows them to draw their will taut around all else that persists.

Note: The present era is replete with artistries of tightness, from the Japanese sensual practice of *shibari* or *kinbaku* in which subjects are voluntarily tethered into bondage and suspended by natural fibres or ropes to form odd diagonal shapes, to the recent 'elastic dance' of a couple in Berlin bound together by skin-tight blankets (showing only facial indentations) and thin straps of white cloth while tilting rigidly across cement columns and stairwells. So it is that mania excels in the logic of originality-through-capture.

Tightness and thrusting; the noose; the horns; secret power; entanglement; binding fates; the tablet; the belly; harshness; ecstasy; fervour; the drums

Part 17
Atelomania (Imperfection)
Peccatomania (Sins, Crimes)
Subteromania (Undergrounds)

Atelomania (Imperfection)

Death, O my shadow who leads me, O my third person...
...Leave your hunting gear at the window and hang your
  heavy key chain on the door.
Mighty one, don't gaze into my veins looking for some fatal
  flaw.
You are stronger than my breathing, stronger than
  medicine...

MAHMOUD DARWISH[115]

The Atelomaniac composes a poetic address to none other than the alleged consummate imperfection of life itself—Death—in a painstaking denotation of terms. Through its crescendo of lines, we hear speaking against the hunter the voice of the civilian for whom several aspects of Death's programme prove unacceptable: (1) that it rushes time—'Death, give me time to arrange my funeral'; (2) that it trespasses on space—'Death, wait for me beyond this earth, in your kingdom'; (3) that it prevents fulfilment or exhaustion of the existential fray—'My life is yours when it has been lived to the full'; (4) that it conceals what lies on the other side of its expropriation act—'No one came back from the dead to tell us the truth';

---

115 Darwish, *Unfortunately, It Was Paradise*, 138.

(5) that it overdoes itself in the realm of thought rather than advancing as radical event—'Sickness of imagination, have a seat'; (6) that it lowers itself to engage in commerce with the struggling human form—'One such as you should not argue with a mortal being'. Above all, though, the poet accuses Death of a cowardly, slinking approach that arrogates life to itself by locating some partial weakness as an excuse to crush the whole—a failed component in the entrails, a localised infection—rather than confiscating its prey through overkill (complete organ shutdown, total cell death). Thus he chastises it for needing 'some sickness in order to kill me'; he tells it to be 'nobler than the insects' and not to 'sit in the doorways like a beggar or a tax collector'; rather than act like 'a traffic cop in the streets', he invites the necrotic sovereign to 'take off that fox mask' and instead 'be powerful, of well-tempered steel'. A fascinating literary-philosophical gesture: to make a checklist of Death's deficient ways, uppermost among which is its own predation on human deficiencies; to simultaneously critique Death and goad it to renounce its timid shortcuts so that it might become 'gallant and knightly, and launch [its] mortal assaults' as a 'clear message from the Unseen'. This scantiness of the end cannot stand.[116]

---

116 All cited lines in this section are taken from the same piece—'Mural', in *Unfortunately, It Was Paradise*—which was intended by the great poet as his last work.

ATELOMANIA

Nevertheless, the Atelomaniac is being deceptive in their poetic formula, for the index of poor designs is meant less to instigate Death to perfection than to highlight the possibility of another singular imperfection: the fact that even at its zenith of transparency and overwhelming power, there are facets that escape Death's quest for absolute collection. Hence the poet derides his enforcer by noting that 'no one has ever utterly died', and also sneers at the creative object's ability to outlast obliteration: 'O death, all the arts have defeated you, all the Mesopotamian songs. The Egyptian obelisk, the Pharaoh's tombs, the engraved temple stones, all defeated you, all were victorious. You cannot trap the immortal. So do with us and with yourself whatever you wish.' Atelomania therefore involves a search for the willed exemption to the rule of the beyond (through the logic of imperfection), just as the omnicidal imagination itself is always already an invitation to envision or fashion that which might survive omnicide (through strategies of immunisation, elusiveness, anomaly, fortification, or recurrence). This is ever the game: to dream the fatal ultimate, and then to dream precisely what could persevere across its closing limit.

Note: There are two underlying motifs in this poetic work that return us to mediaeval Arabian narrative arrangements based on imperfection: (1) the strange domain of manhunting—of the poor, the homeless, the peasant, the fugitive, the sick, the foreigner, the slave, the minority—whose racing subject always embodies an imperfection trying to outrun the coercive forces of law, violence, and death;[117] (2) the disturbing last-recourse strategy of certain women in these stories of the Middle Ages who defile themselves (most often through sexual consort with the most loathsome figure) as a form of contaminative revenge against abusive patriarchs, polluting their beds and thereby instantiating imperfection as a weapon of their own bodies. So it is that *atelos* constitutes both what imperils and what resists fatal jeopardy.

Imperfection and death; the shadow; the third person; the hunter; gazing; the fatal flaw

---

[117] It is an astounding matter of record that certain contemporary dictators have taken to ordering their military officials to use hunting ammunition on protesting crowds and secessionist movements within their borders.

Peccatomania (Sins, Crimes)

> *Clearly there can't be a real crime without the evidence of a piece of bone! Now there, maybe that's the master's secret: he has created a sentence without blood, a simple sentence that kills all pretension! A criminal sentence!*
>
> RÉDA BENSMAIA[118]

The Peccatomaniac operates the roulette table (to lay bets on) and wheel (to spin fortuity) that rotates circumstance from the impeccable to the deplorable. This is the realm of the glitch and the misdeed which, in the hands of mania, becomes a desire for the perfect crime. But what is the exact criterion of the perfect crime, or rather its multiple potential definitions? It could be measured quantitatively: a relative magnification of past infractions (the largest bank robbery, the most kills) or the slimmest probability of success or amount of rewards gained. It could also be measured qualitatively: the infringement requiring the highest level of ingenuity or daredevil ability, or with the greatest overall degree of difficulty or complexity of moving parts. Or else the perfect crime could be the one that elicits the greatest affective impact in terms of shock value, graphic violence, or the notoriety it procures for

---

118 Bensmaia, *The Year of Passages*, 94.5.

the criminal's reputation (the name that engenders awe, fear, horror, or envy). Then again, one could measure its manic perfection by the respected standard of imperceptibility—the escapade of pure slyness, known only to a few and leaving no traces—which would match the call for a 'sentence without blood'. This same 'master's secret' is described by another of our literary configuration who constructs a sepulchre without evidence: 'Then I collected sand and pebbles and scattered them around in order to obliterate the traces of the burial so completely that…I myself was unable to distinguish her grave from the surrounding ground.'[119] Yet others might say that the perfect crime is the one in which the wrongly accused plays a starring role (martyrdom) or the atrocity that vitalises or saves worlds (Promethean robbery). Or better still, perfection as originality: in essence, the surprise malefactor whose wrongdoing has as yet no name or category, being so imaginatively ahead of its time that it will only be called vice in retrospect (a neo-villainy that forces the establishment of a new regulatory code).

Note: These typologies hold for the sumptuous canon of sin as well: we might conceivably start from the ten Judaic commandments—against polytheism, dishonouring of the parent, desecration of the holy day, making graven images, taking the Lord's name in

---

[119] Hedayat, *The Blind Owl*, 34.

vain, murder, adultery, theft, bearing false witness, and coveting the neighbour's wife—and then add the later Christian seven deadly sins—lust, gluttony, greed, sloth, wrath, envy, pride—further compounded by Dante's infernal subdivisions—the unbaptised, hoarders, spenders, agents of sullenness, violence, suicide, heresy, blasphemy, sodomy, usury, seduction, flattery, bribery, divination, political corruption, hypocrisy, false counsellors, sowers of schism, falsifiers, traitors to kin, traitors to country, traitors to benefactors, and traitors to God—alongside the Islamic atlas of *Al-Kabirah* (the gravest sins) including intoxication, idolatry, black magic, figural representation, withholding charity, depriving orphans, fleeing battle, failing pilgrimage or fasting, leaving prayer, lying about prophets, breaking relational bonds, becoming an unjust leader, and refuting divine unity. With all these rubrics established, peccatomania would nevertheless rifle through the semiotics of the heinous in order to wrest forth a new classification of sin altogether—thereby discovering a modus of spiritual tampering not even anticipated by God.

Let us confront a problematic posed to us by the revered storytellers of the ancient world: the first three laws of any nascent civilisation are typically against murder, incest, and cannibalism, and yet most creation stories of these same civilisations situate the origin of existence precisely within the domain of such criminal acts: cosmic butchery, copulation between divine brothers and sisters, the physical devouring of elder god forces by their aspiring children. Quite simply, this tells us that crime is what makes the universe work, or, as another in our literary configuration states, '[t]he universe is a temporary camp in the distance between sin and hell. The sun ascends likewise with a curse, and the day is an irreparable disgrace.'[120] All is affront. But while this may appear a damning articulation, it becomes the exact opposite thanks to the light touch of mania: since creation itself is somehow miraculously a matter of brokenness prior to the inception of law, iniquity before purity, guilt that 'kills all pretension', the ultimate criminal subject would be quite at home in this world, unlike their moral and sociopolitical prosecutors who spread negative fantasies of misconduct, able to manipulate a favourable environment in order to see themselves through the eyes of those who want to punish them (as a valued object of fulmination). Like anyone on their guard, one must inhabit the perceptual register of the tracker, view yourself as they do, enter the thoughts of what hates you most, walk in their mind as they stalk you, step by step, stratagem by stratagem, if only to run circles around them.

Crime and clarity; evidence; the piece; the master's secret;
creativity; bloodlessness; non-pretension

---

120 Shamlu, *Born Upon the Dark Spear*, 109.

Subteromania (Undergrounds)

> *I lay down once more on my 'fugitive's bed'…I knew that in the mad inferno that surrounded us on all sides, it would have taken more than a tank to rescue me. It would have required digging an underground tunnel like the ones that used to be dug in ancient cities under siege.*
>
> GHADA SAMMAN[121]

The Subteromaniac continues our conceptual thread of being chased or on-the-run, for which the author introduces the dual sites of her 'fugitive's bed' and 'underground tunnel' as nether alternatives to reality. She is cornered by the verticality of modern war which dominates street and sky, and therefore mobilises her ancient siege-consciousness to seek the lowest of the low as a last-ditch expanse of the slipaway. But is she more the animal licking its wounds in the crawl-space, the rebel laying low in the hideout, or the gambler playing multiple hands in the underworld casino? To answer this, we must first comprehend the underground as the ideal site of insinuation: it belongs to the whisperer and the eavesdropper; it is the ultra-suggestive zone of the echo, where unnoticed bids are made for perception at each

---

121 Samman, *Beirut Nightmares*, 190.

turn; it turns all thought into scrying (the art of peering into a reflective medium for messages).

Like the legendary Persian Cup of Jamshid (*Jam-e Jam*), said to contain elixirs of immortality, and in whose seven rings one could view the seven layers of the universe, one must turn subterranean insight into power against the sanguinary surface and heavens, for, as a Sufi master once wrote: 'As long as the world-displaying goblet is in my hand, the wheel of heaven on high lowers itself before me.'[122] Notice how this single line coincides smoothly with the above author's depiction of the 'narrow hallway [whose] explosions following one on the other were illumining the depths of my soul', for what we derive from both is the ability to quietly reverse the roles of the pursuer and pursued by dragging everything into the sunken lair.[123] By doing this, all tenors of reality are brought into a dissociative fugue state (strategic depersonalisation and derealisation) in which the low-dweller can lure the others' wandering into retrograde, anterograde, selective, generalised, continuous, or systematic amnesia. The underground therefore becomes its own glossary of self-detaching manias (where one forgets what one came for), and if this somehow fails then one can always simply use the hypogean, downreaching place in its older

---

122 Ahmad Ghazali tr. N. Pourjavady, 'Ġazālī, Majd-al-dīn Abu'l-Fotūḥ Aḥmad', in *Encyclopaedia Iranica*.

123 Samman, *Beirut Nightmares*, 46.

crude manner as a tool of counter-totalitarian violence: to draw usurpers into the recess and then crumble it on top of them.

Underground and the fugitive; the bed; rescue; digging; the tunnel; siege

Part 18
Algomania (Pain)
Pathomania (Disease)
Molysmomania (Contamination)
Narcomania (Drug)
Iomania (Poison)

Algomania (Pain)

> *There's a king who knows no defeat*
> *I pierce his eyes*
> *Two fingers at an angle of absolute pain*
>
> JOYCE MANSOUR[124]

The Algomaniac yields three conditions for the infliction of damage against the diadems of the ruler, as those of bad standing drag the dignified by the riverside of the bruised, the cramped, and the sprained.

First, she is adamant about engaging only the 'king who knows no defeat', confirming the mad subject's desire to match itself against the unbeaten opponent: once again, unlike the sadistic, totalitarian personality, which selects weaker victims and feeds them into pre-rehearsed rituals of sameness, the algomaniac wants to face only the incomparable and the paramount, the one of unchallenged reign, and thereby to conceive a gesture improvised for the most towering stature alone. Like another in our literary configuration who says that 'blood coagulates and pain is the scent of time', she waits for just the right occasion to tip the scales of believed possibility (what they all say cannot be done), to cause pain to the

---

124 Mansour, *Essential Poems and Writings*, 337.

highest pain-bringer and thereby will divarication of the entire pyramidal order.[125]

Second, her tactical approach consists in stealing worlds by removing the perceptual faculty ('I pierce his eyes'), which serves as an attack on the very mythic terms of relation/possession of the kingdom by introducing her enemy to the old philosophical riddle of whether a tree falling in a lonely forest (with no one around to hear it) makes a sound: her revised version is whether a kingdom actually exists if there is no king to see it, thus rendering him over to the pain of the infallible conjecture (that which cannot be proved or disproved).

Third, her mania has perfected a singular technique for this very occasion ('two fingers at an angle of absolute pain'), much like the highly-debated prospect of the death-touch in Eastern martial arts (Chinese *dim mak*, literally meaning 'press artery'), which uses acupunctural knowledge to isolate fatal pressure points on the body. The presumption is that certain sharply-performed or blunt strikes (to the solar plexus or to the neck at the base of the skull) can cause paralysis, stroke, or decreased heart rate to the point of cardiac arrest either immediately or at a delayed interval (five seconds, minutes, days, weeks, or even years later). Thus the death-touch, also sometimes called the vibrating palm technique, is a matter

---

[125] Adonis, *Selected Poems*, 275.

of smothering totality through the exercise of infinitesimal accuracy. Still, it leaves open the question of whether its practitioner must necessarily sacrifice a specific part of herself as well to be capable of taking pieces of the other (the eyes, the head), like those videogame assassins who amputate their third finger in order to conceal a straight-edge blade. Is she a disciple of that manic willingness to forfeit elements of one's own nature so as to prevail against the ultimate, making a deleterious self-cutting deal for that one shot at the throne? To hit gently at the meridians and hence become the assailant of greatest fantasy.

Pain and the king; the undefeated; piercing; the angle

Pathomania (Disease)

> *The walls of my room must have contained some virus that poisoned all my thoughts. I felt sure that before me some murderer, some diseased madman, had lived in it.*
>
> SADEQ HEDAYAT[126]

The Pathomaniac reflects upon madness as a matter of detritus and residue (inheriting the derangement of prior others) that embeds itself into the very living space of the afflicted. Someone came before and rubbed their diseased impressions along the surfaces of things, resulting in a reverse vandalism whereby the walls now exude their hieroglyphic malpractice onto his skin. This reminds us of certain older languages such as Persian or Arabic wherein children can be named after abstract notions (e.g. *Zaman* or *Jahan* for a young boy, meaning 'time' and 'universe' respectively, and *Roya* or *Sanieh* for a young girl, meaning 'dream' and 'second' respectively) or natural phenomena (e.g. *Bahman* for a young boy, meaning 'avalanche', or *Sayeh* for a young girl, meaning 'shadow'), as if the ancients consciously hoped that, via this first act of tribute, the nominated force would pass on its flagrant or subtle powers, its immense or particular properties, to their

---

126 Hedayat, *The Blind Owl*, 103.

offspring. This also reminds us of the nightly routine of the lighting of torches in mediaeval castles: we can follow the image of the servant tasked with walking through long hallways, turrets, and pointed arches, stopping methodically at each wooden stave to wrap it in soaked rags of wax or tallow and always preserving the near-inextinguishable resins of sulphur and lime from the last flame in order to light the following one. Likewise, the pathomaniac follows their own sequential, illuminative procession, carrying touch from one thing to another (until they catch fire), hanging entire futurities on the principles of one-to-one exposure and slightest contact.

In the wake of these pathological depositories, one wonders whether mania can in fact inhabit the space of pessimism in its own unique way: Can it embrace the nihilistic thematics of meaninglessness or decline, given its own intense valorisations of purpose? We have already considered the active version of this premise in the linking of delirium to omnicide (passion that drives all being into the hollow), whereby the fascination for one thing leads to the imaginative or literal obliteration of everything else. But could this vitreous effect (like glass mirrors breaking one after another) also show us the way to turn pessimism into a new form of compulsive fury? Like the great short story writer whose fantasies of the so-called Middle East led him to conceive of the Library of Babel and the Book of Sand—the former with its incalculable permutations of truth or nonsense, and in whose aisles various cults, inquisitors, librarians, or lone seekers would wander their whole lives in futile search of the answer, and the latter whose compendium is bought by an Untouchable and composed in an unknown language, and whose front and back covers forever grow and pour forth ever more pages like a sempiternal torment—we are on the verge of fathoming a kind of abysmal fanaticism through which the appearance of closed totality (the library, the book) leads one into the yawning mouth of catastrophic infinity.[127] For this, a single drop of blood or poisoned thought, a single remnant of disease that functions as an ill-fated coin in everyone's pocket, is sufficient to forge the pessimistic crucible wherein omnicide grants us an unending experience of the end.

Disease and the walls; containment; poison; the murderer; the madman; the lived-in place

---

127 Jorge Luis Borges, 'Library of Babel' and 'The Book of Sand'.

Molysmomania (Contamination)

No single satyr tracks me down
But the verb transforms itself to vermin on my lips

JOYCE MANSOUR[128]

My lot is going down a flight of disused stairs
to regain something amid putrefaction and nostalgia.

FORUGH FARROKHZAD[129]

The Molysomaniac reignites the longstanding question of whether madness has contagious status, in the same way that reality itself sustains its belief-structures through psychogenetic contamination, or whether it might even occupy its own discourse of inoculability. While the strict scientific answer leans toward the negative, there is an obvious performative register in which manic affects definitely wield their own persuasive influence: for it is well noted that figures of obsessive consciousness attempt to sway probability in their favour or against another by devising elaborate exercises in thought (envisioning certain situations), in language (repeating wishes or spells),

---

128 Mansour, *Essential Poems and Writings*, 203.
129 Farrokhzad, *A Lonely Woman*, 112.

in image (constructing sympathetic objects or gazing at pictures), or in touch (collecting things of special belonging, like a strand of hair or prized possession). These are conductive gestures based on the premise that mental accompaniment (walking together in the mind) or remote sensory connections (tracing a fatal line in air with one's hand) can influence the pending chain of events. This stream of visualisations and murmurings is supposed to enhance the productive link between imagination and incident, culminating in the most systematically unscientific practices of association—e.g. the notion that focusing on another's favourite colour will increase the likelihood of crossing paths with them that same day, or that thinking of them continuously will cause them to think of one in turn—as if in an expansion of that strange apperception wherein one can feel oneself being stared at by others. Just as intriguing are the series of connective practices arbitrarily dismissed as ineffective (e.g. concentrating on shapes that resemble the intended form or using certain mimetic substitutes), which provide further evidence of both the extreme flexibility and the precision with which such molysmomaniacal devices are concocted: that contamination can perpetrate itself in a single contour or fragrance, in lazy or full-blown tempos, or even in shades of incognito, but not every straightforward attempt will unlock the mystery of this remote banditry.

Let us return to the original quotes hanging above as adages or runes in service of this antinomy between the well-born versus the speckled existence: Firstly, it is no accident that she mentions the satyr, for thermiomorphic beings (gods in beastly shape) are among the first mythic attempts to understand contamination as a walking, living force. Moreover, when we picture those early cultic adorations of the flute-playing Pan, we see how the right circumstance can propel language/thought ('the verb transforms itself') into a fin-de-siècle or millenarian madness. Note, however, that the key conceptual term behind this dance or kiss of delirium is 'vermin', as vermin are always classified as sullied and partly-mauled forms, like those bats stuck between rodent and winged creature (half-despicable, half-celestial). Moreover, the second passage hits us with the prospect of regaining 'something amid putrefaction' (a contamination amidst contamination): crucially, this one worthwhile extract is to be found stashed among the refuse ('a flight of disused stairs'), or even as a foulness residing in certain overtrodden memories ('nostalgia'), like a war-medal of the defunct cause. We are urged here to honour the resources of decomposition and vitiation (from the word 'vice'): for such are the hidden cartridges of that 'something' that messes up 'everything', like those card games in which a single card can ruin an entire hand, or those rarest of individuals struck by lightning multiple times, or those drug cartel bosses who subject their faces to compulsive plastic surgeries in order to switch identities, or like that untrustworthy book of the Emerald Tablet in ancient Arabian Hermeticism (alchemical teachings of how to garble the *prima materia*), whose alleged author was called 'the thrice-great' (evidence of sequential adulterations), and yet which somehow finds itself translated among the bookshelves of respectable Western scientists and even enters an old psychoanalyst's dreams, where it is sometimes literally portrayed as an emerald table. Indeed, it is the secret to becoming, as a great writer of disquiet once said—the same one who told of a King of Gaps for whom 'All think that he is God, except himself' (frustration of the universe).[130]

Contamination and the satyr; the transformed verb; vermin; the lips; the lot; going-down; the disused stairs; the something; putrefaction; nostalgia

Narcomania (Drugs)
Iomania (Poison)

See *Book of the Opium Den*.

---

[130] This line—'All think that he is God, except himself'—is from Fernando Pessoa, 'The King of Gaps', tr. L. Freire, in *Poesia Inglesa* (Lisbon: Livros Horizonte, 1995), 410.

Part 19
Necromania (Death)
Thanatomania (Death-Magic)
Coimetromania (Cemeteries)
Klaiomania (Weeping)

Necromania (Death)

> *On this side of the wall, a hollow universe, a motionless*
> *and uncreeping universe, spreads out for all eternity*
> *A calm cradle, in which darkness fluctuates from one*
> *galaxy to another galaxy, filling the cold void with the*
> *extract of death*
> *And behind his proud epics*
> *a solitary man*
> *weeps for his own cadaver.*
>
> AHMAD SHAMLU[131]

The Necromaniac combines the figures of the *faqir/fakir* (poor mystic, from Arabic *faqr*, 'poverty') and the figure of the *'amaleh* (poor worker, from the Arabic *'amal*, 'work'), though here referring to those impoverished or toiling not before God, but for Death. The death-mendicant and the death-labourer. The fakir is traditionally a mystic who abstains from material dependencies, living in abject poverty, surviving on alms given by others in the street, and subjecting their bodies to the most vicious practices of self-mortification: they can often be found piercing themselves with blades, placing their flesh against fiery coals, or sitting beneath the scalding heat of the sun, taking vows

---

[131] Shamlu, *Born Upon the Dark Spear*, 21.

of silence or hunger, or remaining motionless or in painful positions for prolonged periods of time (and without bathing or cutting their hair). They are also often subjects of charismatic power, and miraculous deeds are attributed to them, the consequence of their many abasements. The protagonist of the above poem is one who matches this double criterion of endurance and wonder-working, for it is said that 'his hands are devoid of love and hope and future', and yet that each night he 'shaves flowers from jagged stones'. But what does it mean to reterritorialise the fakir as an abstinent servant/lover of Death (with no interest in metaphysical beyonds), one who supplicates to a master of pure physicality (since Death has no use for souls)? To do so is to infuse finality with an unspoken gift: for Necromania here is the obsessive desire, not to kill everyone, but rather to be the only one who experiences death in its radical instantaneity (which otherwise always comes too late for consciousness and sensation). The fakir alone is allowed to accelerate/propel himself toward that near-animatronic state where he can 'weep for his own cadaver', and furthermore perceives this as the most elegant sight imaginable, the seat of sublime possibility itself wherein sadness and delight become indistinguishable beggars on a sidewalk corner. The paradox of the poor-unto-death (richest of all), volcanic in their stillness and all the more alive for their perpetual dying: in short, to be not the proprietor of nothing but instead the proprietor of the nothing itself.

At the same time, however, the poet refers to himself as the *'amaleh* of a self-convened finality—'I was the workman of my own death'—and notes that he casts his prized 'sledgehammer' aside after long years of struggling to 'make the bell-toll of my death even louder'. The term *'amaleh* is typically reserved for the lowest strata of unskilled labourers—those who will do anything for almost nothing, volunteering to undertake dangerous tasks for the most exploitative wages—and who can often be seen carrying heavy loads or perched upon insecure heights, their clothes covered in white clay and chalk. Nevertheless, their primary employment is in construction, as builders and wrecking-crews of walls—and it is no coincidence that the poetic work above is entitled 'Behind the Wall', for in its every line it speaks of an art of demolition. Here, the language of drudgery is everywhere; the daily grind of exertion and strife, although once again on behalf of Death. What does it mean to reterritorialise the domain of labour according to the terms of necromania? If the *'amaleh* are indeed those who wake each morning to toil among near-death experiences—learning how to 'survive both annihilation and its opposite',[132] as another in our literary configuration says—then they are precisely

---

132 Darwish, *Unfortunately, It Was Paradise*, 146.

those whose shovels 'fill the cold void with the extract of death'. Beyond this, they alone bring calcination to the weak pillars of the real that separate life and death; they literally take down the walls, and in doing so allow their immortal boss to expand its mortal industry.

Note: The mystical teacher George Ivanovic Gurdjieff connects these conceptual planes (poverty, work, death) in his own way, though we are interested less in the truth-content of his spiritual claims than in the great necromaniacal fascination that he implants in those aristocrats, intellectuals, and artists who he converted into pseudo-fakirs (demanding intense manual labour from them at his deteriorated mansion in Avon, France). Indeed, Gurdjieff himself used the actual term 'fakir' to describe the first stage of 'The Work' in his so-called Fourth Way, which consisted of extreme physical training based on the 'sacred dances' of arcane calisthenic postures, learned among different mystical orders in his travels through the Middle East and Southeast Asia, which taught initiates to enact the nine-pointed enneagram and thereby to align their bodily movements with the diatonic musical scale.[133] All of this esoteric training, however, hides the

---

133 From Gurdjieff: 'The way of the fakir is the way of struggle with the physical body, the way of work on the first room. This is a long, difficult, and uncertain way. The fakir strives to develop physical will, power over the body. This is attained by means of terrible sufferings, by torturing the body. The whole way of the fakir consists of various incredibly difficult physical exercises. The fakir either stands motionless in the same position for hours, days, months, or years; or sits with outstretched arms on a bare stone in sun, rain, and snow; or tortures himself with fire, puts his legs

death-infatuated turn that intrigues us here: namely, how did Gurdjieff, prone to his own necromaniacal claims of having encountered extinct sects such as the Essenes or the Sarmoung Brotherhood, somehow convince his high-born acolytes to believe that they existed in a state of 'waking sleep' akin to deathliness? Furthermore, how did he captivate them to want to explore the depths of this lost death-state, like those other gurus of reincarnation who would attend fancy dinner parties and regale guests by inducing hallucinated visions of past lives? What kind of manic persona can instil in others this singular fascination to see what has died in them?

Death and the wall; the hollow universe; motionlessness; the cradle; darkness; fluctuation; the cold void; the extract; the weeping cadaver

---

into an ant-heap, and so on. If he does not fall ill and die before what may be called physical will is developed in him, then he attains the fourth room or the possibility of forming the fourth body.' G.I. Gurdjieff, cited in P.D. Ouspensky, *In Search of the Miraculous: Fragments Of An Unknown Teaching* (New York: Harcourt, 1949), 45–50.

Thanatomania (Death-Magic)

> *And writing is your death wish, a desire that flows in words the way blood flows in veins. Are you trying to tell us that writing is breathing an air that is death? Death is silence. Writing is preparation for this silence and a celebration of it. We master the art of silence to recognize the face of death, to learn how to die.*
>
> ADONIS[134]

The Thanatomaniac arrives from an obscure angle to address the age-old discussion on how poetry (with its enigmatic rhythms) differs from all other forms of language, while also reminding us definitively that the question 'What Are Poets For?' belongs neither to modern philosophy nor to contemporary literary criticism, but rather necessarily to those places where the first poets roamed the earth—the Sumerian Temple Hymns of the priestess Enheduanna, the Akkadian Flood Myths, or the Pyramid Texts of the Egyptian Old Kingdoms. Whether wandering between the two rivers of the Fertile Crescent or across the Nile River Valley, their originative ways are answered by the above-cited descendant, who distinguishes the following three touchstones: (1) that

---

[134] Adonis, *Selected Poems*, 278.

the poetic constitutes a form of ritual-magical wish; (2) that the poetic is a sacerdotal domain, belonging to a certain ordained sorcerer-priesthood; (3) that its principal concern is an affirmative practice of 'learning how to die'. This is perhaps what the same poet means elsewhere when declaring that 'I live in the longing, in the fire, in the revolution, in the witchery of its creative poison'[135]—for we are speaking of little else than a writing-act equivalent to death-magic.

Note: By extension, this would imply that all other forms of speech/writing, those that do not prepare such celebrations of imbibed blood and inhaled airs of waste, are relative failures along the same three thaumaturgic lines: (1) they are disenchanted of any wish-potential; (2) they are egalitarian, prosaic modes that can be handled by anyone; (3) they communicate a desperate, pitiful need to live. Thus none of these alternatives can fulfil the project of enlisting words as euthanasia.

Note: There persists a sub-genre of literature about certain texts, rhymes, songs, names, or stories which, if read out loud or even quietly in the mind, supposedly result in the death of the reader, some close kin of theirs, or a random stranger in the world somewhere—which suggests a linguistic unconscious that somewhere still recalls the bond between saying and undoing.

---

135 Adonis, *A Time Between Ashes and Roses*, 121.

THANATOMANIA

But what is the manic component here, which always accentuates a phenomenon or practice to its tensional snapping-point? Would thanatomania be a desire to grasp those spells encompassing the numberless unique pathways of ending, thus turning every designation of this book's *Mania Tabula* into a means of specialised death-fortune (death in forests, caves, labyrinths; death by dancing, razors, mirrors)? Or would poetic thanatomania, conversely, consist in the inscription of an elegy that makes its author the item most craved for Death's timeless collection (the fatally wanted)? Or, lastly, would it consist in somehow reversing the terms' significance to mean playing tricks on fatality itself, conceiving a magical language in which Death would be sent chasing apparitions or lured into granting favours on behalf of its pronouncer? It seems this third possibility would be its own interpretation of 'mastering the art of silence', upon which another in our configuration writes accordingly (with the informal tone of someone who knows the other's face): 'Death, wait for me at the sea gate, in the café of the romantics. Your arrows missed their target this time, and I came back from the dead only to bid farewell to what was veiled within me.'[136] Look at those words that jest with Death in skeins, its nicely wound yarns coiling around the neck of the very prime mover of turns; a poetry

---

136 Darwish, *Unfortunately, It Was Paradise*, 144.

where utterances all have the layout of funeral mounds meant to bait the Last One Coming...an extortion-spell placed upon the agent of infinite finality itself.

Death-magic and writing; death-wish; flowing words; the veins; breathing; silence; preparation; celebration; the face; learning

Coimetromania (Cemeteries)

We will go to the cemetery, to the mortuary, and ask the guardians of the past for permission. We'll take the dead man out to the public garden naked and set him on the platform under the ripe orange sun. We'll try to hold his head in place.

HASSAN BLASIM[137]

As he passed by the cemetery wall, he heard what sounded like a huge blast and the wall came tumbling down. The storm winds were so violent, they were unearthing the contents of the graves and scattering them hither and yon, then depositing some of them on the pavement that ran alongside the cemetery's collapsed wall. The winds had also flung the contents of some of the tombs on to the street outside the cemetery, turning the immediate vicinity into a vast, open grave.

GHADA SAMMAN[138]

---

137 Blasim, *The Madman of Freedom Square*, 13.
138 Samman, *Beirut Nightmares*, 210.

The Coimetromaniac takes up one of two prospective stances. While both are consumed by the dream of opening the cemetery to the world again, the first chooses the manic strategy of infinitesimal insertion, the second the manic strategy of outright takeover. Let us consider the particularity of the first passage, wherein a single dead man is retrieved from the grave and brought back into the heart of the same social reality that banishes the look of Death at the immediate moment of its onset, for its instructions employ the efficient logic of intrusion according to which the presence of a lone corpse is enough to impart an overwhelming sense of deathliness to the environment. Thus they retrieve the corpse from its resting place and station it like a mechatronic puppet in the centre of a public garden, where it mimes vital movements in a way that reminds us of the ancient pharaonic Opening of the Mouth ceremony wherein a sarcophagus or statue of the recently-deceased was used to help reawaken their senses in the House of Gold (allowing them to breathe, eat, and speak in the afterlife). We can imagine the lustration stage, which consisted of the mummy's being faced southward on the cleanest sand while being washed in waters from little sacred jars, then fumigated with various burning aromatics and incense; lastly a priest in panther-skin would approach to apply a sharpened adze and other bladed equipment to the corners of the lips in order to reanimate its sensory abilities. Indeed, the first quote above replays this scenario, converting the manicured gathering places of the modern metropolis into the antechambers of the old pyramid, allowing a naked form with supported head to remind them that no amount of urban planning, and no relegation of the tombs to a demeaning fetishism of the museum, can change the fact that they too remain in the belly of the same crypt. Their avoidance will soon be their recognition (the recognition of a problem in their midst).

The second coimetromaniacal episode, however, comprises a process whereby the cemetery itself is animated to take on the form of a natural disaster: on the one hand, it enlists other elemental forces (trade winds, shale) to help uproot and hurl its contents in all directions; on the other hand, it gradually emulates those meteorological events whose tendency is to blanket, coat, and smother territories (alluvion, soot, sandstorms). The charnel house becomes the universe, at all turns. Space itself becomes an extended mass grave, although one imbued by mad zoetic axioms: this gives those few dour acres a sweeping all-pervasive quality, lets them form a crown or canopy of mortal tokens strewn from side to side.

Note: There is a rare psychological syndrome in which certain individuals hold deep conversations with themselves in the mirror, addressing their mirror image by a different name of its own. This means that the mirror image is either an entirely distinct entity, or that it represents a hypothetical self that has never been allowed emergence, thus making the glass surface a kind of tomb for parallel unrealised worlds. By necessity, this mirror image would have its own coimetromania, and by extension its own take on delirium: (1) that of the one who has lived always in the grave; (2) that of the one who would do anything to leave the grave.

Note: The Fourth Voyage of Sinbad is one that tests the reader's sympathetic view of the pirate's otherwise carefree and adventurous character, for here we are met by a rather gruesome tale that takes place after the sailor finds himself settling on a luxurious faraway island of foreign peoples. He is convinced to take a wife without knowing their custom of burying alive the spouses of those who have died in a large underground vault, and so finds himself cornered by horror once she begins to grow ill and passes away. His smart-talking talents gain him no exemption in this instance, and he is taken beneath to live out his last hours entombed. Even so, there are two versions of what Sinbad does during this subsequent period in the Cave of the Dead: the first describes him finding a heavy femur bone and clubbing to death all later entrants in order to steal whatever food provisions and wealth they bring with them (since this island culture buries people with their riches), while also stripping the helpless bodies of others previously damned to the grave, thus buying him further time to figure out an escape plan. The second version has its origin in a text of the strangest proportions: *The Wonders of India* by Bozurg ibn-Shahriyar al-Ramhormuzi (an alleged tenth-century captain, shipmaster, and cartographer who compiled the exotic accounts of other seafarers he met during his travels from Oman to Indonesia to East Africa). In this book of fantastic digressions, the Fourth Voyage of Sinbad is complicated by a grim new detail: he dwells for many years in the absolute darkness of the burial chamber, taking wives from among the other widows thrown down with their dead husbands' bodies, and even fathering children with them in the pitch-black, until one day he tracks a scavenger animal to a rock fissure that allows him to break outside and rush to a passing boat with all of his confiscated, grave-robber's fortunes. Notice that in none of these accounts does he ever return to rescue his lost wives or children, but rather simply drifts onward to his Fifth Voyage where he battles the Old Man of the Sea without a second thought to the family left behind in the cavern. Is this the face of yet another coimetromania? Does this not unlock a kind of dark vitalism, that of the one who would kill the entire world to save themselves? Or is it not a matter of his hallmark survivalist streak, but rather of an acquired taste for the doomsday setting of the world below? He leaves them there because the vault is its own paradise to those who have adjusted beautifully to its silence, coldness, and gloom.

OMNICIDE II

Cemeteries and the mortuary; the guardians of past; permission; nakedness; the platform; the placed head; the wall; tumbling; violence; unearthing; the contents; scattering; depositing; collapse; flinging; the immediate vicinity; the open

Klaiomania (Weeping)

> *Yet it [the atom bomb] has enabled scientific imagination to write the scenario of the end of the world: an enormous explosion, a gigantic explosion that will resemble the initial formation of the globe with its organized chaos of mountains, wadis, plains, deserts, rivers, seas, slopes, lakes, wrinkles, rocks, all the beautiful variety of an earth glorified in poetic praises and religious ceremonies. After the giant explosion, a great fire will blaze, consuming whatever it can eat—human beings, trees, stones, and other things that can burn—and giving rise to a dense smoke that will blot out the sun for many days until the sky weeps a black rain, which they call nuclear rain, that will poison every living thing.*
>
> MAHMOUD DARWISH[139]

The Klaiomaniac arrives in time for a new aeon: that of atomic mourning. Note that nuclear discourse is a strange choice of topic given the ancient traditions of sadness and death-artistry that are at the clear disposal of so-called Middle Eastern authors: after all, we are tied to a region that invented the first weeping songs, descendants of the earliest witnesses of famine and infant mortality, such that

---

139 Darwish, *Memory for Forgetfulness*, 85.

we wear it well, or, as another in our configuration writes: 'Let the weepers stand and dance. There is still time, still a role for them. I fall in love with their dance.'[140] Meanwhile, rest assured that the same author of the above-hanging quote knows every last syllable and primaeval watchword of this aesthetic inheritance of crying, as he knows his own hands, and that hence there is no shortage of ammunition in this vein from his vast body of work: From the line 'My longing weeps for everything. My longing shoots back at me, to kill or be killed' to the line 'We, too, cry when we fall to the earth's rim. Yet we don't preserve our voices in old jars', to the image of '[a] child now born [...] his cry pierces through the cracks of this place', this one has scripted all conceivable variations of the wailing and the dirge.[141] We are all students of this human bereavement, and we know intimately what happens when the poet lends their manic touch to a throat sobbing for those who have died for nothing and those who have died for something (each their own singular delirium of sorrow).

But we are at the foot of another house, that of the final death-weapon, for which all human destiny seems to be poured into a single object, all tragic affect transferred to a machine for the end of days. What salt tears can be shed here, as the centre of radical sorrow leaves the

---

140 Adonis, *The Pages of Day and Night*, 67.
141 Darwish, *Unfortunately, It Was Paradise*, 4, 61, 58.

condensed inch of the ocular for the condensed inch of the button? The poet recognises two things immediately: (1) that the devastation of the atomic age shares no genealogy with the philosophical-aesthetic dream of omnicide; (2) that the only recourse in this situation is a retelling of the event in madness's specialised terms of cheerlessness. Hence, if the true origins of the bomb are primed by the coldest neurotic-repressive psychologies of order—that all will be vaporised by mere nuisance and unconscious chatter, the blast amounting to little more than a scopophobic exhibition meant to deflect the invisible gaze of judgment from oneself—then the poet must arrive quickly and fashion words of the bonfire (to elevate the act of a 'sky weeping black rain'). Another once tried to tell the Death of God in nobler terms, and so it is similarly with the Death of World: as the all-too-human avenges itself against itself for its millennia of unreconciled interior tensions, deferring its own inner rifts like a catastrophic splitting of the atom, an inhuman or superhuman will to mourning must salvage the otherwise poor story of fission and isotopic betrayal. Klaiomania therefore answers the age of uranium, plutonium, and hydrogen by stringing together the textual nuclei for a counter-nuclear writing: something that synthesises euphoria and dysphoria in a way that honours neither the 'initial formation of the globe' nor the reckoning of radioactive fallout; a motion of the outcry (which cares excessively) to challenge the commotion of the device (which cares for nothing). Let us join those first women who took to the hills and moaned across ruthless space when loved things were taken away—they were never diminished by the violence of circumstance but rather appeared absolutely possessed in their high-pitched howls—for their response to the indifferent outside (of which the bomb is simply a recent extension) reveals the manic role we seek: in essence, a vociferation that somehow simultaneously stands for and against all that ever was.

Weeping and the scenario; explosion; chaos; praise; ceremony; fire; black rain; poison; the living thing

Part 21
Choreomania (Dancing)
Melomania (Music)

Choreomania (Dancing)

> *Dancing with slow, measured movements to the music of the setar, the drum, the lute, the cymbal and the horn, a soft, monotonous music played by bare-bodied men in turbans…and, as she performs her rhythmic evolutions, her voluptuous gestures, the consecrated movements of the temple dance…*
>
> SADEQ HEDAYAT[142]

> *She chanted a song and began to tremble. She sang softly, as if crooning to herself. In her lament he detected the call of eternal yearning that imprisons lost time in the flask of existence and that recovers the lost space that one never reaches by wandering. He reeled. He repeated the refrain after her as he swayed to the right and left…The stillness was humbled. The full moon listened. The bones of dead ancestors shook in hillside graves.*
>
> IBRAHIM AL-KONI[143]

The Choreomaniac avails herself of all movement-potentials—steps elongated, tentative, gnomic even—in order to adjourn the fall of self and other into restrictive worldliness. And yet, while boasting a similar iridescence, the

---

142 Hedayat, *The Blind Owl*, 56.
143 Al-Koni, *The Seven Veils of Seth*, 195.

two passages above appear to attain it by opposite means: the first choreomaniac dances beneath a temple's domes, the second beneath the open night sky; the first dances to an accompaniment of instruments, the second generates the song herself; the first dance is performed for passing strangers ('bare-bodied men'), the second for intimate companions (the husband, the child); the first induces its trance on behalf of some becoming ('rhythmic evolutions'), the second partakes of an ancestral intercourse ('the bones of dead ancestors shook'). Furthermore, the temple dance appears increasingly intent on compressing the entire world into a focused 'voluptuous gesture' of the dancer's own body, whereas the swaying chanter disgorges herself toward cosmic matters ('the full moon listened'). But everything has its respective role in balancing the imbalance of this mania, as the two form perpendicular lines that cross at the most devastating right angle of experience.

Note: We are in a different landscape than that of the historical Dancing Plague, those episodes in which spontaneously gesticulating crowds swarmed the European countryside in their thousands between the years 1300 and 1600, prone to long bouts of uncontrolled ecstatic jumping, wobbling, or lurching—a phenomenon attributed to such varying biological causes as ergot poisoning, hereditary and idiopathic diseases (epilepsy, typhus, encephalitis) and to the lesser-known 'tarantism' of the tarantella dance (named for the belief that victims had ingested tarantula venom), attributed sociopolitically to an extreme traumatic reaction to the Black Death, generalised poverty, and totalitarian rule, attributed theologically to being cursed by angry saints or spirits, and for which later psychoanalysts achieved no consensus but simply renamed the condition in multiple descriptively unhelpful ways as 'mass hysteria' or 'psychogenic illness', 'epidemic dancing', 'collective mental disorder', and 'choreomania'. No, these incidents of mad dancing have their own place in the annals, but here we are seeking a more impalpable caress, one that is no mere response to interdictions but rather is a doomsday activation of its own.

Let us return to the two selected passages in order to reveal their point of congruity: the hidden detail behind each backstory is that both dancing figures, temple-dancer and mountain-chanter alike, are participants in a conspiracy to set animality against the human. The temple-dancer is aligned with the cobra—indeed, her motions are learned replications of the rearing attitudes of the hooded snake—while the latter's trembling is closely affiliated to the grace of the sacred gazelles that graze the neighbouring rock-hills. Both are fatal misanthropists; both favour the destruction of the human by their beastlier counterparts—one dreams of the human's subordination to a fanged species, the other to a being of cloven hoof. But how does one dance for a creature (for its wrath and its victory)? First they make the humans beat drums and sway involuntarily to the music of their own demise, condemning both those of primal lineage and future progeny, and then they lead them, like the pied piper who lured processions of rats and children to their drowning, across bridges where no good could come to them. Some legends say he took them into caves, others speak of steep cliffs, and still others sinkholes: so it is that a rat-catcher easily transitions to a human-catcher. In this sense, the choreomaniac treats the human subject the same way two professional gamblers (who have teamed up beforehand) might cheat an unsuspecting amateur at the card table: more exactly, both lose inconspicuously to one another here and there (throwing hands), in preparation for a rebound-effect in which they will prey upon the novice from both sides and drain their pockets.

Note: The green felt of the card table even matches the hunter's green of the Piper's vest, not to mention the shared performances of frivolity and exasperation through which these omnicidal characters disguise their kill-modes as simple frolicking.

Followed to the letter, this landslide: a careful dance of false munificence and false losses, which warms the disgruntled animal within and awaiting.

Dance and slowness; measure; bareness; rhythmic evolution; voluptuousness; gesture; consecration; the temple; chant; trembling; softness; lamentation; eternal yearning; lost time-space; reeling; repetition; refrain; swaying; stillness; humility; the ancestors; the hillside

Melomania (Music)

> *For which corpse does this instrument moan?*
> *For which hidden dead does this timeless instrument cry?*
> *In which cave*
> *in which history does this bowstring and cord move, this unknowing claw?*
>
> AHMAD SHAMLU[144]

The Melomaniac paints a picture of conspiracy operating behind the curtains of creation itself, in what is apparently a three-part argument. The first premise is that someone had to be killed for the sake of the world's origination, or rather for the thought/experience of world to even attain the shape of possibility, and that this constituted a wholly unwilling sacrifice. So it is that we are confronted with the prospect of building our homes on an unmarked grave ('for which hidden dead'?) and the long-held secret of a history buried out of sight ('in which cave'?), just as we are told of an unnamed corpse whose spilled blood (against their will) made viable the very actualisation of existence. Indeed, the tones of the melomaniac are both requiem for and sonic speculation upon the identity of this first casualty: its chords tempt

---

144 Shamlu, *Born Upon the Dark Spear,* 126.

us to the mad hypothetical prospect of an alternative creator who might have elicited altogether divergent outcomes if given the chance. Was divinity initially a dyad (of twins, nemeses, or mutually irrelevant figures) that was only later violently uncoupled? What might the murdered partner have done differently, what would their disallowed universe have looked like, and why exactly was their assassination a matter of necessity in order for inception to take place?

The second premise is that the only remaining testimony is to be sought in the realm of sound: such is the role of the 'timeless instrument' that replays the record of the shameful, draconian act (that God killed in the void); its notes tighten like a straitjacket or tourniquet in order to preserve the accursed occurrence and recurrence of this decision. Thus 'the bowstring' plays on behalf of the entire undeveloped world of that alter-companion whose death brought about this life. Nor is this the first time the above poet has connected music with the executed: elsewhere, in the prisons, he compares the facial expression of those condemned to death sentences to 'a wayward note turning and turning upon the holes of the flute, in search of its home'.[145] It seems there is a kind of orchestral remnant exclusive to those shot in cold blood on behalf of self-perpetuating structures.

---

145 Shamlu, *The Hour of Execution*, 12.

The third premise of this manic blueprint is that the musical instrument does more than simply lament the collateral damage of the alternative world-founder: it revenges itself on the unatoned and demands penance from all residents of sky and earth. In this sense, the melody is pure threat (to the pernicious, the hijacker). To this melomaniacal subject, all sound is like the hum of a plague of locusts; all pitches and every scale point back to the rustling of sackcloth and ashes meant for the guilty judge. All harmonies speak to the disharmony of the first breath; all songs are the undersong of the same payment-seeking demand, 'this unknowing claw' that scratches on behalf of reprisal and redress for the spare god.

Note: There are three potential types of threat: (1) those where one leaves the consequences of an action totally unknown (irruption); (2) those where one makes certain that the consequences of an action are known and weighed in exact terms (proviso); (3) those where one makes explicit the fact that there will certainly be consequences, but consigns to sheer vagueness the where, when, or how of this backlash (intimidation). Each has its own radically bittersweet taste.

Note: The poet who penned the above selection descends from an older language in which profanity has been refined over thousands of years, whether the swearing concerned is directed at body, spirit, fate, or family. But here we are interested specifically in those curses that call death upon their target. The most common in this category is *khaak bar sar* ('dirt upon the head'), which conjures images of the other's being covered by a freshly-dug grave, whereas more ingenious versions declare *takhte beshuran* ('let them wash the bed'), conjuring images of the dead's removal from atop stained sheets that require scrubbing, or *roo aab bekhandi* ('may you laugh on water'), spoken as a reply to those who mock unwantedly, and conjuring images of their floating corpse frozen in laughter on the surface of a lake or swamp. To connect to our opening theme, though, note that all three of these vulgarities—the shovelling of soil, the wiping of bed linens, and the gurgling of the drowned—evoke our auditory senses above all others (we hear them, first and foremost). Now allow a manic consciousness to redirect this procedure in two unorthodox ways: (1) by turning the death-threat into a song; (2) by aiming the death-threat at the metaphysical centre of all things. Is it too much to imagine, then, that the melomaniac inhabits a kind of deicidal desiring-machine, thereby perceiving music as a death-wish for the creator?

> *Music and the corpse; the moaning instrument; the hidden dead; timelessness; cry; the cave; the unknowing claw*

Part 22

Dendromania (Forests, Branches)

Nebulamania (Fog, Mist)

Brontomania (Storm, Thunder, Lightning)

Spectromania (Ghosts)

Dendromania (Forests, Branches)

> *The trafficker had lost his way (that's what he told us), so he said we had to spend the night in the forest. We got into our sleeping bags, shivering from the cold... So they left us in the forest, dead to the world. When we woke up we realised we'd been tricked. We started looking for the river so we could cross into Hungary ourselves. God started making the fog even thicker. He seemed to be doing it deliberately.*
>
> HASSAN BLASIM[146]

The Dendromaniac weathers the many schemes of both humans and gods to traverse that uninhabitable backwoods where neither race is welcome. This is the place where both exercise their treachery: the trafficker leaves them stranded in the dirt; the divinity sprays mist into their faces—and yet the thickets and underbrush themselves remain uninvolved in such affairs. How many strangled bodies have secretly been buried among its orchards, how many half-formed prophets drawn to the groves and turned mad to satisfy God's boredom? Still, the trees ignore everything; the branches hang in open air like paralysed spines that refuse the demands of the

---

[146] Blasim, *The Iraqi Christ*, 93.

world's movements. They remain the most unimpressed, despite being aspects of the growth, such that the forest is simultaneously the zone of the left-for-dead and that of the only-way-out (while itself taking no part). The night-traveller therefore becomes conscious of the fact that they walk in a place of no obligation, where the sticks and dead autumn leaves say nothing to halt fated abandonment, trickery, or cruel obstacle from being carried out against the guilty and the innocent alike. Moreover, the forest is where one finds it increasingly difficult to see through the thickening atmosphere, to stay together, to catch one's breath, or to keep up with companions. Nevertheless, it is also somehow the only path through the uncontested reign of ill-being (to the other side).

Another figure in our literary configuration writes: 'I try my best to understand you, but I am lost like a shadow in a forest of skulls', thus revealing the forest's connection to misunderstanding (the uncomprehended).[147] Another writes: 'Our neighbor in the oak forest is the owner of an old lute. He carries time with him disguised as a mad singer', thus revealing the forest's connection to a delirium born of deceptive temporalities (the anachronistic).[148] Still another writes that she 'asked wild rabbits one night in that green flowing forest', thus revealing the forest's

---

147 Adonis, *The Pages of Day and Night*, 90.
148 Darwish, *Unfortunately, It Was Paradise*, 67.

connection to an alternative language of wildness (the uncommunicated).[149]

But what it all amounts to is that the forest offers a 50-50 split to save or kill those who enter the bramble, timber, and moss: this necessarily positions us in a logic of the coin-flip or toss-up (reaching the waterfall or devoured by bears).

> *Forest and the trafficker; losing-way; night; cold; the left-behind;*
> *the dead-to-the-world; realisation; trickery; looking;*
> *crossing; thickness; deliberateness*

---

149 Farrokhzad, *A Lonely Woman*, 96.

Nebulamania (Fog, Mist)

> *At night*
> *when a dizzy breeze whirled*
> *past the suffocating skies,*
> *when a bloodied mist pervaded*
> *the veins' blue roads,*
> *when we were alone with our trembling souls,*
> *a sense of existence, an unwell existence,*
> *pulsated in veins.*
>
> FORUGH FARROKHZAD[150]

The Nebulamaniac senses in the trailing fog that something is unhealthy in the substance of things. Has something gone wrong, or has it always been wrong? She is the bothered one, as mania searchingly attunes her inner turbulence to outer disturbance, her eyes stricken with the ability to perceive blood in the white mist. She is never more certain than when dizziness overtakes her; she is never more aware of this 'unwell existence' than when her soul begins to shake and dissolve into the compromised air. Her sentience is elevated through betrayals of her own body. Her confusion signals proximity to

---

[150] F. Farrokhzad, 'Summer's Green Waters', in *Sin: Selected Poems of Forugh Farrokhzad*, tr. S. Wolpé (Fayetteville, AR: University of Arkansas Press, 2007), 36.

answers behind the clouding. Her personal sickness is the sickliness of all, her mental fog an echo of the world's own increasing surrender to radiation and valley fogs, as if initiated in the practices of those 'fog catchers' of ancient cultures who placed their trap-vessels along the low grounds to collect water. Nausea, headache, suffocation, trembling: a syndrome unveiling that all is syndrome.

This is the whirling of which she speaks (from down by the glade and the creek), which slowly blocks her carotid artery from delivering blood to the brain, granting her the clearest consciousness (of the nebula) right before she faints into unconsciousness. These are pressing questions for the manic imagination: Why does existence want her to know that it is unwell, and for her to grow unwell alongside it (to understand its secret complex)? What does it mean to interpret smog and wisps as tragic anticipations of the beginning of the end (the invalid's onset)? What should be mere plays of humidity, water droplets, or volcanic activity are not enough to explain the haze; what should be the simple vapour of cooling dewpoints is in fact a prognostic factor writ universal (telling how long is left).

Another in our literary configuration writes 'heavy the miasma in a carnivorous field', and that she 'wanders in hideous galleries of human mists', thus confirming the fog's connection to the misshapen, the unfavoured, and meat-eating.[151] Another writes that 'the answer is the road, and the road is nothing but vanishing into fog', thus confirming its connection to the untrodden and perhaps impassable trek.[152] Another reminds us of those dervishes of the annihilative circle—'You're whirling, you're whirling, you're whirling about yourself and you're the only one not to see that you're whirling around a void!'—thus confirming mist's connection to the mystic's final pirouette and circumvolution.[153] Lastly, still another leaves us with the following declaration: 'You were the desert when I shackled the ice within you. Like you, I split into sand and fog. And I scream you are a god, in order to see his face'—thus confirming mania's ability not only to elevate itself to extreme thresholds of omnipresence, but also to inject godliness into the veins of others through violent consolidation (the shackle), enunciation (the scream), fragmentation (the split), and perception (the face).[154]

In conclusion, what happens when mania and hypochondria collide, though now driven by delirious thirst rather than fear, and when it turns out the hypochondriac was right all along in detecting sickness everywhere? Is this somehow even richer than the accelerated vision of those Decadents who saw the sprawling presence of

---

151 Mansour, *Essential Poems and Writings*, 281, 337.

152 Darwish, *Unfortunately, It Was Paradise*, 40.

153 Bensmaia, *The Year of Passages*, 42.2.

154 Adonis, *A Time Between Ashes and Roses*, 91.

skeletons and gangrene among living bodies, as predictive poets of the done-for and the over-already, by turning illness into both a spook and a kind of pledge? To thereafter vow oneself to view all as if through the opalescent or milky white intumescence of the cataract, hence drawing the soft or dense fog directly into the lens cortex of one's own eye. Note that an important book remains to be written on the varied blights of philosophers, writers, and artists—those whose destinies were visited by tuberculosis, malaria, syphilis, migraines, polio, smallpox, typhoid, scarlet fever—so as to extricate a certain vigilance and cunning found only among those who have felt the manic fog of affliction. It gives insight into those who wrote, composed, performed, or sculpted while unable to see straight; it gives insight as to why the terms 'endemic' and 'miasmatic' prove synonyms to this day, and what might have been learned from this time spent among emissions and polluted air.

Fog and dizziness; breeze; whirling-past; suffocation; pervasion; the veins; aloneness; sense; the unwell

Brontomania
(Storm, Thunder, Lightning)

> *Let wise men*
> *bring us saviors from abroad.*
> *Let them be men of lightning.*
>
> ADONIS[155]

> *Isn't it be better to be insane*
> *Under thunder*
>
> JOYCE MANSOUR[156]

The Brontomaniac invites us to a council of male and female elders both wise and insane, who dispute the future through the prism of a single concept: *vanity*. They face some critical hour of pandemonium, although their deliberations lead them in two extreme directions: the first speak of vain men approaching with a warlike din (the champions); the second speak of all efforts being in vain (the madwomen). In either instance, we are in the rat's nest of a certain ataxia (disorder) for which only the undisciplined storm offers aid (meeting chaos with chaos).

---

155 Adonis, *The Pages of Day and Night*, 37.
156 Mansour, *Essential Poems and Writings*, 311.

The first poet tells us to fight; the second tells us to enter derangement beneath the blizzard. But are these necessarily different things, or can we locate an alternative experience of struggle that would rely upon this very *infuriation* of mind? If we return to ancient epic literature to uncover those rare combatants known for their capacity to *rampage*, which joins vanity and fury as another concept of excess, then we can imagine someone whose war-movements resemble low and high-pressure systems or those shelf-cloud formations that gather over tropical islands and dark seas alike. Thus the first poet elsewhere writes that 'I bathe my wounds in thunder',[157] just as the second writes of a night storm gifting her 'the sparkling eye with a strange flowering',[158] for mania allows this thematic overlap of war, storm, and madness in the emergence of a fusillade (a series of fired shots in rapid succession or simultaneous barrage).

Or, to follow another expression: so is it that the maniac might also achieve the 'Ninth Wave', a longstanding sailing term referring to a wave of soaring proportions that follows a sequence of incrementally developing waves, and which forms terrifying walls of water around the boat-vessel (blocking all view of the sky). Let us capture this image in order to redefine thought as precisely that

---

157 Adonis, *The Pages of Day and Night*, 41.
158 Mansour, *Essential Poems and Writings*, 205.

which causes shipwrecks, inaugurates ice ages, and respects neither law of property nor perpetual right to terrestriality: in other words, to turn consciousness itself into a nucleus of awesome precipitation and discharge.

Storm and wisdom; the saviour; men of lightning; insanity; the underneath

Spectromania (Ghosts)

> *Everyone who visits the hole soon learns how to find out about events of the past, the present, and the future, and the inventors of the game had based it on a series of experiments they had conducted to understand coincidence. There were rumors that they couldn't control the game, which rolls ceaselessly on and on through the curves of time. He also said, 'Anyone who's looking for a way out of here also has to develop the art of playing; otherwise they'll remain a ghost like me, happy with the game…There are two opponents in every game. Each has his own private code. It's a bloody fight, repetitive and disgusting.'*
>
> HASSAN BLASIM[159]

The Spectromaniac entertains us with a story for the ages: a shopkeeper being chased by masked gunmen finds himself falling into a deep hole, where he discovers a bare-chested, grizzled old man sitting next to the dead body of a Russian soldier. The old man asks this newly-fallen someone cryptic questions (whether he believes in God), offers cryptic advice (suggesting he should pray for colourful animals), makes cryptic predictions (that he will one day eat the former and another fallen will

---

[159] Blasim, *The Corpse Exhibition*, 76.

eat him or use his energy to fuel their battery systems), tells cryptic origin stories (that he himself was a writer-inventor from the time of a mediaeval caliphate who was attacked by thieves for bringing lanterns to the city at night), tells cryptic transformation stories (that he has since become a jinni and a ghost), and explains cryptic details about the nature of the hole itself (that its creators were studying the phenomenon of coincidence before they lost control). Moreover, the old man lights endless candles while rambling about musical event-chains and claiming a certain omniscience toward all who become hostages of the vortex in which they find themselves: he expounds upon this with an air of mixed indifference, amusement, and impatience, all the while reading aloud from a Book of Hallucinations with the line 'We are merely exotic shadows in this world.' Eventually the old man dies, and the thief is left alone for what feels like hundreds of years (eyes open, mind asleep) until a wounded young woman falls into the hole with multiple futuristic devices attached to her body. Breathless, she asks the now-ancient narrator who he is, and he responds 'I am a jinni' like the one before him, while slowly seating himself next to the old man's corpse.

Recent narratology has developed rhetorical and ontological definitions for 'metalepsis' (when a character slips between logically-exclusive worlds), although these are thrown into more complicated variations when mania exerts its stomping influence on the domains of the telling and the told. In most literary examples, paradoxical intrusion across the presumed boundaries between fictional, actual, or counterfactual worlds produces a looping effect of strangeness, but here the fantastic subsides into the fatalistic from the first passage. The old man is the concurrently-realised destiny of the fallen man of the present: they originally appear from different temporal dimensions, and yet the ghostly hole is where all zones/selves lurk within one another. Metalepsis is therefore not necessary here (no transgressive crossing) in the wake of more radical face-melting strategies. Perhaps this is the inference to be drawn from another in our literary configuration who writes that 'every hydra I swallow transforms itself into a ghost', for it is less a question of sliding levels than of sheer possessions (of the whomever, whenever, however).[160] It is therefore a mistake to understand the spectre as a visitor from an alternative elapsed time: instead, it is what builds itself a caldera (like a volcanic mouth) to feast on all moments and events in order to continue. Phantasmatic power is what nourishes itself through multiple meals of time, space, story, and identity: so it is that the old man is found slowly nibbling the corpse of the Russian soldier,

---

160 Mansour, *Essential Poems and Writings*, 237.

for the hole itself is nothing less than an eternal drip-feed (intravenous becoming).

Somewhere few scholars have thought to probe the archives of metaleptic creativity and transmedial migrations (long before their official theorisation) is among sectarian denominations or minority offshoots of religious traditions (such as Shi'ism in the Islamic world, not to mention those mystical orders for whom unnatural narratology was the given starting point). Against a backdrop of persecution, and with miracle overtaking logic to rise to the top of their hermeneutic hierarchies, these movements often experimented with storytelling devices that allowed prophetic figures to communicate with myriad divine, angelic, demonic, phenomenal, or extra-universal characters beyond their own space-time constraints. Note that these encounters were neither considered an overstepping, in the sense of a vertical or horizontal jump, nor intended to enhance the playfulness or humour of a structured narrative world, but rather aspired to envelop all existence in fictive layerings that entertained no barriers of impossibility. In the most compelling ways, these expelled factions (in their tragic dispositions) stumbled upon a descriptive disorientation very similar to that ascribed to the Death of God: in effect, that there remains no lateral, ascending, descending, forward, backward, or sideways motion to speak of anymore, so that every proceeding storyteller (born from the paranormal ditch left behind) is also the gravedigger of all temporal and spatial quotients.

Note: Can there even be true metalepsis in the absence of metaphysics, or at that point is it all just the same non-circulating air of the hole? Here though, metaphysics is smartly rendered inoperable not by elimination of the highest but by elimination of the in-between.

Let us return to the story's spectral mineshaft and ask how it might allow a surpassing of even so-called multiple personality or dissociative identity disorders, in which drastic splitting typically arises from early traumatic experience, for mania seeks something ever more sinuous for its purpose. First, the hole is not the self-contrived consequence of an abused psyche; rather, it is the contrivance of others (the inventors of the game). Second, the hole is not intended to house victims of malevolent will but rather unwitting players of concomitance, arranging them like a row of black orchids in a cult devoted to the curve. Third, all four hole-dwellers (the soldier, the old poet, the present narrator, and the futuristic woman) were not struck by violent forces but rather fell in the process of evading them (chased). Fourth, dissociative plurality attempts to form a protective shield around the hurt one, whereas the hole only compounds vulnerability before horror into a limitless reception of all conceivable circumstances. Fifth, dissociative disorders tend to render the central host (the original identity) the only personality who remains unconscious of the existence of the others, whereas here the host (the long-residing one) at any given instance is the all-seeing innkeeper of all other falling personae (he knows their every intention, movement, secret). Fifth, the psychoanalytic aim of reintegration (unifying the varying personalities through intercommunication) is here obsolesced by the hyper-imbrication of characters in ghostly deposits and palaeoflows. Hence, we are not skipping across ontological states but rather entering the sedimentological structures of a magma chamber or reservoir of conglomeration that resembles the ultra-sutured version of a Cubist mess: for this marks the crevasse where identities, realities, and illusions collude in manic style, like those snake-pits or wolves' dens where all sleep within one another, forming ominously undifferentiated shapes of the helix, through the act of phantom-narration. This is a study in how certain manias turn the incidental into the inseparable (coinciding as co-insides).

Note: There are those rare conditions when madness, or rather going-mad, proves the most pragmatic course of action (to follow adventitious ways). How else can one survive the crazed King Minos into whose maze every nine years are sent seven young boys and girls to be eaten by the Minotaur? Is the hole not the labyrinthine exploded beyond mere spatial convergence to include all other subsidiaries of experience, where all roads lead to the same disembodied centre?

> *Ghost and everyone; learning; event; the inventor; the game; the experiment; coincidence; rumor; the uncontrollable; ceaselessness; the curve; art; remaining; repetition; disgust*

Interlude: Book of Poor Games (Philosophy of Play)

They destroyed my toys, O father.
When the gentle wind played with my hair, they were
 jealous
They flamed up with rage against me and you.

MAHMOUD DARWISH[161]

One might ask whether omnicide brings with it a signal of insurrection or one of extinction. And yet even breathing the words 'insurrection versus extinction' transports us into a malevolent game, one that hassles us by being based again on this single concept: *the ultimatum*. The very question itself, staged as a fatalistic either/or, assumes a significant breach in the continuum of things, and so we must immediately ask ourselves whether this breaking-point represents a threshold (transitional arch, portal), a precipice (tightrope, cliff's edge giving onto certain death), or a crossroads (forked path, impasse), since each reading entails different methodologies and possesses its own dramatic implications. Beneath whatever veil,

---

161 M. Darwish, 'I Am Yusuf', tr. A. Amireh, <http://www.naseeb.com/villages/journals/1-palestinian-poetry-oh-my-father-i-am-yusuf-68387>.

though, the catastrophic imagination always places us in the experiential domain of a decision-toward-loss, and so it might be worth considering the strangest of games, those in which one is bound to lose—or even wants to. (Ludomania: obsession with games)

I. THE GAME BEGINS

> *I like to play with little things*
> *Pink unborn things beneath my eyes' madness*
> *I scratch I sting I kill I laugh*
>
> JOYCE MANSOUR[162]

We were once warned by a philosopher to 'beware the other's dream, because if you're caught in the other's dream you're done for', and perhaps we should also extend this logic to waking in another's game.[163] What we call existence, are we playing for it, with it, or against it? It seems that two camps have developed in modern thought: on the one side, those advocates of 'being-in-the-world' who treat this sphere as a dwelling; and then the more resigned 'world-without-us' configuration who speak of the sheer indifference of the universe. And yet

---

162 Mansour, *Screams*, 30.

163 G. Deleuze, 'What is the Creative Act?', in D. Lapoujade (ed.), *Two Regimes of Madness: Texts and Interviews, 1975–1995*, tr. A. Hodges and M. Taormina (Cambridge, MA: MIT Press, 2007), 312–24.

INTERLUDE: BOOK OF POOR GAMES

few seem to consider the more aggressive possibility of our 'being-against-the-world'—for what if the more fascinating course is to contemplate an existence that is out to get us, and thus compels us to react to it adversarially as cut-throat or nemesis? For our purposes, however, it does not matter if the host itself cares nothing for whether we persevere or fade away, or whether it might indeed be pursuing a deep vendetta to ensure our ruin. We must proceed according to the latter assumption for purely tactical reasons.

In those rare instances when insurrection and extinction become simultaneously viable hands at the card-table, we notice a series of incidents emerge: (1) the rise of *vanguardism* (undergrounds, secret societies, avant-garde circles) in which the creative instinct attempts an immense overthrow of the world through cryptic channels and unforeseen turns; (2) the rise of *fanaticism* (cults, sectarian factions) in which the onset of epochal futility and general depletion of purpose is energetically countered by ravenous paradigms of extremity: nihilistic voids are thus filled by new militancies, as doomsday visions often thrive in times of famine, conquest, or plague; (3) the rise of *abstraction*, in which certain rogue individuals place their bets on untimeliness, distance, solitude, and delirium in the face of disaster: in doing so they restore the storyteller to their rightful function (which is never to provide distraction, but to be a harbinger of disappearance by literally speaking 'the end'); they also restore the philosopher to their rightful function (never to provide meaning, but to inspire the will to madness by compounding perplexity). Together, they form a certain insoluble game—that of miniscularity versus the ordinance.

All trails bring us back to that most treacherous concept of 'play' in this discourse of insurrection versus extinction. Many decades ago, a brilliant treatise was written delineating four fundamental types of games, cited in our first volume: (1) *Agon* (games of skill—chess, archery); (2) *Alea* (games of chance—lotteries, roulette wheels); (3) *Mimesis* (games of role-playing—childlike pretending, masquerades, costume-parties, video games); (4) *Ilinx* (meaning 'whirlpool' or 'vertigo', games of sensation—skydiving, rollercoasters, virtual reality, childlike spinning until falling dizzy).[164] Beyond these four categories, however, we can add a fifth manic-omnicidal type, games of *subversion* (demolishing structures—falling dominos, vandalism, hacker culture), and a sixth, games of *masochistic defeat* (i.e. those in which the greatest affective pleasure resides in losing or being caught—haunted houses, tag, the knife-game of spread fingers). Nevertheless, do not all of these intricate classifications necessarily assume a human-centric definition of the game, and a

---

164 R. Caillois, *Man, Play, and Games* (Chicago: University of Illinois Press, 2001).

INTERLUDE: BOOK OF POOR GAMES

sentient or teleological projection of the opponent, thus foreclosing the possibility of our being stranded in the waves of an impersonal and inhuman force? Not in the least, for whether there is actually thought, desire, intention, or volition behind the event, we are still entitled to perceive ourselves as being in something else's crucible, and are well-served by doing so, for the desert has its own exclusive modes of passage that one must learn adaptively to survive, such as crawling inside the emptied stomach of one's camel to avoid freezing—as do the forest, the mountain, the jungle, the island, the sea, and outer space (each sets its constraints mercilessly). Mediaeval Iranian poets called this concept simply 'the wheel' (that which turns of its own drifting accord).

Coming back to the original question of insurrection or extinction, we are therefore compelled to consider the seemingly countless aspects and detailed realms of play, and to re-fathom the aforementioned concepts through such acute prisms one after another:

- Games of Endurance in which the game's objective is simply to hold out for as long as one can before eventual defeat; a trial of withstanding surrender. Notice how we even marvel at those of exceptional old age, as if lasting were an accomplishment in itself: to simply hang on for a prolonged stretch of time.[165]

- Games of Cheating in which one can circumvent rules or skip stages. Notice how most people unconsciously conceptualise death in this manner, comforted by delusions of invincibility: deep down everyone thinks they will be the only one to live forever, thereby foiling the finisher's rest by dint of some accidental exemption.[166]

- Games of Unclear Progress in which it is concealed whether one is winning or losing until it is too late and the result is officially revealed. Lotteries follow this criterion of instantaneous announcement.[167]

- Games of Self-Endangerment in which one willingly

---

[165] There is an old saying in various cultures that our relation to mortality itself is like playing a great master: that we are inexorably destined to lose, but still want to give it a good game (in the meantime). Examples of such endurance-testing procedures are: the rodeo (where riders count the seconds before being kicked off wild bulls); tug of war (where teams pull large ropes to gauge their relative strength); children's breath-holding or staring contests; or, at a more cosmic level, the prediction of the red giant sun, where supposedly in 5 billion years the star's outer layers will scorch the oceans and consume earth and the other planets in our solar system—a realisation that trivialises all action, reducing it to a short-lived venture.

[166] Piracy has cheating built into its very cultural substructure: sidestepping, theft, deception, and betrayal are all assumed parameters.

[167] Waiting ultimately becomes an essential experiential facet of these games—for instance, the lottery dictates that one buys the ticket (in advance) and then remains stalled in some helpless unknown until the climactic occasion arrives.

forfeits pawns along the way, or sometimes even moves in the direction of peril.[168]

- Games of Sudden Shifts in which one is losing the whole time, until a miraculous comeback in the last phase (jackpot); or, vice-versa, where one lets everything ride, only to fall victim in a single flick of the wrist to the depletion of an amassed fortune (snake eyes).[169]

- Games of Wild Betting in which one forsakes calculation and submits to the futility of programmatic approaches. Thereafter, all movements are determined by negligence, in the hope that the old Spanish swordfighter's saying proves true: that the most dangerous opponent for a master is a total amateur, since someone with minimal training will follow the proper forms and be easily undone by the master's superior technique.

---

[168] Certain animal species have the instinctive ability to double back when hunted, thus confusing trackers by disturbing the sequential legibility of their traces. Some early psychoanalysts also advised our turning back into the nightmare's centre, meaning that we should run in the terror's direction or even bite down on the apparitional figure of fear.

[169] Casino culture houses both elements of suddenness: spontaneous victory can be found in the flashing reels of the slot machine, and spontaneous destitution in the bad dice-throw of the craps table. Another example of this is the Mongolian game of Shagai, usually played with the cleaned astragalus or ankle bone of a sheep, on decorative rugs, where the pieces are flung or shot like dice with four sides representing the horse, sheep, goat, and camel, each allotted its share of luck, and with a highly unlikely fifth landing-side of the cow possible only on uneven ground. The same devices are also used for fortune-telling rituals, gifts, and offerings.

But there is always an unpredictable particle in the know-nothing who resorts to wild swings.[170]

- Games of Superstition (ritualised wildness). Superstition admits no belief in law, unity, or reason; it embraces the notion of chaos, yet adds the qualification that certain methods or choreographies somehow harness arbitrariness better than others (learning to play to the anarchy of things). To that end, one can even refine one's relation to luck (via practices of intuition, reaction time, hypothetical thought, and by studying the routes of the ricochet).

- Games of Narrow Victory, Landslide Victory, or Pyrrhic Victory based on varying protocols of 'satisfaction', and also differing definitions of 'excess'.[171]

- Games of Changing Levels or Roles in which hierarchies, positions, and identities continually shift, periodically

---

[170] Again, Jorge Luis Borges's 'The Library of Babel' comes to mind, with its architectural infinity of enigmatic books and hallways of lost lifetimes: some go mad, some form occult devices, some devise highly intricate hexagonal numerologies and interpretive schemas, but some exasperated types eventually start deciding where to look based on the mere falling of metal disks. They sit in corners and allow the twisting instrument to determine whether to turn right or left, high or low, aligning motions according to intentional randomness.

[171] There is a certain megalomania that sometimes unleashes itself during gaming campaigns. It often results in a euphoric subject who conceives of themselves as the greatest player to ever grace the game (the paragon), and each opponent as the second most talented player in existence (the arch-rival), for this mindset vivifies all potential outcomes.

INTERLUDE: BOOK OF POOR GAMES

restoring players to a zero degree. Musical chairs; costume-parties; those card games of rotating kings.[172]

- Games of Distraction (based on temporary escapism: the masquerade, rave, or hallucinatory trip that always guarantees return or homecoming) versus Games of Concentration (play that demands all-consuming immersion; games that become the world; games that take forever; games in which obsession drowns out the player's loyalty to any past whatsoever, inviting oblivion and radical forgetting of all else).[173]

- Games of Clues/Signs in which we search for hidden tells, reading near-imperceptible patterns: the puzzle; the riddle; the scavenger hunt; games of immanent deciphering and discovery.[174]

---

172 We might think here of the tea party in *Alice in Wonderland* and its constantly-switching seats, but also another short story of Borges titled 'The Lottery in Babylon' in which identity is renewed each night as people draw lots to swap titles/destinies. Thus, in any given bout, one can become the apprentice, gladiator, dancer, god—unchained to fulfill all potential desires or fantasies, at the simple cost of a willingness to accept being a plaything of others' wishes in those devaluating rounds where things go the other way (the slave card).

173 Fairy-tale arcs typically conclude with the child's return to the real, though for illicit purposes of smuggling in remainders of the unreal (they always remember the flecting diversion), whereas an example of the latter (all-enveloping play) can be found in Herman Hesse's *Glass Bead Game*, which describes a futuristic activity of extreme sophistication, one developed by neo-esoteric schools that bind together all variations of thought through unexpected connections. Here, everything becomes the all-synthesising code.

174 Note that the inventor of the puzzle or riddle is a benevolent torturer, in that they ultimately hope for its solution.

- Games with Dealers (where we encounter mechanistic intermediaries: the tarot card reader; the blackjack dealer; the supposedly impartial). Notice that the dealer is often blamed for the cards, and this is indeed a correct intuition, because they do serve the house, and the house must always win, though the evil of their collaboration is dulled by the more metallic look of probability.

- Games of Territoriality (where the specific locus is chosen by one side, thereby affording experiential or psychological advantages).[175]

- Games of Boasting (in which bravado, swagger, and competitive taunting are integral) versus Games of Courtesy (in which respect, formality, or even ceremonial silence are demanded).[176]

- Games of Infinity (endless lives; reset) versus Games of Finitude (all-or-nothing; one-shot deal). As a formulation that seamlessly threads together these two precepts, the Japanese leagues of the ancient Chinese game Go are reputed to have a special room called Yugen-no-Ma

---

[175] This also adds to our discussion the important component of the crowd or audience that offers vicarious reinforcement.

[176] War harbours both concepts, depending on timing/circumstance: the hour of the rallying cry versus the hour of humility, truce, or mercy (collection of the dead).

(a word with connotations of shadow, subtlety, obscure elegance, 'mysterious depth' or 'mystery at the light of day') into which only the highest-level masters are allowed entrance, and where they are rumoured to channel hallowed ancestral senseis.

- Games of Addiction in which the game increasingly becomes an obligation, need, or neurotic compulsion. This occurs when the ludic figure declines from *techne* to technics, which, as another philosopher once said, entails a failure to let 'the earth be an earth'.[177] It is also distinguished by the decline of pleasure into mere release from pain—in which case one might say that human existence itself, and particularly its drive to perpetuation, is the first game to fall sway to this addictive degeneration.[178]

- Games of Style in which each player develops a singular performativity, something distinctive or improvised, and where victory itself depends on realisations of originality, craft, or rarity. Here players must become inimitable or iconic in order to prevail.

---

[177] M. Heidegger, 'The Origin of the Work of Art', in *Poetry, Language, Thought* (New York: Harper Perennial, 2013), 17.

[178] Is the omnicidal dream itself a proposed antidote to this first drug-game (curing the desperate need to keep living)?

- Games of Entering the Opponent's Mind (hyper-anticipation). First Question: Is the opponent cunning or whimsical? Here one should definitely consult with those early pagan thinkers who contemplated dealing both with scheming gods (operating from plans) and temperamental gods (volatile, impulsive)—one requires a correct identification of the gamemaster as either diabolical overseer or unreliable force, for this will decide whether one is reading furtive steps or moods.[179]

And there are never-ending lists of other foreseeable and unforeseeable types: Games of Avoidance, Dodging, or Fleeing; Games of Alliance, Assemblage, or Admixture; Games of Betrayal (cutthroat), Decoys (smokescreen), or Barriers (obstruction); Games with Animals, Avatars, or Honorary Titles; Games of Reversal or Sacrifice; Games of Charade, Pseudonym, or Special Attire; Games of Paradox; Games of Folds; Games with Masters, Judges, Guides, or Hosts; Games of Middle Passages, Shortcuts, or Diagonal Movements; Games of Erasure (where one forgets they are playing); Games of Trial and Error (where one learns only from others' defeat); Games of Balance, Tumbling, or Entropy; Games of Plague or Emergency;

---

[179] The billiards player must superimpose an anticipatory gaze upon the pool table being surveyed (the aiming line, the angle of incidence or reflection, backspin), both toward the opponent's range of options and their own, being several shots ahead of reality. Thus it is no coincidence that elite shooters are often called 'sharks'.

INTERLUDE: BOOK OF POOR GAMES

Games of Countdown; Games of Domination (pyramidal force, tournament) vs. Games of Shared Wins (gala, tribal war); Games of Speculation, Journey, or Maps; Games of Calling, Passwords, Noises (bells, sirens), or Unusual Terms; Games of Tempo or Reflex; Games of Admission (selective, by invitation) vs. Games of Accidental Discovery (open entry); Games with Intermission (half-time, break, rest) vs. Nonstop Games (marathon); Games of Disintegrating or Stacked Objects; Games of Confinement (shrinking spaces, melting planks) or Vastness (widening orbits, javelin throws); Games of Near-Death Experience (daredevil, bloodsport); Games within Games (Russian dolls); Games of Suspicion (paranoia); Games of Lost Turns (penalty) or Extra Rounds (overtime, sudden death); Games of Wrong Rooms, Deadends, or Warnings (biohazard/radiation symbols); Games of Collectibles (spoils, premium); Games of Geometric Ability (angles); Games of Second Chances.

II. THE GAME IS LOST

It no longer occurred to me to try to escape or to ask them what they wanted from me. I felt that I was carrying out some mission, a binding duty which I had to perform until my last breath. Perhaps there was a secret power working

> *in league with a human power to play a secret game for purposes too grand for a simple man like me to grasp.*
>
> HASSAN BLASIM[180]

We remember that many have pronounced philosophy an *ars moriendi* (art of dying), and that just as many have insisted that the only philosophical question worth asking is whether to kill oneself. Yet how do we elude the integral criterion that a game must be voluntary, when we were not invited to join the pastime of being in this world, which by definition means that we *cannot* be in a proper game? That is, unless there is actually a way to make it so after the fact: no doubt this is how the advent of extinction gives us the absurd freedom to wrench existence into the realm of the voluntary (not at its origin, but at its terminus): stated simply, we do have the power to stop playing the game, or to lose it on purpose.

With that premise established, is there not an ecstatic dimension to this equation as well, one that bids us seek for the intimate relation between fatality and eternity? We might summon here the one whose Drunken Song exclaimed to death: 'Was *that* life? Well then! Once more!' and whose Vision and Riddle defined ecstasy as that bizarre outer boundary where one simultaneously cries 'How could I bear to go on living, and how could I

---

180 Blasim, *The Madman of Freedom Square*, 8.

INTERLUDE: BOOK OF POOR GAMES

bear to die now.'[181] To enter this ever-revenging circular imagination, however, one must abandon rigid logic and instead take a deranged walk with the Arabian *samira* (evening conversationalist): for example, Shahrzad from *The Thousand and One Nights*, who, in order to keep staving off her own execution at dawn, each eve recounts those cliffhanger tales of intrigue and cruelty that indefinitely extend the duration of the end. In other darkly meditative corners, there are those who similarly credit the thought of suicide with carrying them through many a bad night, with exact quotes being something along the lines of 'Without the idea of suicide, I would have surely killed myself.'[182] So it is that those of us who frequently deal with end-of-days poets and philosophers of the lost cause can explicate this trick once again: that the recurring narration of doom in fact ensures our suspension in a kind of infinite finality. In effect, it keeps the claw at bay; it buys us time before the absolutism of the final breath by making the last moment everlasting.

Nevertheless, this fatal-eternal paradox requires us to distinguish between the many chambers of game-oriented loss itself, for which only a condensed diagram is provided below:

---

[181] F. Nietzsche, 'Thus Spoke Zarathustra', in *The Portable Nietzsche* (New York: Penguin, 1982), 272, 430.

[182] Emile Cioran, interview with Christian Bussy, 1973.

OMNICIDE II

Games of Intentional Loss

- Affective Loss, where sensory intensity is highest for the player who fails; games of hide-and-seek or chase, where all the exhilaration is compressed into the moment of breakdown. This is the thrill found only in dread, the gasp of (1) being-caught, (2) the close-call.[183]

- Strategic Loss, where the rewards to be had in defeat supersede the formal decision of the game.[184]

- Artistry, where one seeks the aesthetic challenge of losing in unparalleled fashion.[185]

- Glory, where one defines climax as spectacular death upon the field.[186]

---

[183] Again, this refers to the aforementioned will to masochistic defeat. Adventure, in both its classical and unique sub-genres, combines precisely these two principles in a pendulous convention: that of always being on the run (the fugitive) and just barely evading menace (the escape artist). Astonishingly, one can also find this excitation in that maniacal infant's toy, the jack-in-the-box, where a grinning joker springs loose at the apex of some eerie melody.

[184] Speculative finance contains this option of strategic loss through negative betting against markets (choosing unpopular stocks, forecasting price declines) and other predatory short-selling techniques.

[185] Consider those auto-destructive movements that set fire to or poured acid on their own artistic products, or the Japanese author Yukio Mishima, who planned his own ritual beheading in an arcane theatrical scene of troubling detail.

[186] As noted elsewhere, many ancient societies perceived heroic glory as something equated with dying in ways that attain immortality—affirming Seneca's line that 'Life without the courage for death is slavery'—which itself follows the same paradoxical logic of monstrosity in horror: Are the vampire, ghost, zombie, or mummy not precisely those who perish in the most brutal conditions in order to

INTERLUDE: BOOK OF POOR GAMES

- Bribery, where one takes a fall for reasons of alternative compensation.[187]

- Nihilism, where one purges or incurs loss in order to clear the way, although without delineated horizon, whether from simple exhaustion with the state of things or as a means to aerate the terrain of possibility.[188]

- Martyrdom, where one loses in order for something else to win. Martyrs whose sacrifice is a conscious payment or trade, committed to seal another's triumph; or those servile characters who betray the human race in order to aid the rise of the inhuman (alien, wolf, image, demon, machine).

- Conspiracy, where one offers oneself as bait—the easy

---

achieve supernatural status as the undying? Moreover, consider those precarious fighters who upon becoming champions increasingly begin to tempt loss: they flirt with critical error (dropping their hands down or behind their back); they make conditions harder (looking sideways or keeping one eye closed); they take actions that make the guarantee of retaining titles more unlikely (intentionally fighting with their back against the wall or cage). Such recklessness is a chasing of the great upset, for this embodies the final stage of exaltation: after all, the standard of becoming godlike (apotheosis) is not only to be able to create and dominate a world, but also to be able to destroy or forfeit it.

187 As Ibrahim al-Koni warns: 'You don't play around with spirits. Do anything else, but not that.' For it is indeed better to consort with spiritual agents through bribery than through direct challenge, nor is it entirely heretical to interpret the Devil's fall as a temporary side-deal with the divine that brings eventual prizes (al-Koni, *The Bleeding of the Stone*, 122).

188 This is almost akin to thieving God's propensity for flooding or burning cities, landscapes, and full worlds in order to reset the game of creation.

target; the waiting-to-lose—in order to lure others into the grip of the larger waiting pack.[189]

- Playing Multiple Hands, where one makes several incursions and retreats, combining paradigms of irregular warfare and criminal versatility, staging eruptive plots here and there in scattershot formations—not a centralised revolutionary process but rather a procession of disparate, fragmented, shape-changing escapades. Extinction also benefits from these (non)settlements of flux by wagering itself on only one activated trigger coming through in order to collapse the totality of the real. Such is the chronic advantage of evil: not everything has to go right; just one stake has to hit and catch fire—the use of indeterminacy and the lone exception to crash the game in its entirety.

- The Long Game, where one specifically loses in the short term in order to seek a windfall in the longer run: the shaky logic of rebels who believe that the final successful revolution will redeem all prior struggles, thereby justifying casualties and blood ad infinitum along the way; or those great creative loners who wore the mantle of historical losers in their eras, risking alienation or

---

[189] Children's street gangs use this asymmetrical strategy in superior fashion, manipulating the appearance of innocence in order to overwhelm with later numbers.

INTERLUDE: BOOK OF POOR GAMES

persecution in order to engrave their names onto the gameboard of existence against all odds.[190]

- Disguised Loss, where one cleverly dissimulates strength or simulates weakness in order to reverse situations and wield surprise: e.g. those prophets, assassins, and martial artists who wore the robes of the beggar or acted physically crippled in order to seem vulnerable and thereby seize control of the game. Thus the disguise negotiates a bridge between pseudo-abjection and violent revelation, a kind of anti-bluff, advertising a lesser power than what truly lies beneath.[191]

Against this backdrop of the vanquished, we might also recall that the earliest civilisations—Babylonian, Sumerian, Egyptian, Persian—devised creation fables and apocalypse fables in the same stride: the two were imagined alongside one another, marking a remarkable closing of the circle at the very juncture of its opening. We have to ask what these ancients—who encountered mortality at every turn in the jaws of environmental quandaries—suspected

---

190 Antonin Artaud refers to this unstoppable echo of those condemned or the crucified (in their own time) as a revolt against the nothingness that 'laughs at us at first, lives off us later'. A. Artaud, *Selected Writings,* ed. S. Sontag (Los Angeles: University of California Press, 1988), 516.

191 In Kung Fu traditions, the Drunken Fist or Drunken Boxing school of *zui quan* derives from the Taoist myth of the Eight Drunken Immortals, where fighters imitate, feign, or enter actual intoxication and employ techniques of successive feinting, stumbling, swaying, and bobbing to catch their opponents off guard.

intuitively about this human experiment with time, consciousness, and destiny, and how this could have led them to invent the first games. It also allows us to speculate on how the concept of inevitability fuses with our discussion of risk, play, and hazard—not to mention an entire network tied to carnivalesque indulgence (the banquet, the feast, the amusement park, the circus, the bonfire, the festival). Beneath their surfaces of frivolity, we somehow always sense that we are watching an end-of-the-world show.

Furthermore, in entertaining these many corridors of loss, we stumble upon the potential for a paradoxical inversion of our original two themes: Insurrection as a gateway to extinction (have we not seen the revolutionary promise that mutates quickly into gulags and death camps?), extinction as a form of insurrection (is there not at times a rebellious potential hidden in devastation?). Oedipus's defiant gesture of tearing out his own eyes makes him the blesser and curser of cities in his later years; and the same is true of Cain, the first human, born outside the garden because his parents themselves are the subjects of a lost game or failed test, and whose status as primordial lawbreaker wins him the touch of the accursed wherever he roams. Interestingly, the Devil's bet against God is itself also a story in which a failed rebellion is tied to an extinctive effect: the Devil becomes the agent of Hell (extinction-zone of the soul), but is still a gambler caught forever in a computational race against the divine (philosophy of spite) to steal as many hands and hoard as many human spirits as possible, like cards or gamepiece tokens, until Judgment Day. Hence the boundaries between insurrection and extinction—the saving of the world and the killing of the world, the roar of the masses and the mass grave—are invariably blurred.

To conclude this book of poor games, let us be tempted by the vague image of a third god (one of stone-cold neutrality and irreversible desertification): a figure with zero interest in good or evil, creation or endtimes, origin or futurity, punishment or salvation, life or death, who would have slept through Genesis and would turn a blind eye to Armageddon, and with equal indifference toward the collection/distribution of souls that comprises the race to apocalypse. Their sole temporality would be that of the aftermath; their sole spatiality would be that of the wasteland; their sole desiring-function, to rule over the non-world that arises from it. Let us wonder what it would mean to perceive such omnicidal games of insurrection and extinction before the inexistent altar of this figure—the brooding one, the undecided—which might require us to inhabit the silhouette of the anonymous player: the blank domino; the wild card; the skeleton key that opens all doors because of its radical smoothness. More on this another time, though.

Part 23

Chronomania (Time)

Atemania (Ruins)

Petramania (Ancient Monuments)/

Geomania (Stones)

Osmomania (Smells, Odours)

Chronomania (Time)

but don't give way too quickly,
don't let up too quickly,
don't give yourself to the sentence too quickly,
better to have fear, to face the void, than the wanton
*　　abandon of the sentence!*
give oneself the time and make the time last,
make the sentence endure, make it endure pain,
make it suffer under the time of thought

RÉDA BENSMAIA[192]

The Chronomaniac takes an almost agricultural approach to creativity, resuscitating those methods of cultivation that rely on the harshest means (crop burning, fallowing, pesticidal measures). Chronomania is therefore the use of extended time in the service of slowly-inflicted pain, though always with an eye to future harvests. This makes one the exactor who attains manic audacity by going all the way through deprivation, accepting the lesson that sometimes things grow only by cruelty. And what does it mean to compare writing or consciousness to the process of crop burning, where residual straw from the last reaping is set afire in order to prepare the rice

---

192 Bensmaia, *The Year of Passages*, 48.9.

fields for reseeding, in the process emitting a particulate matter of black carbon pollutants born of incomplete combustion? And how would one apply to the domain of thought or textuality the ascetic practice of laying a field fallow, first initiated by Mesopotamian farmers around 6000 BC who began to rotate land usage, systematically leaving arable plots unsown in certain years in order to allow them to recover between seasons? Or does the author's counsel to 'to have fear, face the void' refer to those rarely-used schemes of intentional flooding (carried out to ready soil for drought years)? Then again, perhaps the instruction to 'make the time last' refers to something like the gentler cultivation technique of bonsai pruning, where an array of concave cutters, shears, and clippers are brought to trim miniature trees and train their trunks or leaves into the desired shape (often by clamping or wiring branches and roots). Lastly, the impetus to 'make it endure pain' reminds one of the secret ancient Scythian practice of 'breaking' wild horses, where those Iron Age nomads along the northern coast of the Black Sea would first mount stallions in rivers or snow banks in order to allow them to wear themselves out against the resistant elements, only then to ride them at the point of exhausted submission. Note the philosophical realisation that strikes us here: it is not the horse's wildness that makes it an excellent instrument of violence, but rather its tameness. The thrashing is not actually dangerous; the gallop is the perfect incarnation of a war-machine.

Note: This thematics of 'giving oneself time' and not 'letting up too quickly' can even be tracked into the human domain of cosmetics (as severe cultivation of the face): hours spent punishing the skin with often repulsive or toxic ingredients—fish scales, whale vomit (ambergris), dynamite (diatomaceous earth), crushed beetle shells, snail ooze (mucin), placenta, rust—in order to prolong youth (its own time-extension principle). Another manic embarkation of bewitching appearances based on acrid strategies, for the re-creation of the self often requires one to become the gradual looter or pillager of one's own resources.

Note: Speaking of this relation between time and the labour of propagation, was this not also the cultivation method inadvertently employed by the father of psychoanalysis himself, who one by one cut off those disowned sons and daughters of his famed school, depriving them of titles, affiliations, and support when they contested his theories, thereby freeing them into that autonomy in which their greatest counter-insights then flourished? The shunned generation, we should speak their names as gleanings of a brutal harvest: Otto Gross, the anarchist psychoanalyst who challenged Freud's allegiance to the civilising mechanism of repression and instead encouraged hedonistic fulfilment of all kinds, influencing the early avant-garde while he himself was committed to asylums and ostracised from Vienna circles, and ultimately dying in the streets of Berlin in 1920, frozen and starved; Sandór Ferenczi, who remained the ever-obedient student until Freud's death, waiting until after the latter's passing to publish his more controversial theories such as that of an 'alien will' capable of 'incessant protestations that she is no murderer, although she admits to having fired the shots' and of a megalomania that sees her consumed by 'a feeling of being bigger and cleverer than the brutal force', and even subtly complementing those manias through which 'the mentally ill person has a keen eye for the insanity of mankind',[193] whereafter he was maligned by the new generation of Freudian loyalists and his writings were placed under strict censorial control of the Freud archive; Otto Rank, the most favoured pupil, taken under the master's wing at the early age of twenty-one on account of his literary-artistic insights, and even invited to co-author various sections on mythic symbolism in *The Interpretation of Dreams*, but then scorned by the master and his peers for developing his 'here-and-now' therapeutic procedure and for daring to suggest the possibility of a pre-Oedipal phase in a single sentence of a public talk,

---

[193] S. Ferenczi, *The Clinical Diary of Sandor Ferenczi*, ed. J. Dupont (Cambridge, MA: Harvard University Press, 1985), 17, 19. For an excellent short meditation on Ferenczi's concept of the 'alien will', see Reza Negarestani's text 'The Psyche and the Carrion', in *Abducting the Outside* (Falmouth and New York: Urbanomic/Sequence Press, 2023).

for which crime he was compelled to forfeit his post as Vice President of the Psychoanalytic Society and Editor of its journals; Carl Jung, who famously bore the brunt of Freud's disapproval when he began experimenting with ideas of intuition and the collective unconscious, a presumed heir apparent left to a massive psychotic breakdown full of apocalyptic visions that lasted six years; and Sabina Spielrein, whose convulsive brilliance and daring as a thinker of destruction (preceding later elaborations of the death drive) was often compromised by Freud's twisting games of prejudice, leading her to return to the Soviet Union where she established the first ever Kindergarten based on Freudian principles, and who was later shot dead along with her two daughters by fascist soldiers occupying her town. Was there not a crude botanical or pastoral approach to discipleship at work here, in this long vacillation between generosity and renunciation, this fatal culling between Chronos (Father Time) and chronomania (the time of deviant offspring)? Were they not all made promises of legacies and rewards before being confronted by the 'wanton abandon' of their master? Did they not all 'suffer under the time of thought', even though their singular talents emerged precisely when they had been left burned, fallowed, clipped, broken, or smeared?

> *Time and giving way; quickness; the sentence; fear; void; abandonment; lasting; endurance; pain; thought*

Atemania (Ruins)

I had nearly reached the river Suran when I found myself at the foot of a barren, stony hill…The level ground was covered with vines of morning glory, and on one of the hills stood a lofty castle built of massive bricks…All at once I saw a little girl appear from behind the cypress trees and set off in the direction of the castle…I remained petrified, unable to make the slightest movement…It occurred to me that this was the hour of the day when the shadows of the castle upon the hill returned to life, and that this little girl was one of the old-time inhabitants of the ancient city of Rey.

SADEQ HEDAYAT[194]

The Atemaniac demonstrates the reverberant power of ruins by placing us before a particular site: that of the castle. It is a castle from whose descriptive characteristics we can derive many assumptions: (1) the fact that we 'reach' its lower ridge casts us in the role of visitor, meaning that we do not belong there, cannot anticipate it ever following the logic of a proper home, and are expected at some point to leave; (2) the fact that the ground is 'covered with vines' tells us that we face something overrun by time, as weeds burgeon through windows and up walls,

---

194 Hedayat, *The Blind Owl*, 76.

testament to a nonhuman life-order of vegetation; (3) the continued 'loftiness' of the structure refers to a disturbing category of things that impress even when dead or obsolete, and the 'massive bricks' confirm the great suffering experienced by those servants or slaves who slung upon their shoulders those thick plates designed to generate an aura of impregnability; (4) the abrupt emergence and flight of the little girl plays to the two key criteria of apparitionality (appearance and disappearance), a dual ability that simultaneously paralyses and beckons forth; (5) the narrator's becoming 'petrified' is an exudation principle whereby the stone materiality of the castle converts the onlooker into something stone-like as well; (6) the reference to 'the hour' of shadows returning to life alludes to a secret animistic temporality, though it is only a transitory resurrection allowed by the ruins.

Above all else, though, the identification of the little girl as an 'old-time inhabitant' and shade of the bygone city means that she was there for the initial naming of the place. We must imagine the mania of those first name-givers who would often abide by no etymological rationale or epistemological basis, but instead contrived some new meaningless sound in a gesture of outlandish creation (the tantrum). Nothing less than a language of thunderous nonsense—to call the river *Suran* or the province *Rey* merely because of a spontaneous sensory attraction—which history then repetitively echoes into familiarity so as to conceal the otherwise insane origin of the declaration. But the young shadow-child of the ruins has come back to give us elocution lessons: she restores all trespassers to the passionate, guttural absurdism of that first shriek of antiquity that would break across a thousand tongues before one day itself breaking down into ruination. She reminds us that all expression is neologism, if one only travels back far enough.

Note: The ghost of the little girl illustrates a further incredible capacity in madness that is worth exploring: the ability to entertain all kinds of metaphysical possibilities without ever forming a metaphysics as such. In particular, this is done through an encounter with abstraction that takes place outside those problematic domains of theology and philosophy consumed with authentic belief, and which instead restores the images, narratives, and ideas of metaphysical phenomena to those domains of storytelling, poetics, mysticism, thought, and art that treat the otherworldly as a matter of vision, style, sensation, narrative, speculation, or hallucinatory aesthetics. 'The skull of God bursts, and no one hears', writes one figure; 'I am God most of the time, when I don't have a headache', writes another; and still a third one sets himself '[t]o kill God in his major reflection, the Moon'.[195]

---

[195] G. Bataille, *Inner Experience*, tr. S. Kendall (New York: SUNY Press, 1988), 41; F. Guattari, *Chaosophy*, ed. S. Lotringer (New York: Semiotext(e), 2008), 51; E. Jabes, *The Book of Questions Vol. II*, tr. R. Waldrop (Middletown, CT: Wesleyan University Press, 1983), 61.

These statements are not testaments to a metaphysics: rather, they are deimaniacal strands of imagination that wrestle with celestial questions or unseen creatures (in all their complexity, distance, euphoria) without ever being tempted to build a metaphysical refuge. One should not fear the critique of metaphysics as a literal forbidding of all talk of strange things, thus entering the paranoiac disavowal of the accused (taking it as seriously as its own fanatics): indeed, it is only those manic enthusiasts (who no longer fear metaphysics) that are capable of projecting new things onto ruined worlds—of dreaming the dead gods again and seeing age-old shadows come to life.

Ruins and reaching; the foot; the ground; covered; vines; loftiness; the castle; petrification; the hour; the shadows; return; the old-time inhabitant

Petramania (Ancient Monuments)/ Geomania (Stones)

> *Tombs had collected atop other tombs, and their stones had crumbled, covering other stones. Buildings had collapsed, burying the tops of those preceding them. The bones of the latter-day dead were heaped on the skulls of earlier decedents, rising to lofty heights in a structure that deserved to be called a sanctuary rather than a mountain. It towered into the sky, where it stood as a beacon to people of their own futility, bearing witness to them every day of the destiny that awaited them and their descendants.*
>
> IBRAHIM AL-KONI[196]

The Petramaniac places us before another important spatial form—that of the tower—although here its monumentality is made rancid by its being assembled from heaps of bones and shattered stone tombs. The tower is therefore no longer a symbol of ascendant destiny but rather one of descendant destiny, a soaring omen of 'futility' for those still striving in any fashion whatsoever. This is the architectonics of the catacomb and the ossuary (ancient Persian *astodan,* 'bone-receptacle'), where skeletal remains

---

[196] Al-Koni, *The Seven Veils of Seth*, 45-46.

are both interred and displayed for all time, and yet this version is neither subterranean nor sacredly distanced but rather takes the shape of an immense pile stretching upwards into open air. A morbid verticality the uncomfortably exposed sight of which can be felt in the very pores of whoever lives in its proximity—as the mounds grow week by week, month by month, like a spearhead of human downfall. Not a resting-place but a codex, and yet one that tells of nothing save the bare facticity of what it represents.

And where exactly does mania intersect here with monument or stone? First we must inquire after that mad ruler who ordered the construction of such a tower honouring nothingness (the something that became nothing), for their delirium is of the same nature as those recently-discovered deep-sea fish species whose ultra-black colour makes them impossible to photograph. Despite the many spotlights and strobes of their underwater studios, marine biologists can still capture only the vaguest silhouettes of these fang-toothed creatures, describing these image-encounters as something like 'staring into a black hole', for the fish have developed an evolutionary camouflage surpassing even ultra-black butterflies and birds of paradise, whereby the specialised cellular dispersal of melanosomes creates a darkness-pigment that deflects photons. This protects them against bioluminescent predators hundreds of metres down, and against the camera, whose flashes are hopelessly trapped in the structural layers of the creatures' skin (which absorbs over 99.7 percent of all light) in a process similar to that revolutionary nanotech material known as Vantablack, whose forest-system of carbon tubes produces a coating that permits no reflection and erases the appearance of spatial depth (almost disappearing). Once again the primordial and the futuristic converge, the rare fish specimen and the Vantablack compound, the ancient genus and the new synthetic, the oceanic and the laboratory—and perched ominously at their temporal midpoint is our tower of accumulated stones and human debris. For the monument's technique of forming caches through collapse and burial does to Being precisely what ultra-blackness does to Light: it forever entraps the potential illumination of the existential within the insubstantial reserve, never allowing it to escape and therefore rendering the bones and chipped rocks impervious to representation. All is space-time deformation: where sanctuaries are supposed to inscribe their contents as monoliths, here they participate in an ambient particle fallout. The skeletons can no longer be recognised or even described specifically; they have disappeared into the mere shapelessness—not quite mountain, column, bank, or dune—where ontology finds itself looking through the lens into its own black hole.

OMNICIDE II

Monuments/Stones and tombs; collection; crumbling; collapse; bones; skulls; the decedent; the sanctuary; the mountain; the tower; sky; beacon; futility; witness; destiny; awaiting; the descendant

Osmomania (Smells, Odours)

> *So then, the corpse would stay with us. And before long it would begin to decompose and stink. As a consequence, we would soon have a new catastrophe on our hands…'He's no longer your father,' I told him. '"He" is now a corpse. And we've got to do something to keep ourselves from being asphyxiated by the stench once it begins to rot.'*
>
> GHADA SAMMAN[197]

The Osmomaniac assaults subjectivity by allowing aromatic traces to mark the obsolescence or dysfunction of the personal pronoun. 'He's no longer your father', she writes, much in the same way that the Death of God was first announced to us via the odour of decaying flesh: 'Do we smell nothing as yet of the divine decomposition? Gods, too, decompose.'[198] It is a race against time that in fact harbours a race against self, as the lineaments of the stench confirm transition into the domains of the nonhuman or the thing (or even an omnicidal disrepair). For mania, however, this is no denigration: rather, the logic of acquired tastes is such that increased sensitivity turns receptors from aversion to tolerance to appreciation.

---

197 Samman, *Beirut Nightmares*, 228.
198 F. Nietzsche, *The Gay Science*, ed. W. Kaufmann (New York: Vintage, 1974), 181.

Thereafter, one begins to seek out ever more unique combinations and details, like those perfumers who have gone as far as to include in their preparations the bouquets of smoke, wood, gasoline, metals, gunpowder, animal musks, glue, starfish, caviar, hay, saffron, tar, blood, goat hair, and leather book bindings.

We can picture the perfumer's world of polymer needles, droppers, and vials, imagine them sitting at the perfume organ blending samples and formulas into various compositions for the expert nose, or even envision this liquid-vaporous aesthetic back in its initial settings (Mesopotamia, Egypt, Rome, Cyprus, the Arab and South Asian palaces), submerging ourselves in the early workshops of alembics (from the Arabic *al-inbiq*) likely invented by Cleopatra the Alchemist of Alexandria (third century AD) whose books flaunt the eternalising symbol of the Ouroboros (the snake eating its own tail) coiled around the words 'the all is one'. Is it so callous, then, to assume that such manic experimentation might eventually lead one to try the scent of rotting entities, and to the conversion of the corpse into an olfactory ornament? This is not the contemporary technological gesture of converting a passed loved one into a diamond or jewellery piece (objects of permanence), for here the dead remain in a zone of ephemerality, that of the wafting and the fine fragrance, only to be mourned once more, though in a different kind of grief, once the bottle is finally emptied.

OSMOMANIA

But then dangerous questions begin to follow: Might the particular type of death (the fashion of pain or cessation) have some slight influence on the redolence? The scent of the one who died in bed alone; the scent of those who have been stabbed; the scent of one fallen from a fatal height. Such fluctuations take us across an osmomaniacal canal to something closer to old potion-making, where the ingredients might include tears of the widow, eyelashes of the orphan, and knucklebones of a wise man or murderer. Could the manner of derogation find its way perceptibly into the spice, sweat, or spit of the other, such that enlightenment, sociopathy, or premature loneliness might transfer their flavours into the individual body's oils? So it is that mania can turn even the 'asphyxiating' form into an extravagance of high living.

Smell and the corpse; decomposition; stink; soon; catastrophe; the no-longer; keeping; asphyxiation

Part 24
Politicomania (Power Structures)
Misomania (Hatred)
Haematomania (Blood)
Phobomania (Fear)
Polemomania (War)

Politicomania (Power Structures)

> *The streets are narrow*
> *the shops are closed,*
> *the houses are dark*
> *the roofs toppled downward,*
> *the sound has fallen*
> *from the tar and the kamancheh*[199]
> *they carry dead bodies*
> *from street to street.*
>
> AHMAD SHAMLU[200]

Politicomania may assume three conceivable shapes: (1) the desire to overtake all power structures; (2) the desire to overthrow all power structures; (3) the perception that oppressive power looms all around (immanent totalitarianism) and enchanting power is available everywhere (immanent resistance). All three manic arcs would require an anarchist fantasy of universal proportions—as another says, 'I have ashes for all the sultans'—although here, this will to all-unrest is accomplished by the most subtle figure: the rhyme-maker.[201]

---

199 The *tar* and the *kamancheh* are two stringed instruments prominent in classical Persian music.

200 Shamlu, *Born Upon the Dark Spear*, 43.

201 Adonis, *A Time Between Ashes and Roses*, 69.

The above writer remains a legend of free verse in their homeland and beyond, having shattered metric conventions in the very region that invented poetry, leading the avant-garde into unconstrained airs. And yet there are rare occasions upon which this figure accedes to rhyming. These few compositions have the feeling of absolute gravity encased in a negligible package—the more childlike the cadence, the more grim the overall tonality; the more lyrical the imagery, the more ominous the final repercussion. Often entitled 'Nocturnal' like the above selection, these pieces are almost always deeply revolutionary in nature, and yet they adopt a grander occultic perspective on the state as a magical apparatus that can only be unsung by a magical verse, thus establishing a correlation whereby the more each stanza approaches a nursery rhyme stylistics, the more apocalyptic its content. In fact, one of his most famous works, 'The Fairies', establishes this same disorienting link between a child's rhyming fable (about three naked weeping fairies) and an omnicidal catalogue replete with visions of chains, slaves, sickles, thorns, jinxed stars, fireworks, and the Devil's house, such that the most innocent announces the most guilty. This is how the symbolic order is unmade; this is how a simple double-couplet seals a cradle-to-grave pact with the zero-degree. For the rhyme is seductive (breaking indoctrination); the rhyme forges a semblance of absurd unity (treating words like wall-panels or fitful statuettes);

the rhyme conceals violence (seemingly harmless in its turning of tongues). Rest assured, though, the rhyme can bring down worlds.

The fact that 'they carry dead bodies from street to street' is a sign that the governing organs cannot keep up with the insurgents—they find themselves carting martyred limbs in wheelbarrows at every hour of the night, while the city caves inward in self-imposed lockdown. In this respect, the rhyme here resembles an old killing methodology of the Turkmen-Sahra provinces of Iran in which murdered bodies were rolled in *namad* rugs (dyed wools stitched with geometrical swirls or images of war), thereby allowing easy transport while also hiding the atrocity from public view and soaking up the victim's blood. Once more, an onslaught wrapped in something wonderful, a gesture of intentional misuse (like the rebel-poet's rhyme) to molest the dusty regimes over and over again.

Power structures and the street; narrowness; closure; darkness; toppling; silence; the dead body

Misomania (Hatred)

> *Night has fallen, there are no more enchanted evenings...*
> *you think you can be done with your fears by taking refuge*
> *in all the seaweed and kelp of your slavish thought, you're*
> *insomniac, you wait for daybreak, you ruin your eyes...*
> *from afar you look like a bird of prey, up close you remind*
> *me of a baby, and there's all this disorder, the disorder of*
> *the city...all the rats of the city get up at the same time as*
> *you, you say hello to them, you write for them...May be*
> *hyenas, may be wolves! Or just hatred! Human fear and*
> *hatred! Deep down! Very deep!*
>
> RÉDA BENSMAIA[202]

Misomania may assume two conceivable shapes: (1) the desire for hatred itself (as an electrifying affect); (2) the attraction to hated or hateful objects and figures. Note that the author accredits the moment when mania and hatred converge to an omnicidal occasion ('no more enchanted evenings'), and yet initially the drive is one that gnaws inward: the body is made haggard over and again ('you ruin your eyes'), consciousness overworks itself in insomniac stretches, and thought itself goes walking amongst mouldering bare life (seaweed). This is the

---

202 Bensmaia, *The Year of Passages*, 129.

phase of 'refuge', the author tells us, and yet we would be wrong to comprehend it as a hiding place rather than as a pressure chamber: indeed, this is how anger gathers and builds; its recession into depths has nothing to do with inner subjectivity, but rather here depth constitutes a boiler oven in which the hate-affect can roughen and become the perfect irritant.

Soon enough, however, the correct temperature for bursting is achieved, and with this, hatred manufactures its own literary genre: *the rant*. There is a careful staging to this movement into misomaniacal writing: the first dimension consists in splitting the same depth (in which the 'I' had been tearing itself apart) into an interior and exterior portion through mockery, such that one aspect taunts the other ('up close you remind me of a baby') to form a new coefficient of kinetic friction; the second dimension consists in starting to push this magnitude outward, projecting hatred as a series of sliding or rolling surfaces against so-called outer reality ('the disorder of the city'), such that resentful perception begins to spread indiscriminately, coating everything in its path; the third dimension consists in introducing *the slur*, as the once-higher forms of the human are misanthropically reduced or demoted to forms of odium ('all of the rats of the city'); the fourth dimension consists in allowing hatred to send languages of calumny reeling into chaotic expression, to unclasp itself from the control of its original speaker, thus signalling the important reference to those 'hyenas' known for their cackling laughter, as ranting approximates the rapid staccato and high-pitched giggle vocalisation of a predatory creature; the fifth and final dimension now consists in dragging all existence backward into the mire of hatred alongside itself, into a certain spherical nastiness, where all things rankle together at the very bottom ('Deep down! Very deep!').

> *Hatred and night; disenchantment; fear; refuge; seaweed;*
> *slavishness; insomnia; the baby; disorder; the city;*
> *the rats; the hyenas; the deep down*

Haematomania (Blood)

> *From within*
> *they would attack one another;*
> *men would slash each other's throats with knives*
> *and sleep*
> *with prepubescent girls*
> *in beds of blood.*
>
> *The bleeding ancestry of flowers*
> *has committed me to life.*
> *Are you familiar with the bleeding*
> *ancestry of the flowers?*
>
> FORUGH FARROKHZAD[203]

The Haematomaniac's code, like those formulations of power and hatred before it, is predicated on a profound sense of conflict, although here it is one that draws its dividing-lines in blood. On one side are those agents whose belief in bloodlines (closed identity) leads them to blood-letting (unidirectional violence), the autocratic coercion of the knife held against undefended veins, thus revelling in the reddening of their sheets with victims' plasma; while on the other side are those mistresses whose

---

203 Farrokhzad, *A Lonely Woman*, 50, 162.

vow to 'obey the four elements' ends with their trickling (open experience), thus subjecting their own chests to the alternative brutality of the natural. Such is the cost of partaking of the so-called 'bleeding ancestry of the flowers', of which we can apparently learn only one paradoxical thing: that it simultaneously teaches one to become the absolute cover-up artist (upholding life while operating beneath the limelight of true 'familiarity') while also making one the cynosure of all eyes (centre of attention, focal point, guiding constellation). Haematomania, then, consists simply in celebrating this misunderstood donation of the antecessors and primogenitors whose attractive brilliance distracts the onlooker from the infinite cuts across their bodies. It is the assessment of exactly how much they must bleed (somewhere silently) in order for existence to go on.

Blood and within; attack; slashing; the throat; knives; pubescence; the bed; ancestry; flowers; committed life; (un)familiarity

Phobomania (Fear)

Bewilderment is his country, though he is studded with eyes.
He terrorizes and rejuvenates.
He drips shock and overflows with ridicule.
He peels the human being like an onion.

ADONIS[204]

The Phobomaniac is not one passively consumed by the delirium of fear, but rather one who deliriously wields fear to attain the most astonishing levels of impact: to become the most fearsome, and thereby scare everything (including themselves). This obviously begs the crucial methodological question of how one might turn one's own subjective image into an unforgettable moment (to make a terrible impression), and we can comb through the specific terminology of the poetic passage above for an answer: namely, it seems based on conveying 'rejuvenation' (the terror of the beginning), 'shock' (the terror of the first), and 'bewilderment' (the terror of the unprecedented). This peeling process is therefore an overture to the unacquainted mind, to the world of appearances before or after names and ideas, the young time of the world, enjoined by a troublemaking

---

204 Adonis, *Selected Poems*, 23.

figure resembling the Euphrates Valley god with eyes encrusted all around the head (the earliest visualisation of omniscience) yet who traps enemies in the confusion of divine winds and nets.

Above all else, the construction of such a visage requires precociousness (element of the infantile), for rejuvenation assumes the juvenile, like those pirates who wore sparklers in their hair during battle to convey a lunatic-child aura to their enemies. It is the will to radical carelessness, or even omnicidal silliness, the presumptuous behaviour of that which 'overflows with ridicule', but which nevertheless makes the boldest statement—for mania is often precisely this decanter ('he drips') mixing flagrancy and disarrangement. We stand dumbfounded before such gazes, in fear of those who assail us while smiling for no reason.[205]

Fear and bewilderment; the eyes; terror; rejuvenation; shock; ridicule; peeling

---

[205] Recall that one of the origin-points of literature (Aesop, collector of fables) rests in the grinning face of someone depicted often as a figure of light madness or mental-physical disability (represented as man-child, hunchback, or simpleton). Nevertheless, those same fables house some of the longest-lasting fears of human imagination, though disguised in animal shapes and talking objects—so let us not underestimate what this grin means, or what ferocious things it can do when given the chance.

Polemomania (War)

> *S is elated by war: it has allowed his repressed violence to emerge and ally itself with chaos. In war he gives his horses free rein, unsheathing the hooves of a song that scatters not dust but bullets. And in war he returns to the era of ancient mountains, to shepherds' pipes that make the distant dance, to chivalry and the din of self-conceit and the splendor of the first knights in armor. Briefly, in war he finds the battlefield of winds that unsheathe him, a fresh sword in a fencing match against enemies who have already passed through.*
>
> MAHMOUD DARWISH[206]

The Polemomaniac authorises us to ask two fundamental questions: (1) What is the relation of madness to the dream of a golden age?; (2) What is the difference between the compulsion to war and the compulsion to serve the many imaginaries of war? To answer both questions, we need only look to the aberrant time-travel of the above passage in which a war-crazed figure transports himself to a supposed antiquity of javelins and paladins, which bears a marked resemblance to those first literary sources of the novel genre brimming with manic inferences—the

---

[206] Darwish, *Memories for Forgetfulness*, 83.

mad quixotic knight bearing swords against Spanish windmills, or that eleventh-century Japanese tale with chapters entitled *Maboroshi* ('illusion') and *Kumogakure* ('vanishing into clouds'). For here there is a fascinating technique of metachronism at work, a chronological error through which something is assigned a date later than the actual event: more exactly, the polemomaniac views their own Being through this metachronistic lens as if born too late, like a reverse-ghost haunting the back-then from the vantage of the now, their battle-lust stranded in an undeserving present and so found scavenging elsewhere, in things 'already passed through', always hoping that some grand combative gesture might awaken a new age worthy of the elder art of war. This premise of bad timing subsequently allows them to contemplate an elaborate narrative universe that will fill the temporal void, circulating desire through abstract yet vital figments from various golden ages—'Skulls pour blood, skulls get drunk and hallucinate', another writes[207]—with a perfect understanding of how desires become images, images become stories, stories become affects, and affects become dauntless actions upon the world (note: this is the creative period of inception in theology and ideology as well, the vaporescent instant before they stiffen into vapid orthodoxies). But mania resists dogmatism by simply staying

---

207 Adonis, *Selected Poems*, 380.

in the intricate state of war, for 'wars teach us to love the details', and indeed the exuberance of images soon spills over into the realm of identity (self-image) as mind becomes a diary of misplaced happenings.[208] This is how an individual turns into a walking *solecism*, both in the principal senses of the word—a grammatical mistake in speech and writing, a deviation from socially acceptable modes of decorum—and in the unspoken existential sense of breaking the very codes of being-alive. At this point we are far beyond minor catachrestic breaches in manners, etiquette, or diction: rather, we face the impropriety and radical inconsistency of someone who wages war in our world as if living in another moment. Yes, we are speaking of the Unhesitating one, who escapes the inhibitive psychology of violence by promulgating visions that 'make the distant dance', for no doubt is allowed when war serves no larger cause than itself, i.e., war for its own sake (and expedited by a flipside concept of the today or tomorrow).

> War and elation; emergence; alliance; chaos; free rein; unsheathing; scattering; return; the ancient; the distant; din; splendour; armour; the match; the already-passed-through

---

208 Darwish, *If I Were Another*, 19.

Part 25
Geumomania (Taste, The Mouth)
Aceromania (Sour Things, Bitterness)
Limomania (Hunger, Thirst)
Geliomania (Laughter)
Zoomania (Animality)

Geumomania (Taste, The Mouth)

The Geumomaniac extends us the opportunity (which we shall take) to pay tribute to a modern author who taught us his parasitic philosophy of meals. Consequently, all ten members of our literary configuration are here invited as honoured guests to offer a single line that might inaugurate our own specialised manic itinerary of dinners and tastes.

> *I kissed her legs; the skin tasted like the stub-end of a cucumber, faintly acrid and bitter.*
>
> SADEQ HEDAYAT[209]

First is the Meal of the Unexpected: here nothing tastes as it should, so that the mind pays the price for its attempts to encapsulate encounters before the fact (all promise of set associations is suspended).

Note: Mania is one of the only existential conditions in which one experiences a euphoric uptick when confronted with a surprise or blunder, growing stronger as assumptions are upended.

---

[209] Hedayat, *The Blind Owl*, 113.

OMNICIDE II

I can stick my tongue out, there's nothing to put on its taste buds, nothing to make it salivate, nothing to edify it, a useless muscle.

RÉDA BENSMAIA[210]

Second is the Meal of Blandness: here all things are flavourless, tasting of lack and disappointment, as the mouth becomes a deadened organ incapable of enjoying even a single morsel (disbanding all concepts of superiority or difference), for the host prefers the tepid slice and the watered-down drink above all else.

Note: Mania is one of the only existential conditions that can actually feast on the deficient, subsisting on fallen overripe fruit or empty plates, thriving on the disagreeable crumb or even in starvation.

You cook me in the cauldron of your prayers, you mix me with your soldier's soup and the king's spices.

ADONIS[211]

Third is the Meal of Petty Kings: here the rulers hold court dining upon the innards of great poets, adorning their long tables with the torn limbs of those who have questioned their titles, forming a broth of sameness from the skin and fatty tissue of firebrands.

---

210 Bensmaia, *The Year of Passages*, 61.
211 Adonis, *Selected Poems*, 51.

GEUMOMANIA

Note: Mania is one of the only existential conditions that gambles on its ability to survive unharmed by fatal humiliation, confident in its becoming auratically magnified for all time by these occasions of momentary painful consumption—for the mere fact of one's having touched life, it presumes, is enough to influence the ages according to one's will.

> *I love the taste of your thick blood. How I savor it in my toothless mouth.*
>
> JOYCE MANSOUR[212]

Fourth is the Meal of the Outworn: here guests devour the essence of other things, but to their own gradual detriment, their cheeks growing gaunt and their teeth falling out, their frames emaciated and their eyes yellowed by insatiability, though loving every dash of blood, however small, that wrecks them.

Note: Mania is one of the only existential conditions in which one becomes increasingly heedless of one's own mental-physical deterioration, at the expense of one's desire for any external object, vision, or becoming, often sacrificing one's individual beauty and taking on awful facial wrinkles in order to savour the target of this other destiny.

---

212 Mansour, *Screams*, 37.

OMNICIDE II

The journey of a form along the line of time...returning from a feast in the mirror.

FORUGH FARROKHZAD[213]

Fifth is the Meal of Mirrors: here guests stare into floor-to-ceiling mirrors while eating, watching themselves throughout as a series of quirks—the way fingers curl around silverware, the slight inexplicable pause before food touches lips—but forgetting that they see not themselves but rather their inverse image on a backwards or contrary journey.

Note: Mania is among one of the only existential conditions to name the mirror-image a foreigner, nemesis, or opposite counterpart, deciding on alliances or death-threats based upon the logical conclusion that it must have antipathetic tastes in every conceivable instance.

The scorching south wind sucked the tears that trickled slowly down his cheeks.

IBRAHIM AL-KONI[214]

Sixth is the Meal of Elements: here guests (or rather trespassers) are drained slowly by their starving elemental hosts (wind, earth, fire, water) as each atmosphere thirsts

---

213 Farrokhzad, *A Lonely Woman*, 112.
214 Al-Koni, *The Bleeding of the Stone*, 36.

GEUMOMANIA

for something particular in its human or animal sojourner, taking its excessive share for the room-and-board of all entrants.

Note: Mania is one of the only existential conditions that never assumes entrance into Being as a free ride; the manic one always counts themselves as an out-of-towner, ever suspicious of a world that drinks their tears as nutriment or alimentary ration whenever possible.

> *I would make a meal from my own body's flesh for the hungry companions.*
>
> AHMAD SHAMLU[215]

Seventh is the Meal of the Desperate: here guests are caught in a state of pure dearth, in thinning and attenuated forms whose palates have reached the last resort and have recourse to anything whatsoever, to the point where the companion offers them an arm to gnaw upon or a leg with which to glut themselves.

Note: Mania is one of the only existential conditions that gravitates toward figures of marasmus (severe malnutrition, from the ancient Greek *marasmos*, meaning 'withering'), for it has an acute perception of those things that are supposed to look or be otherwise, and offers up its own fury as handout, fare, or barely-edible cuisine.

---

[215] Shamlu, *Born Upon the Dark Spear*, 20.

> *He trembles like a person who is burning…but no one hears him screaming that the bees are coming out of the mouth of that witch.*
>
> GHADA SAMMAN[216]

Eighth is the Meal of Witches: here guests are treated to the miraculous ability of witches to produce stinging entities from their own throats, moving them across the burned roofs of their oral cavities (as if mouths were caves for swarming creatures) and among the waiting bodies of those seated around the altar or den.

Note: Mania is one of the only existential conditions that constantly turns the tables of supposed hierarchies in a sorcery of function, transforming the once-sacred being (the human) into crumbs or table-scraps for those forgotten life forms (ants, bees) that gorge together, with a million quick bites.

> *I drink a glass of the wandering merchant's wine.*
>
> MAHMOUD DARWISH[217]

Ninth is the Meal of Exotic Vendors: here guests desire only delicacies hailing from the most faraway places, fashioning their diets along the lines of inconceivable

---

216 Samman, *The Square Moon*, 142.
217 Darwish, *Unfortunately, It Was Paradise*, 149.

GEUMOMANIA

refreshments, although this philosophy of leisure, luxury, and frill always requires the introduction of a dangerous stranger onto the scene: the merchant.

Note: Mania is one of the only existential conditions that manages both import and export trades concurrently, buying and selling the under-supplied item in alleyways, both seeking from others evidence of an unusual possession up their sleeves and constantly playing dealer to its own collection of extraordinary samples.

> *You should have died of hunger and thirst there in the room. But evil men like you are lucky.*
>
> HASSAN BLASIM[218]

Tenth is the Meal of Ingested Beloveds: here guests are required to perpetrate the most intimate evil by eating what they love most, endowing all desire with a drastic epicurean consequence such that objects of obsessive longing find themselves attached to a gastronomic destiny in the pit of the stomach.

Note: Mania is one of the only existential conditions that equates wanting with literal devouring, like those religions whose followers drink the blood shed by their messianic prophets or those tribes who ritualistically swallow the flesh of their chiefs—to the extent that we

---

218 Blasim, *The Madman of Freedom Square*, 35.

can imagine the chronomaniac ingesting the gears of the clock, the bibliomaniac crumpling pages from old volumes into the jaw, the thalassomaniac drinking vials of salt water, and the catroptromaniac shoving small pieces of glass along the gumline. This is how the manic figure becomes the ultimate embodiment of the host: by turning their own interior body into a dining hall for the favourite guest.

> *Taste and the kiss; acridity; the tongue; the buds; salivation; the cauldron; mixture; thickness; savouring; the journey; return; the feast; sucking; trickling; the cheeks; flesh; the companions; the witch; the glass; the merchant; wine; the room; evil; the lucky*

Aceromania (Sour Things, Bitterness)

> *The embryo of the story:*
> *it can take at any moment, it can turn sour, it can spin*
>   *off-track, if it takes, it's horrible, but if it doesn't take,*
>   *it's horrible too,*
> *Total surveillance over the rhythm that takes*
>   *or doesn't take,*
> *At any moment, everything can turn to vinegar.*
>
> RÉDA BENSMAIA[219]

The Aceromaniac advises us of a certain sensitivity that comes into play at the cusp in every narrative, an expressive axle by way of which the line of thought suddenly hinges or twists one way or another. And yet, in perfect accordance with the logic of doom, whatever direction it takes leads to an ultimate souring of the imagination. Thus, to become a savant of the turning point is to learn to somehow ascertain the moment of germination or spoiling, and we reference this image of bacterial cultures not as metaphor but rather as a diagnostic device that apprises us of a unique process of fermentation. When

---

[219] Bensmaia, *The Year of Passages*, 52.3.

does the lavender or alkaline mind fall into acidity? What stipulations must encircle the still-unborn story for it to go from upright to putrescent, from so-called sanity to that acetic delirium where one says 'Alone I taste rotten meat', or that one's only wish is to pour the 'bitter wine of my life down the parched throat of my shadow'?[220] For answers, we could look to the applied science of zymology (or zymurgy), which observes the biochemical accumulation of non-toxic slimes, but better to study those old peasant grandmothers of the villages who store pickled mixtures in bottles under the floorboards or in unreachable corners of their closets and pantries for year upon year. They become masters of astringency, mustiness, tartaric and pyrogallic persuasions; they are the figures of 'total surveillance of the rhythm that takes or doesn't take'; they conduct the dynamics of microorganisms and long waiting; they share familial practices of preservation, allowing vinegar to play sovereign in the breaking down of natural sugars. To treat consciousness similarly would be to hold watch over the multiple pathways of its turning 'horrible', desiring those selective thoughts that, like citric juices, cause an initial rejection response but then increasingly lure through their sharpness: moreover, it would be to carefully scrutinise both rational and imaginative notions with a kind of anti-spatial attunement to

---

220 Mansour, *Essential Poems and Writings*, 109; Hedayat, *The Blind Owl*, 47.

the 'off-track' and an anti-temporal attunement to the 'at any moment' where sourness emerges and becomes the jar, text, idea, or world.

> *Sourness and the embryo; the take; the turn; the off-track;*
> *the horrible; rhythm; vinegar*

Limomania (Hunger, Thirst)

> *If the river runs dry it will be filled with the blood of those who love it…The spectre of the future takes the form of a terrifying desert. We won't go back to the jungle to fight. This time we'll go to the desert and slaughter each other. Our new ice age will be a thirsty desert.*
>
> HASSAN BLASIM[221]

The Limomaniac exhibits one of the potential routes to an omnicidal future (by famine or drought), although in the above passage this fatalistic desertification is also connected quite brilliantly to the many levels of insanity: the short story from which it is excerpted tells of a village whose people always speak in cryptic ways in order to avoid bad luck, giving vague non-answers to all questions, for in this village there once lived an old woman who fell into madness upon the death of her only child, a fisherman drowned in the river, after which she took her herd grazing into the outer dunes (first mania), losing herself, living in a secluded tent for five years, and upon finally returning, has taken on the demeanour of a joyful little girl, ignoring others' words, succumbing to a compulsion to swim in the same river for hours

---

221 Blasim, *The Iraqi Christ*, 102.

while singing ancient songs (second mania), and always sleeping among the animals at night (third mania). Soon after her arrival, however, the villagers start to observe the horrid outgrowth of several death-trees, 'born-dead' trunks that shoot their decrepit underground roots into poisonous branches hundreds of feet into the air, in the process rendering the land arid for a mile around. Faced with a nearing horizon of starvation, the villagers bring a mad shaman back from exile to locate the source of the murdered soil (fourth mania), and he quickly detects that the death-trees arise from the old woman's stare (wherever she looks, they spring forth as an extension of her thought or gaze—fifth mania). After multiple failed attempts at ritual cleansing, pleading, and blindfolding the old woman (sixth mania), the villagers accept the awful necessity of banishing her altogether, and tie her arms and legs with rope one night and send her down the long river in a boat toward some indeterminate shore (seventh mania), although they leave one solitary tree standing in her memory, upon which no birds or insects ever alight. As the narrator makes his decision to immediately leave this village of enigmatic tongues, the apparition of a little girl approaches and hands him a milk-soaked flower, commands him to chew it that same evening and leave the pieces 'in a place you have forgotten to miss' (eighth mania). For starvation is precisely the experience of missing the self or world that was once full, before the time of raw need—a longing only possible from the vantage of dryness or of a glacial epoch.

All of this is recounted in order to trace the lineaments of a new delirium of hunger/thirst not based in human fear; note that here we must abandon the phobiacentric syndromes identified by psychoanalysis around the experience of malnourishment, whatever their excesses, especially those that misappropriate the term 'mania' to suit their neurotic purposes: polyphagia or hyperphagia (sensations of voracious hunger), pica (named strangely after a bird that eats anything, referring to abnormal craving for non-nutritional objects—e.g., pagophagia, eating of ice; tricophagia, eating of hair; geophagia, eating of clay or ashes); cibophobia or sitophobia (morbid aversion to food); dipsomania (unstoppable compulsion to drink, usually alcoholic liquors). No, these diagnoses are not of the same experiential register as the aforementioned tale of the old village woman whose ecstatic imagination wills the onset of mass hunger and thirst—elsewhere the same author writes that 'the idea of hunger seeped into my mind like a quicksilver snake'—for in the latter case we are dealing with a host who serves up barrenness as a form of desire.[222]

To understand this distinction better, let us turn to a dangerous question: If most ancient civilisations did

---

222 Blasim, *The Iraqi Christ*, 51.

indeed include gods of famine and drought in their mythic-cosmic structures, most of them also developing elaborate rituals of pacification in response, paying their accursed shares to these destructive divinities in order to protect the land from pestilence or scorching, were there ever individuals or minor cult-formations that adoringly followed these deities? The answer is yes, there are obscure accounts of such limomaniacal worship, but even more interestingly, the reason for their doing so is neither moral nor practical (such gods could hardly be expected to spare their own followers, after all), but rather stems from an affinity for the deities' physiognomic appearances, affects, moods, and sensations, based on the storied accounts to which they were culturally exposed. Furthermore, this attraction to the fascinating bodies and motions of such gods of slow misery is enough to also answer the age-old philosophical problem of why one might knowingly choose what is not good for oneself (for mania subscribes to no moral foundation of the good life, but only to a search for the ultimate experience, whatever shape it might take).

Although monotheistic traditions borrow from the limomaniacal appetite, often depicting their own prophets and saints as lean or even bone-thin, their rib cages jutting out from beneath pale skin, again it is the ancients who concocted a truly wondrous aesthetic for the divinities of scarcity. They give us visions of an ontology of gnashing teeth, with zero stake in psychological repression, but rather which trample continents through a superabundant will to carnage (wrought from outside within). In the Zoroastrian tradition, the god Apaosha was represented as a terrifying black horse that assaults the white-golden horse of rainfall, whereas the early Mesopotamians speak of Erra (later Nergal) as the 'Lord of affray and slaughter' related to deadly hunger, a god of war, plague-stricken earth, and underworld whose indiscriminate killing sprees are often linked to boredom, and who is represented in the iconography of monument stones and relief carvings as a lion or a mace with the head of the lion. On the Greek side, while certain central gods such as Poseidon or Demeter could occasionally bring drought and famine by passively restraining their own powers (provision of water and harvest), Limos was herself the active apotheosis of the starved world, dwelling at the frozen outer limits of Scythia, able to drive kings mad with hunger, making them eat their own hands by breathing emptiness into their stomachs; she is portrayed with sublime visual complexity in the following passage:

> Her hair was coarse, her face sallow, her eyes sunken; her lips crusted and white; her throat scaly with scurf. Her parchment skin revealed the bowels within; beneath her hollow loins jutted her withered hips; her sagging breasts seemed hardly fastened to her ribs;

her stomach only a void; her joints wasted and huge,
her knees like balls, her ankles grossly swollen.[223]

Lastly, we look to the Chinese goddess Nuba, shown sometimes in green robes but most often naked, capable of moving at supernatural velocities, who wars with rain and wind deities by paradoxically creating trails that impede their progress; a divinity of pure speed who inflicts slowness upon her enemies, and against whom peasants conceived rituals in which one of their number would (un)dress mimetically as the goddess and play-act her retreat, or in rare circumstances would exhume and whip the newly-buried corpses thought to be used as her famine-vessels.

For a select few, however, these myriad sculptures, tales, and elegant or wild ceremonies had the reverse effect of generating a limomaniacal interest, enough to build temples such as the House of E-meslam in Kutha to quietly solicit those whose epithets translate as 'the burner', 'the raging king', and 'the lord of the high summer sun': rather than seek to placate the latter or evict them from the real, they mouthed dialogical prayers to these forces of sparseness and desiccation (to want what leaves wanting).

Hunger/Thirst and dryness; filling; blood; spectrality; future; desert; jungle; fighting; slaughter; the ice age

---

[223] Ovid, *Metamorphoses*, tr. A.D. Melville (Oxford: Oxford University Press, 1998), 195–97.

Geliomania (Laughter)

> *Still holding my hands before my face, I involuntarily burst into laughter. It was a more violent laugh than the previous one had been and it made me shudder from head to foot. It was a laugh so deep that it was impossible to guess from what remote recess of the body it proceeded...*
>
> SADEQ HEDAYAT[224]

The Geliomaniac coaxes themselves into seeing in everything a reverse hyponymy—a semantic relation in which the meaning of one word is included in the meaning of another, although here we speak rather of a jester's philosophy in which meaninglessness is enveloped in meaninglessness. Such is the recurring laughter that we find across numerous pages of the text quoted above: the laugh of the old man in the painting, the laugh of his deranged uncle, the laugh of the hearse-driver, the laugh of the odds-and-ends seller, and finally the laugh of the narrator himself staring in the mirror. It seems that each encounter is a bell-toll or omen of the impending last stage (when he wears all faces at once); they all have an aspect of foresight and imminence in their hair-raising echo. This is not the hysterical cry of the one who laughs

---

224 Hedayat, *The Blind Owl*, 127.

at nothing in particular, but rather the manic showmanship of the one who laughs at every particularity, who prefers the world as immanent joke, and perceives each identity and event as histrionic entertainment; whose laugh is at once the breathtaking multiplicity of every joke ever told and the breathtaking finality of all jokes becoming one punchline (the last laugh). Geliomania is therefore the signature of a certain syncretism: it brings every mishap together into a conspiracy of aerodynamic lightness; it allows existence to become blameless before comedic paronomasia (play on words).

At the heart of any philosophy of becoming is the ability to surprise oneself (with unknown power): however, this is not the reawakening of an inner unconscious strength but instead the summoning of an extraneous newfound ability gained by risky pursuit (what was not there before). Such is the value of the expressions 'involuntary burst', 'impossible to guess', and 'remote recess' in the above excerpt: they serve to successively clarify a function that never belonged to the narrator prior to the metamorphic shudder. The sudden originality of that laugh whose pitch shocks one's own ears, the odd look in the mirror-image's eyes that one does not recognise as oneself—indeed, this is the dominion of mania alone, above all former explanations, and hence the crowning puzzle-piece to an entire intellectual-artistic line of those who have sought the existential answer to a single question: that of how one becomes more than this.

Nevertheless, it also eases the way for the omnicidal imagination: for the world that closes in laughter is nothing more than a formal gesture of the curtain-call. Thus, when another in our literary configuration writes similarly of a figure who 'leaned back and shrieked with laughter, the echo ringing strangely through the unknown caves', we may read this as confirmation of a certain fatal hilarity, a doomsday posture or howl of that knowing clown who has seen through to the end of things, to the point where mad humour is the only affect left standing before the infamy of an all-encompassing illusion. And so it is not hard to fathom how the subject of absolute bemusement could also become the henchman of the world's undoing—the cheerful one; the livid one.[225]

> *Laughter and the face; the involuntary; violence; shuddering;*
> *impossible depth; guessing; the remote recess*

---

[225] There are others who connect this semi-laughing sound to apocalyptic experience: 'I hear the ruin of all space, shattered glass and toppling masonry, and time one livid final flame.' J. Joyce, *Ulysses* (New York: Dover Publications, 2009), 2.7–10.

Zoomania (Animality)

The Zoomaniac extends us the opportunity (which we shall take) to pay tribute to a mediaeval author who taught us his mystical philosophy of the seven valleys by convening a fatal conference of the birds. Consequently, all ten members of this literary configuration are here invited to offer a single line that might inaugurate our own specialised manic assortment of animalities and bestiaries (compendia of beasts).

> *I had become like a screech-owl, but my cries caught in my throat and I spat them out in the form of clots of blood.*
> SADEQ HEDAYAT[226]

The First Creature is the Screech-Owl: being of shrill nocturnal calls, whether for mating purposes or to signal extreme territoriality, whose trill (known as a bounce song or tremolo) consists of low whistles and ever-dropping pitches designed to ward predators away from the nest. But in its manic form, the screech-owl abandons its defensive, retaliatory tendencies and instead takes on an emetic quality: it spits out bloody remnants of its own interior self onto the forest ground, thus showing how the manic

---

226 Hedayat, *The Blind Owl*, 123.

imagination becomes unfettered by territorial instinct (making the inside unbearable).

> *Don't you see? Mules are everywhere! Even the greatest writers can't get along without them!*
>
> RÉDA BENSMAIA[227]

The Second Creature is the Writer's Mule: being of crossbred species and chromosomal blending, whose resilience, docility, and stamina makes its body ideal for the harshest working conditions, its hardened hooves able to climb rocky terrain and carry loads or passengers for long periods, its calm temperament making it the chosen animal for transporting explosives in wartime. But in its manic form, the mule abandons its deterministic sterility and instead begins to proliferate trains of new foals across the mountain trails: it multiplies infinitely here, in the rugged places, while at the same time becoming increasingly selective in its cargo, allowing only visionaries of the writing-act to mount and dismount at will, taking them where they need to go (much like those trusted steeds of heroic legend who alone could find the roadless path), thus showing how the manic imagination often prompts the notion of a necessary secondary agent to guide the way.

---

[227] Bensmaia, *The Year of Passages*, 93.

ZOOMANIA

I ride a salamander's back abroad and breathe embers.

ADONIS[228]

The Third Creature is the Riding Salamander: being of the damp habitat and the slender amphibious tail, whose existence is an odd combination of shyness, skin toxicity, and regenerative processes; once believed to be aligned with elemental fire (and hence represented in many folkloric and occult literatures as emerging from pure flames). But in its manic form, the salamander abandons its cold-bloodedness, which formerly made it impervious to burning, in order to actively 'breathe embers' upon the surrounding world: much like the scorpion and the frog referenced in the lines that follow, the salamander here takes on not anthropomorphic traits but rather alter-animalities, and furthermore abandons its skittish character to accept riders, thus showing how the manic imagination (as in certain fairy tales) allows otherwise impossible forces to be harnessed.[229]

---

[228] Adonis, *The Pages of Day and Night*, 41.

[229] This manic tactfulness corresponds to the lesson of Nietzsche in *Thus Spoke Zarathustra*, another figure of delirious animal companions: 'It is not enough for me that lightning no longer does any harm. I do not wish to conduct it away: it shall learn to work for me.' F. Nietzsche, *Thus Spoke Zarathustra*, in *The Portable Nietzsche,* ed. W. Kaufmann (New York: Penguin Books, 1976), 401.

OMNICIDE II

I explained to the striped cat...And the octopus born with flaying arms.

JOYCE MANSOUR[230]

The Fourth Creature is a hybrid of Cat and Octopus: being of the nine lives and of the nine minds, of the retractable claws and the contorting arms, walking tiptoed across edges and blasting backwards along sea bottoms, mastering both quick reflexes and camouflage, curiosity and complex plotting, creature of the thin-slitted glowing eye and the bulging socket, the self-grooming paw and the blue bloodstream of the soft-bodied ones. But in its manic form, the cat-octopus transfers its anti-social fighting instinct (such creatures usually tear at one another in alleys or in dense ocean dens) to the hearing of poetic 'explanation': the radical ingenuity of both animalities is used to turn them into listeners, thus showing how the manic imagination believes it can soothe even the most aggressive forms of being (via its own ever-present aura of aggression).

Note: As with those hybrid deities and mythic creatures that adorned the walls of ancient temples, manic amalgamation raises the concrete question of what happens when multiple compulsions—e.g. the cat's delirium and the octopus's delirium—simultaneously

---

230 Mansour, *Essential Poems and Writings*, 93.

inhabit the same consciousness, whether they can indeed cohabit, how the transition is made between them or how they assist one another, how they decide which mad amenity is to take its turn next. The descriptive terms 'striped' and 'flaying' are themselves like valves giving us some indication of the orienting mechanism at work: namely, that it operates either by gently painting an asynchronous streak across an underlying facade (the brush), or by fiercely stripping off the layered skin of subjectivity whenever required to call forth the other (the whip).

I had become the pelican of the wasteland.
FORUGH FARROKHZAD[231]

The Fifth Creature is the Wasteland Pelican: being of the elastic throat, of those pouches that carry gallons of water, adept at both dynamic soaring and low-altitude skimming of the water's surface, flying against winds without expending energy by manipulating changing draught-pockets in order to rise, drop, and dive suddenly. But in its manic form, what was always a seabird of ease instead chooses inhospitable atmospheres, going where it is least accommodated, through the desert inlands where it can no longer fly in V-formation or single-line flocks, subject

---

231 Farrokhzad, *The House Is Black*.

to the hungriest incarnations of its principal predators (the coyote, the cat, the human), thus showing how the manic imagination often makes things harder on itself (altitudes that require the greatest energy expenditure).

> *Magic overflows from their eyes...The thought torments me, that I've never in my life held a live gazelle in my hands.*
> IBRAHIM AL-KONI[232]

The Sixth Creature is the Magical Gazelle: being of short-burst speeds, of the light frame and of the agile leap (enemy of the fast cheetah), famed subject of romantic Arabian poetry (from the original Arabic *ghazal*) for its graceful movements and beautiful curved horns, that creature whose thin scapulae (shoulder blades) were covered in notches by Palaeolithic cultures of the Levant for symbolic design and message-transmission, and who can shrink their own hearts and livers in order to stay alive in the hottest savannahs. But in its manic form, the gazelle becomes the repository of an uncalming magicality, no longer abiding by the legs that flee at first sighting but now harbouring allure in its eyes, inciting in all onlookers a growing desire to hold it closer, to clutch its presence, thus showing the manic imagination's ability to turn itself into something graspable, something against which

---

[232] Al-Koni, *The Bleeding of the Stone*, 45.

others press themselves impetuously: to turn captivation into an impulse to hold captive, and to do this by converting a single feature, detail, or limb into the sole gravitational centre of the will to embrace.

> *And this mountainous, iron-willed lion of a man, thus infatuated, trekked across the blood-soaked field of destiny.*
> AHMAD SHAMLU[233]

The Seventh Creature is the Bleeding Lion: being of muscularity and of the heaving chest; apex predator. But in its manic form, its metaphoric universe of majesty is supplanted by a broken will to overthrow the kingdom: like those haunting mountain ranges whose first ancestral princes are said to have flung themselves down from on high, a refined model of mad vertigo exclusive to the majestic, the lion moves against its natural destiny; the roar soon becomes the whimper of the fatally wounded, the long-sleeping becomes the ever-plodding, thus showing the manic imagination's ability to turn dominant power into self-ejecting vulnerability, to turn the light-sensitive vision of the perfect hunter into the introspective vision of oneself as damned quarry, to rob the circus tamers of their centrepiece and to instead seek

---

233 Shamlu, *Born Upon the Dark Spear*, 82.

conditions under which ferocity wins only the grasslands of spilled blood.

> *I could still hear the mournful, collective voice of the 'pet people' in their cages…These creatures' relationship with sun and moon, forest and jungle, with the seas, the night, the joys of changing seasons and freedom…*
>
> GHADA SAMMAN[234]

The Eighth Creatures are the Animals-No-Longer: beings robbed of their instinctive animality, whose relations to material landscapes and to their own physical expressivity have been forever disrupted by the human perversions of the pet shop or the zoo. But in their manic form—for mania also often perceives itself as a being-caged—the self-forgotten are able to form a 'collective voice' which evokes sympathetic hallucinations in others, thus demonstrating the manic imagination's ability to turn subjugation into passion play, like those recreated scenes of prophets' suffering that send believers into dramatic trances or those tragic statues of death-warmed messiahs known to cause epileptic seizures.

---

[234] Samman, *Beirut Nightmares*, 13.

ZOOMANIA

I must bear the weight of the earth on my shoulders
alone, and become an enraged bull.

MAHMOUD DARWISH[235]

The Ninth Creature is the Enraged Bull: being of the dangerous temper and of the killer-instinct, whose grand physique has throughout time made it at once a creature of heavenly worship (zodiac), of ritual feasting (divine sacrifice), and of spectacle-killing (bullfight). The Apis Bull Cult and Serapeum of Saqqara; the Colossal Bull's Head of Persepolis; Moloch the bull-headed Phoenician-Carthaginian god of child sacrifice, or Baal the Canaanite lord of storms; the gruelling contest of the Spanish bullrings, their caped *toreros* freezing in sculptural poses. But in its manic form, the bull is neither elevated to pantheonic status nor impaled before cheering human masses, but rather identifies itself with the mythic syndrome of Atlas, titanic figure condemned to lift the heavens upon his bare shoulders, thus showing how the manic imagination envisions itself similarly as upholder of celestial globes (of singular desires), both as punishment and as eternal duty, converting rage into the expenditure involved in carrying entire worlds on its back. For is the suggestion of a person bearing the full weight of the universe not already a pure manic image?

---

235 Darwish, *Unfortunately, It Was Paradise*, 153.

Note: The above passage also confirms mania's potential to influence consciousness to switch sides and strike alliances with animality over the human race.

> *I would stumble upon another species of...insects called Reduvius, though they don't actually kiss each other. These only like the mouths of sleeping humans. They crawl across the face till they reach the corner of the mouth, where...they secrete poison in microscopic drops.*
>
> HASSAN BLASIM[236]

The Tenth Creature is the Kissing Reduvius: being of stealth-related names (assassin bug, masked hunter, nymph) owing to its ability to disguise itself in dust particles, though itself an insect of incomplete metamorphosis. But in its manic form, the Reduvius's venomous toxins and saliva (normally used to immobilise stabbed prey while draining their body fluids) herald paradigmatic reversals of that biased humanist mentality wherein killing insects 'is the only act of violence which remains unpunished even within us. Their blood does not stain our hands, for it does not remind us of our own.'[237] Instead, the manic imagination imposes a magnifying effect on its

---

236 Blasim, *The Corpse Exhibition*, 30.

237 E. Canetti, *Crowds and Power*, tr. C. Stewart (New York: The Noonday Press, 1960), 210.

ZOOMANIA

philosophy of the infinitesimal: to allow the smallest thing (the insect's kiss, bite, secretion) to digest the everything. *Note*: So it is that a simple bestiary might conceal an omnicidal text, and that a single animal can be ascribed the right to end the world.

Animality and screeching; crying; the blood-clot; the everywhere; getting-along; riding; the back; explanation; the striped; flaying; magic eyes; holding; the mountain; trekking; the field; mournfulness; collectivity; the cage; weight; rage; the kiss; the corner; sleep; secretion; microscopic poison

Part 26

Haphemania/Chiraptomania (Touch)
Dermatomania (Skin)
Amychomania (Claws, Fangs, Horns)
Mechanomania (Machines)
Ergomania (Work)

Haphemania/Chiraptomania (Touch)

> *Time passed,*
> *time passed and night fell*
> *over the acacias's naked limbs,*
> *night slithered on the other side*
> *of the window panes,*
> *and with its cold tongue*
> *sucked in the remains of departed day.*
>
> FORUGH FARROKHZAD[238]

The Haphemaniac reminds us of the infinite ways in which one can be touched, later in the same work referring to someone 'whom a glance caressed', and to being 'nailed to the scaffold', and describing how 'the tracks of your five-finger branches, which were like five words of truth, have remained upon her cheeks'. Each of these three images (of the caressed, the nailed, and the imprinted) possesses a temporal specificity with respect to how long the touch imposes itself and how long its effects last: herein lies the significance of the above verse's repeated warning about time's passing, for the night's falling, slithering, and sucking motions are also each overtures to a chronometrical shift. Chronometry (study of the

---

238 Farrokhzad, *A Lonely Woman*, 127.

measuring of time) as opposed to Chronology (study of the arrangement of time): for the intent is to cultivate a kind of touch before and after which nothing else remains.

This clockwork haphemania is perhaps best understood by reference to three strange phenomena: (1) the history of food-tasters (Persian *pish-marg*, literally meaning 'pre-dier'), commissioned by paranoid leaders to ingest substances before they themselves partake, so as to detect slow-acting poisons; (2) the Japanese *wakaresaseya*, a professional seducer hired to sabotage an ongoing relationship by beguiling the client's lover, whether for the sake of extricating oneself from a contested divorce, avoiding the messy confrontation of a breakup scenario, or wresting the lover from the spell of another affair; (3) the ocular condition known as long-term *mydriasis*, whereby an injurious physical incident (concussion, stroke) or shocking experiential encounter (hallucinogenic drugs, traumatic witnessing of violence, or in rarest instances recurring nightmares) leads to an unusual dilation of the pupils. These are three distinct variations of manic touch that leave the realms of sensation and subjectivity like tarred surfaces by virtue of their interindividual reaction-times: the food-taster (the one who touches first); the paid charmer (the one who touches second); the mydriatic patient (the one who is touched suddenly yet forevermore). Hence, whether we speak of the testing of imperial plates to pre-warn of assassination attempts, the employment of private agencies for the sake of relationship dissolution, or the abnormal hugeness of the black inner circle of the eye, our concern remains that of understanding how mania handles the world and thereby perfects touch according to its own affective timekeeping: in essence, it is a matter of measuring one's influence as the hands of a deranged tactile clock; of taking strangers to 'the other side' of chronological windows through a single contact with madness, whether meant to graze them momentarily (the night of abandon) or to clinch them in some omni-braced state that demands an entire existence (the lifelong hook).[239]

> *Touch and time; passing; nightfall; nakedness; the window; coldness; departure; the remains*

---

[239] Certain recent psychological studies trace the ability of mania to make acute physical impressions (its touch) on the body or look of the manic subject. For instance, although the article remains beholden to the standardised categories of bipolarity, euphoric versus dysphoric mania, and hypomania versus full-blown mania, the interesting prospect of mania's transformation of the eyes is examined in J. Wheeler, et al., 'Bipolar Mania Eye Image Classification', *SMU Data Science Review* 1:1 (2018). Still, we would be even more interested in a study that identified mania's impact on the appearance of the other: Is there something uniquely discernible in the eyes of the individual who has come into sudden contact with a manic figure?

Dermatomania (Skin)

Did you say you're a poet?
Where do you come from? You have a fine skin.
Executioner, do you hear me?
You can have his head.
    But bring me his skin unbruised.
    His skin means so much to me.
Take him away.
Your velvet skin will be my carpet.

ADONIS[240]

The Dermatomaniac falls into the same market as those animals whose exotic hides are prized by illicit collectors: their supposed powers are bolstered by anecdotal suggestions as to how they must be absorbed. The combination of a flatline formula and a vitalist formula: one must swallow the skin of the dead being in order to actuate some rare becoming, so that murderous indiscretions furnish the basis for enhanced perceptual-motor gifts. Violence as existential luxury. 'His skin means so much to me', rasps the executioner's boss. And so it is that the mania of the poet winds its way quickly into

---

[240] Adonis, *Victims of a Map*, 89.

the thoughts and veins of the poet's enemy (a costly form of victory).[241]

Note: The multitiered etymology of the term 'ablation' has some intractable value in our discussion of mania here (resembling the above philosophy of skin-removal). The word can mean: (1) the surgical resection of tissue; (2) the melting or evaporation of ice from glaciers; (3) the dwindling of meteoric material in flight caused by thermal or aerodynamic pressures. Thus the dermatological (the excision of epithelial lining) shares a common thread with the topological (the uninhabitable terrain of the arctic) and the cosmological (the hostile projectiles of outer space). But let us propel this manic philosophy of removal yet further by recalling two distinct figures who separated themselves from the world: (1) Empedocles, who flung himself into the mouth of a Sicilian volcano believing he would be reincarnated as a god; (2) Simeon the Stylite, an ascetic saint who spent thirty-seven years living atop a single pillar in Byzantine Syria in order to gain distance from the human realm and proximity to the heavens. One swallowed by lava, another swallowed by the sky, both participating in a doctrine of being taken away. Such gestures bring to mind the Iranian rural

---

241 Elsewhere, in a work entitled 'Beginnings of the Body, Ends of the Sea', the same poetic author writes that 'I want us to become a language of euphoria, an alphabet of limbs' [Adonis, *Selected Poems*]. Thus we see that this is no incidental connection: that euphoria (a manic disposition) is embedded in a language that functions like the skin of an inflictive body (what latches on).

practice of tea-drinking wherein a white sugar cube is held between clenched teeth and the hot beverage poured through the narrow opening, thereby carrying the sweet flavour down into the throat with each sip. Does omnicide therefore connect to the desire for gradual ablation, or better yet, the desire to eat the very object of removal (to become that which feeds on extracted things)?

Skin and fineness; the executioner; the unbruised; meaning; velvet; the carpet

Amychomania (Claws, Fangs, Horns)

From now on I shall write with claws!
RÉDA BENSMAIA[242]

It's not my fault if your nails grow longer.
JOYCE MANSOUR[243]

I feel the beak of a vulture in the vicinity of my liver.
AHMAD SHAMLU[244]

The Amychomaniac searches through whatever closet of sharp objects—claws, fangs, horns, nails, hooks, beaks, thorns—might bring them the sensation of scratched life, thus leaving us chasing after a philosophy of laceration, scoring, and grated nerve-endings. Although each of the aforementioned items deserve their own customised phenomenology, the two overarching principles here relate to a philosophy of imminence and immanence (like the simultaneous narrowing/aggravation of an asthmatic's chest). Accordingly, the three passages convene at the same juncture, erasing all semblance of moral

---

242 Bensmaia, *The Year of Passages*, 66.7.
243 Mansour, *Screams*, 55.
244 Shamlu, *Born Upon the Dark Spear*, 19.

responsibility: whether accidental or malicious, this *amycho*-scape remains an inextricable facet of existence itself (it is what happens, inevitably and everywhere). It comes with the territory of moving through a barbed-wire world: thought defined as the scraping gesture of consciousness; desire defined as the pointed or serrated implement. For there is only ever the will to abrasion.[245]

> *Scratching and the decision; the conclusion; non-fault; length; feeling; the vulture; the vicinity*

---

[245] For a more detailed philosophy/poetics of the knife-sharpener, see chapter 'The Sharpening' in J.B. Mohaghegh, *Inflictions: The Writing of Violence in the Middle East* (London: Bloomsbury, 2012).

Mechanomania (Machines)

> *I found myself thinking of my body as material that could be pierced by a bullet, or broken, or burned, or torn to ribbons. I don't know why, but it made me think of advertisements for watches that are 'unbreakable' and 'waterproof,' and I felt envious of them. It grieved me that the human body is so fragile, that life is unrepeatable.*
>
> GHADA SAMMAN[246]

The Mechanomaniac takes the first step toward converting their own flesh-and-blood body into machine by virtue of mere comparison: they admire the durability of the machine; they envy its reproducible patterns and components; they crave its utter lack of psychology. If mania is enemy to both human subjectivity and psychological structures, then one could not find a better paragon than the mechanical apparatus. The second step, then, is to fashion consciousness into axle and wheel by surrounding oneself with factory-like atmospheres—the noise, the oil, the applied force of pistons, brakes, timing devices, and springs—like the Persian Banu Musa brothers, three sons of a caravan-robber whose trailblazing *Book of Ingenious Devices* (850 AD) is not only credited with the invention of

---

[246] Samman, *Beirut Nightmares*, 9.

the first programmable machine but also revealed a rich flair for pneumatic and aerostatic control (the automatic flute, the alternating fountain, the self-trimming lamp) as forms of neo-enchantment. This mechanomania was only heightened later by their Arab-Kurdish scientific descendant al-Jazari (1136–1206 AD) whose fantastic experiments with hydropowered peacocks, waterwheels, castle-clocks, self-opening gates, delay systems, humanoid tea-servers, and hydraulic musicians (drummers) earned him the title of having constructed the earliest humanoid robot and the first programmable analogue computer. There is a certain undeniable madness in this tinkering with 'trick vessels' across mediaeval Asia, a fixation with contrivance and an underlying search for the secret of the 'unbreakable' life. So it is that one can unlock a specialised delirium salient only in the kinematics of the automatic world, for whoever said that the novel discovery of the avant-garde (automatic writing) was truly an encounter with some a priori unconscious rather than with the emergent consciousness of a machinic self, albeit in a preindustrial Eastern sense: a trick vessel made of double compartments and trap doors? Who is to say that all those avant-garde manifestos are not simply their own Books of Ingenious Devices?

Moreover, where a great early psychoanalyst once diagnosed a type of paranoid schizophrenic delusion wherein subjects believed themselves to be oppressed by some sinister 'Influencing Machine'—i.e., a literal persecutory contraption, its pathology-inducing levers and spinning globes operated by obscure overseers—perhaps the manic version of this would be to perceive oneself as the inventor or technician of one's own influencing machine, but in this case with wires capable of manipulating or electrifying reality so as to move it toward more powerful ranks of possibility—never 'passivity phenomena' but rather a magic lantern projecting images of hyperactive rapture.[247]

Machine and body; piercing; the unbreakable; envy; non-fragility; repeatability

---

[247] V. Tausk, 'On the Origin of the Influencing Machine in Schizophrenia', *Psychoanalytic Quarterly* 2 (1933): 519. Note that this same figure was also the very first to dedicate study to the subject of war deserters: i.e., those who dodged the traumatic ideology of war-machines through an alternative manic automaticity of the renegade.

Ergomania (Work)

I wish to live. I have work to do on this volcanic bit of geography.

The boredom of keeping watch exhausted him.
Then he bequeathed his daily work to me and begged me to save the city from your song.

MAHMOUD DARWISH[248]

The Ergomaniac takes us back to an initial premise of this book: the danger of the one with unfinished business. Nevertheless, there is a slight qualification to be made between the two excerpts, for the first reflects an individual duty to execute some lingering work, while the second describes a burden handed over from another who has failed to complete the deed. And yet there are two further problematic details associated with the latter (bequeathed) assignment: (1) the predecessor's exhaustion had no tragic or noble quality about it, like that of a martyr's sacrificial falling-short, but rather stemmed from the conceptual archenemy of work itself (boredom); (2) this is no casually relinquished project, for the stakes are apparently nothing less than the salvation of the city itself.

---

248 Darwish, *Unfortunately, It Was Paradise*, 139, 158.

He must hold guard; he must take his station; he must walk the upper walls and keep vigilant watch throughout the night so that others are not slain in their sleep. And what happens to him there, all alone on the ramparts? He focuses on his work through the manic gesture of talking directly to the dream of an invading figure: in a reversal similar to that of the child's imaginary friend, here the imaginary foe appears before his eyes and whispers threatening sentences around him ('your song'). His work is to stand ready, to fasten his gaze to the vague outer perimeters, and to speak endlessly (in dire warnings) to the one who would undo the work of this place. The mania of the defender, the mania of the tasked: this paradox of how only a 'volcanic' condition of madness could produce the ethos of the unwavering.

Work and the wish; the volcanic; boredom; the watchful; exhaustion; bequeathing; everydayness; the saviour; the city

Part 27
Nihilomania (Nothingness)
Eremomania (The Desert)
Taphemania (Being Buried Alive)
Athazagoramania (Forgetting)

Nihilomania (Nothingness)

*and fountains of blood were gushing forth
from the distressed temples of my desire,
when my life was no longer anything*

FORUGH FARROKHZAD[249]

*Alone...alone, just as I always had been. Planet Earth
was like one immense 'zero', and I myself was standing at
'point zero' once again... I felt like myself. I felt alone. And,
as a result, I felt on top of the world...Time had taught me
that 'zero' was actually the largest number in my life. It
didn't represent loss to me. It had always been a point of
departure.*

GHADA SAMMAN[250]

The Nihilomaniac is not the one with nothing to lose, but the one with only the nothing to lose (and who therefore guards it preciously). This figure will go to any length, sacrificing everything, to maintain this nothingness: consequently, the nihilomaniac reconciles the primordial dialectical tension between presence and absence simply by siding with absence, or rather bartering presence for

---

249 Farrokhzad, *A Lonely Woman*, 123.
250 Samman, *Beirut Nightmares*, 372.

absence, fighting everywhere for the void and making it a point of fatal preference.

Yet in phenomena these dimensions often overlap: How does one accurately differentiate presence from absence in some particular thing (a person, object, space, force) in order to observably favour the right granules in each encounter with outer reality? Ironically, did psychoanalysis not originate precisely in the effort to build a method to detect these holes, gaps, and lacks across the fabric of consciousness (even if it mistakenly classified them as problematic deficiencies rather than delicate motivations), and as a method to reach the zero-points of all human experience (although it mistakenly classified them as deterministic concatenations rather than as multivectorial projectiles)? In order to suppress something, one must first know where it dwells centrally (approach of the psychoanalyst); in order to protect something, one must first know where it moves dispersibly at all times (approach of the nihilomaniac).

Note: A perfect example of the conversion of this nihilomaniacal strand into a method would be the early Arabic linguists who etymologically bound the word *sihr* (spellbinding, enchantment) to *sahereh* (sorcerer) to *sahar* (the latest pre-dawn phase of the night) to *sahara* (restrictive damage to the lungs or heart buried in the chest cavity), for all reside across space-times of unawareness and in the vacuous corners of the apparent world.

NIHILOMANIA

Thus attempts to fascinate, conjure, charm, bewitch, enamour, ravish, dazzle, mesmerise, tempt, or curse, in addition to nocturnal shading and hard-to-access internal organs, all revolve around this dangerous triple-letter root (*s-h-r*) that stems from the manic desire to reach into chasms, to turn the hidden into pedestal, fountain, and pinnacle of the world, to recognise the 'no longer anything' as the true ward of 'gushing' and 'departure', to dress oneself in the radical nothing and turn its converting power upon whatever still believes itself to be something. It is the antonym and veto, but also the locked box of all occulted fantasies. Delirium of the non-entity.

> *Nothingness and the fountain; gushing; distress; the temple;*
> *the no-longer-anything; aloneness; the planetary; immensity;*
> *zero; the top of world; the number; the always; departure*

Eremomania (The Desert)

> *Every Bedouin in the desert would rather hide a bullet in the pupil of his eye, ready to use it to defend his children at the dreadful moment the enemy launched its invasion of the desert...Isolated though the Bedouins were, in their southern wilderness, news of the invaders still came to them on the winds, as rumors always do among desert tribes—rumors of marriage and divorce, and scandal, of death and the birth of new children. Nothing's ever secret in the desert, no matter what lonely spot you choose.*
>
> IBRAHIM AL-KONI[251]

The Eremomania would drink the sands if possible, and yet this same thirst is predicated on a mad transversal whereby the infatuated is also the most traitorous. Elsewhere he tells us that '[t]he Desert has never betrayed us. It is we who have betrayed the desert', for it is through a paradoxical rite of unfaithfulness alone that one may assume the crown of its geo-militancy.[252] In essence, the custodian of the desert must be *the deserter*.

To the same degree, the Bedouin of the above passage, the lunatic who conceals bullets beneath his eyelids and

---

[251] Al-Koni, *The Bleeding of the Stone*, 24.
[252] Al-Koni, *A Sleepless Eye*, 32.

listens to breezes for the footsteps of would-be conquerors, the lunatic who tells the desert's secret (that it keeps no secret), is also a perfect atychimaniac (obsession with failure). We must therefore imagine a figure whose cyclothymia (circling moods) and parathymia (disordered moods) involve some intense fondness for bad outcomes, failed enterprises, or lost souls, one who sees utopias in dystopias, always on the lookout for the victims of poor decisions, those who have fled in desperation to the flats, to the parched world, to become broken trinkets of the red god.

Desert and the Bedouin; the hidden bullet; defence; the invader; isolation; the winds; the tribes; rumour; scandal; birth; the never-secret

Taphemania (Being Buried Alive)

> *They buried life! Death clutches the living, no expression will have ever been so ironically revolutionary: by taking his own life, by burying himself alive, Hedayat became the vigil of what is alive in us, in being buried alive in opium, Hedayat became the implacably living testimony of every force that struggles against death...By burying himself alive, Hedayat ended up making incarnate the vigilance of life... allows us to look at life directly, from the deepest pit of the tomb.*
>
> RÉDA BENSMAIA[253]

The Taphemaniac here presents us with one of those extremely rare instances when one player of our literary configuration explicitly calls upon another of its authors, repeating their proper name like an incantation (for that is exactly what it is)—a remarkable philosophy of intimacy hanging on a necromancer's premise: that death arrived too soon for this one. He joins him below, then. He projects himself beneath the ground to launch this one accusation: that an elder visionary was buried alive.

(*Note*: Some of us have actually visited the worn-out apartment in Paris where this master scrawled his dark

---

253 Bensmaia, *The Year of Passages*, 72.3.

masterpiece, sentence after sentence, page after page, before laying down upon the floor and turning the gas stove on to perish in a carbon monoxide haze.)

And he says his name in a backslide—Hedayat (literally meaning 'Guidance' or 'The Leading')—over and again, until it hurts, until something breaks inside, and one feels oneself down there beside him, his coat still warm, his pulse still lightly throbbing, in order that we might become incarnations.

Burial Alive and the clutch; irony; revolution; the vigil; the implacable; testimony; struggle; the incarnated

Athazagoramania (Forgetting)

Jagged and limitless
in the duration of foregone times
columns of bones
vacant eye-sockets
naked ribs
a mouth
   without a single scream arisen
all its teeth fallen out,
the foreign-straying hiss of a melody of forgotten epochs
in the drone of an archaic wind
   unceasing still
      from a whenever antiquity.

AHMAD SHAMLU[254]

The Athazagoramaniac is the one who turns time, consciousness, and being into objects of the slipped mind, whose sole desire is to forget everything, all that was ever told or seen, to go walking along moors, to awake in the limitlessly unoccupied, and to be forgotten in turn by all who ever crossed their path before. Following those ancient fighters who would circumscribe themselves within a fatalistic ring and promise violence to whatever

---

[254] Shamlu, *Born Upon the Dark Spear*, 133.

trespassed across the line, so does the manic figure draw a circle around themselves, with the implication of another oblivion: to turn all that enters into the stranger in a strange land.

Note: We are aware today of the multiple meanings of the term 'black mirror'—from ancient sorcerers who believed that faraway occult lairs of (un)reality could only be perceived through black volcanic glass shards, to the seventeenth-century invention of the Caude Glass Lens through whose portable boxed mirror painters could test the tonal gradations of colours, to the all-pervasive influence today of virtual flecks cast across shiny or textured matte touchscreens.

Note: We can confirm mania's ability to sometimes accomplish 'chirality' or chiral effects (wherein identical mirror-image objects or molecules are unable to be superimposed on one another). Meanwhile, the psychoanalyst Jacques Lacan's own dual obsession with mirrors and with the topology of Borromean knots led him to conceive of 'the symptom' as a *sinthome*—no longer an interpreted message sent from the unconscious but a meaningless expression of the subject's enjoyment of their own unconscious. But what if we rethink topology in terms of the mystic Jalal al-Din Rumi's manic theory of 'reflection', via a story about Chinese versus Roman artists ('Roman' being a codename for Sufi mystics). According to this tale, two contingents of great painters were sent from these two rival kingdoms to the Sultan to determine which civilisation possessed the better aesthetic practitioners. Each side was given a grand parlour room (facing one another) in which to compose their works, at which point the Chinese artists began rapidly crafting the most elegant patterns across their immense plane, while the Roman artists were given orders by their masters to simply polish their wall over and over again, inexorably burnishing the surface to the point where it shone like a perfect night sky. When the time arose to display their finished products, the Chinese artists revealed a tableau worthy of their highest formalised training, adorned with a hundred colours, whereas the Romans (Sufis) dropped the separating curtain to reveal only a radiant reflective canvas that somehow projected an even more magnificent version of the original Chinese image. So it is that the symptom can be read in the manic terms of exteriority, neither as transmitted signal of the repressed nor as spontaneous enjoyment of the unconscious, but rather as the subject's rejoicing in the delirium of consciousness/identity flung toward an outer image-world of more fascinating proportions and tints. It is the exacerbated variant of the identical, thus leading precisely to the 'chiral' rise of a non-superimposable mirror-image object.

Note: This is not what the edited technological simulation does, but rather what it can only pretend to do in its totalitarian transparency, in its obscene promise of idealisation of the inner self, for manic talent belongs only to a pretender-subject willing to impel itself into outer hallucinatory silhouettes and to recognise the existential superiority of the figment. Hence the symptom should instruct us in the arts of becoming-unreal and becoming-forgotten through the construction of black-mirror instruments and spaces, the topography of the altered and the far-reaching and the going-incognito, which require not the elucidation of rusted archetypes but rather the glistening of new obscurities.

Forgetting and jaggedness; limitlessness; the duration; the foregone time; bones; vacancy; nakedness; fallout; foreignness; drone; the archaic; the unceasing; the whenever antiquity

Epilogue: Book of the Liar (Philosophy of Deception)

Man prays for evil as he prays for good, for man is hasty…
THE QUR'AN [255]

Once again, Omnicide is no sordid utopian-dystopian ideology of the solid world, but rather a light-footed, creative-destructive inkling of the fact that all experience fades, betrays, and ends. To attain this, the omnicidal figure must acquaint themselves with Deception as a philosophical art form of the highest order, circulating between dream, nightmare, mirage, fantasy, hallucination, simulation, vision, memory, enigma, image, story, wish, and apparition (ghost, shadow). They must unravel the particular techniques of distortion, riddle, and encryption that make up the vast arsenal of the liar, just as they deliver acute insight into the performances of stealth, manipulation, seduction, and intelligence behind acts of great deceit. For Deception radically alters our understanding of everything through carefully-designed prisms of affinity and of the two-faced, play and violation,

---

[255] Chapter 17, *Sūrah Al-Isrā* ('The Night Journey'), *The Koran Interpreted: A Translation*, tr. A.J. Arberry (New York: Touchstone, 1996).

enchantment and disenchantment. Following the supposed last words of a mediaeval Persian assassin (the Old Man of the Mountain)—'All is illusion, thus all is permitted'—the deceivers dedicate themselves to those typologies of artifice that bring thought to its extreme limits of dying and renewal. For what are the most subtle procedures of insinuation (and their faint interplay of proximity and distance)? Which vocabularies are most effortlessly tied to persuasion and influence, rumour and extortion (whether conscious or supraconscious)? What images induce curiosity, entrancement, infatuation, obsession, or self-ruin? What are the strange ethics of transformation, vulnerability, and subversion upheld by the charlatan, the trickster, or the saboteur?

Note: There are sacred shrines built along the ocean coast of North Africa containing the tombs of venerated saints and meant for pilgrimage, but with centuries of neglect—fluctuating tide levels or gradual erosion of the stone foundation—those hallowed sites have found themselves slowly submerged and carried out into the black waters. There is a double mysticism at work in such reburials at sea, these white-shrouded holy bodies of lost mausoleums drifting into the depths (they play tricks upon the sacred). We must learn to look like them.

Note: There are ninety-nine supposed names of God in the Islamic tradition, each signalling a distinct attribute, yet when brought together forming an almost pantheistic

EPILOGUE: BOOK OF THE LIAR

heterotopia of titles or parade of inscrutable masks. Some of these names are obviously benevolent—*Ar-Rahim* ('The Merciful'), *Al-Muhaymin* ('The Protector'); *Al-Hafeez* ('The Guardian'); *Al-Rafih* ('The Exalter')—whereas others occupy a tenuous borderland between nobility and neutrality—*Al-Musawwir* ('The Designer'); *Al-Fattah* ('The Opener'); *Al-Basit* ('The Expander'); *Ar-Raqib* ('The Watcher'); *As-Sami'* ('The Hearer'); *Al-Muqit* ('The Nourisher'); *Al-Latif* ('The Gentle'); *Al-Jami'* ('The Gatherer'); *Al-Mujib* ('The Answerer'); *Al-Hadi* ('The Guide'); *Al-Baith* ('The Awakener'); *Al-Warith* ('The Inheritor'); *Al-Batin* ('The Hidden'). And still others plunge into the dark side of divinity, where radically destructive aptitudes loom: *Al-Qahhar* ('The Subduer'); *Al-Khafid* ('The Humiliator'); *Al-Muzil* ('The Degrader'); *al-Muntaqim* ('The Avenger'); *Ad-Dharr* ('The Afflictor'); *Al-Mumeet* ('The Death-Bringer'). And then, beyond the ninety-nine official names, strewn across a handful of Quranic verses yet only emphasised in apocryphal discourses, there appears the designation *Al-Makr* ('The Plotter/Deceiver'), referring to the strategic laying of plans or cunning schemes that entrap enemies. Moreover, it is often taught that each heavenly angel was gifted with and therefore embodies just one of the ninety-nine righteous traits expressed by the names, while the demonic race of angels (*shayatin*) each carry one of the aforementioned violent potentialities. This in turn corresponds to another elegant belief:

that all angelic beings were born of sunlight whereas Satan was the only creature in existence created from God's moonlight—i.e., that evil is a touch of something else, the reflective effulgence of the satellite. Lastly, some esoteric orders suggested that the ninety-nine aliases, when arranged together correctly as manic alter-egos, would form an arcane, combinatory one-hundredth autonym or eponym, a supreme theophoric handle (*ism al-'azam*) whose very enunciation commands the almighty to respond or even turns its human speaker into a god of some kind. We must learn to sound like them.

Note: The greatest conspiracies of all time are exceptional orchestrations of three paradoxes: secrecy and transparency (philosophy of the gesture); abstraction and viscerality (philosophy of omnipotence); malice and intimacy (philosophy of betrayal). Within the first paradox, these groups must master imperceptibility in their entrance and tracelessness in their exit, while also harbouring no unconscious (only fanatical will): thus the secretive ones also possess a militant clarity of ambition, like the vampire who stalks with anonymous, elusive movements while driven by an unmistakable thirst in the veins. This coagulates into a perfect execution of the gesture, such that we can recall two particular works of the twentieth century, each of them a sort of literary instruction manual devoted to elaborate micro-techniques: the first with chapters entitled 'The Gesture of Shaving', 'The

EPILOGUE: BOOK OF THE LIAR

Gesture of Smoking a Pipe', and 'The Gesture of Turning a Mask Around'; the second with chapters entitled 'Instructions on How to Cry', 'Instructions on How to Climb a Staircase', and 'Instructions on How to Kill Ants in Rome'. To understand why such books are even written, why this sub-genre exists, is to take a step toward the power of deception. With respect to the second paradox, conspiratorial blocs cinch together the omnipotence of thought (developing numerologies and orphic systems) and the omnipotence of the body (developing idiosyncratic rituals and daggers), in the same way that voodoo practitioners construct an abstract-visceral doll to simultaneously torment mind, flesh, and soul—or more precisely, themselves invent the soul precisely in order to torture it. And the third paradox somehow mixes the worst intentions with the greatest familiarity or affection, realising that true betrayal requires closeness above all else, as with that poet of malicious intimacy whose opening hex reads: 'I have cursed your forehead, your belly, your life / I have cursed the streets your steps plod through / the things your hands pick up / I have cursed the inside of your dreams.'[256] So it is that these three paradoxes of conspiracy are able to animate fantasy; more than this, they weaponise fantasy to wrest reality back into

---

[256] H. Michaux, 'I Am Rowing (Poetry for Power)', in *Darkness Moves: An Henri Michaux Anthology, 1927-1984* (Berkeley, CA: University of California Press, 1997).

suspicion, doubt, and ambiguity: their gatherings are a blade of imbalance; their paranoid stories of the enemy are blades of imbalance; their trances, war-cries, and berserk retellings of the outside are themselves blades of imbalance. We must learn to dream like them.

So it is that these pages culminate with a series of unfinished, fractal diagrams of the multiple dimensions of the lie—tracking obscure codes of concealment, veiling, and conjuration—which stand like open wounds inviting further injury. Diagram 1 breaks deception into several molecular sub-concepts; Diagram 2 articulates varied typologies of deception; Diagram 3 outlines conceptual figures who deploy and inhabit deceptive identities; Diagram 4 sketches a sequence of deceptive techniques aligned with the misleading of perception; Diagram 5 lists a number of specific spaces, objects, and body parts that help forge deception's theatre of operation.

DIAGRAM 1: DECEPTIVE SUB-CONCEPTS

Manipulation (mastery, craft, artifice)
Distortion
Riddle
Encryption
Stealth
Seduction (style, immersion)

EPILOGUE: BOOK OF THE LIAR

Desire (attraction, repulsion, disequilibrium)
Intelligence (diabolical perception)
Enchantment (intensity, awe, projection)
Unknowing (disorientation, forgetting)
Imagination
Intimacy
Betrayal
Guile
Violation
Subtlety
Secrecy (allure, secretion)
Subterfuge (procedure)
Insinuation
Proximity
Distance
Language
Persuasion (intimation, suggestion, contagious movement)
Influence (contact)
Rumour
Extortion
Consciousness (vigilance)
Curiosity
Intuition (anticipation)
Interruption (diversion, digression, twitch, stutter, pause)
Entrancement (private delirium)
Infatuation (intrigue, fixation, captivation, obsession)

Self-Destruction (unravelling)
Transformation (strangeness)
Vulnerability (exposure, sensitivity)
Subversion
Concealment (masking, disguise, dissimulation, camouflage, mystification)
Misinformation (false divulgence, hearsay)
Complexity (contrivance)
Manifestation
Confusion (disorientation, perplexity)
Disappearance (erasure, exit)
Conjuration (amorphousness, pretending, costume, masquerade)
Impossibility (miracle)
Appearance (idolization, intimation, awe)
Disappearance (withdrawal, return)

DIAGRAM 2: DECEPTIVE TYPOLOGIES

1. Lies of Death, War, Love, Dream, Game (potential transversals)
2. Lies of Status (the ruler, the icon) versus Lies of Wretchedness (the ascetic, the prophet, the outcast)
3. Lies of Tone (aggression, lightness, mockery, indifference) and Rhythm (speech, breath, narrative)
4. Lies of Voice (volume, emphasis, labyrinthine eloquence, mystifying silence)

EPILOGUE: BOOK OF THE LIAR

5. Lies of Posture (relaxed, intense), Gesture (signal), and Appearance (dress, gaze, accessory, style)
6. Lies of Instrumentalism (functionality, the means) versus Pathological Lying (mythomania/*pseudologia fantastica*, the habit) versus Aesthetic Lying (pleasure, the craft)
7. Lies of Neurotic Desire (power, belonging, beauty, preservation) versus Lies of Ecstatic Risk (adventure)
8. Lies of Specificity (the one thing) versus Lies of Vagueness (the unknown)
9. Lies of Simplicity (one-dimensional compression) versus Lies of Intricacy (layering)
10. Lies of Formality (hierarchy, sanctity, jargon) versus Lies of Informality (humour, slang, vulgarity)
11. Lies of Youth to Elders (fraud, neglect) versus Lies of Elders to Youth (abuse, protection)
12. Lies of Enticement (temptation) versus Lies of Inhibition (fear) versus Lies of Provocation (incensement)
13. Lies to the Collective (universality, good) versus Lies to the Individual (particularity, evil)
14. Lies of Rare Opportunity (urgency, last chance) versus Lies of Indefinite Potential (feigned neutrality)
15. Lies of Denial versus Distraction versus Intrigue
16. Lies of Invention (fabrication) versus Exaggeration (adulation) versus Diminution (slander) versus Omission (hiding)

17. Lies of Coming Utopia (revolution, transcendence, escape) versus Impending Dystopia (doom, catastrophe)

18. Lies of Reward (the promise, the vow, the debt, the gift, the offer/proposal) versus Punishment (the penalty)

19. Lies of the Fantastical (fairy tale, carnival, freakshow, bestiaries) versus Hyper-Realist Lies (shock images)

20. Lies of Play (skill, chance, mimicry/role-play, sensation, sabotage, masochistic defeat)

21. Lies of Intentional Self-Delusion (fluidity, to believe oneself)

22. Malicious Lies (hurt) versus Social Lies (courtesy) versus Entrancing Lies (vitalism)

23. Lies of Familiarity (the intimate) versus Lies of Anonymity (the stranger)

24. Lies of Miraculous Illusion (the impossible) versus Conceivable Lies (the everyday)

25. Collaborative Lying (mass hallucination, conspiracy) versus Solitary Lying (sorcery, visionary delirium)

26. Lies of the Superior (the master, whim/wrath) versus Lies of the Inferior (the underling, aspiration/resentment)

27. False Messengers (whisper, gossip, rumour)

28. Salvaged Lies (return of old myths, superstitions, ideologies) versus New Lies (surprise, novelty)

29. Lies of Adolescent Development: pretending (lies of play); denial (lies of cover-up); self-aggrandizement (lies of identity); rumour (lies of cruelty)

EPILOGUE: BOOK OF THE LIAR

30. Lies that Grant Entrance (infiltration) versus Lies that Unbind (elusion, circumvention)
31. Lies of Mood (atmosphere, sensation)
32. Lies of Self-Training (the simulated arena, espionage, the nightmare)
33. Lies of Elevation (euphemism, metaphor) versus Lies of Degradation (malediction, onus)

DIAGRAM 3: DECEPTIVE CONCEPTUAL FIGURES

The Liar
The Charlatan
The Trickster
The Cheater
The Imposter
The Heretic
The Alchemist
The Saboteur
The Storyteller
The Occultist
The Seducer
The Courtesan
The Confidence Man
The Criminal
The Hustler
The Spy
The Madwoman

The Actor/Artist
The Poet
The Ringleader
The Hypnotist
The Gambler
The Perjurer (false witness)
The Forger
The Fugitive
The Costume-Maker
The Conspirator
The Coder
The Sphinx/Riddler
The Propagandist/Demagogue
The False God
The Piper
The Siren
The Predator/Prey
The Deviant/Dealer
The Game-Master
The Escape-Artist
The Fortune-Teller
The Smuggler/Pirate
The Mystic
The Mirror-Image
The Puppet-Master/Ghost-Writer
The Traitor
The Prodigal (oath-breaker)

EPILOGUE: BOOK OF THE LIAR

The Rogue (disgrace, scandal)
The Hypocrite (duplicity)
The Villain (nemesis, spite)
The Seer (shaman, astrologer)
The Samira (evening conversationalist)
The Eavesdropper

DIAGRAM 4: DECEPTIVE TECHNIQUES

1. Nonsense (oddity, randomness, accident, unnatural combination)
2. Esotericism (hierarchy, intimacy, the arcane)
3. Foreignness (the somewhere, the elsewhere, the nowhere, the accent)
4. Treason (hostility, sabotage, the enemy)
5. Complicity (the oath, the accomplice, the servant)
6. Secrecy (extortion, the unspoken)
7. Sacrifice (forfeiture, grieving)
8. Fragmentation (chasm, splintering)
9. Profanity (malediction, the curse)
10. Threat (menace, the ultimatum)
11. Excess (overdose, the rant)
13. Distraction (barrage, decoy, the palimpsest)
14. Subtraction (obscurity, silence, the half-formed)
15. Reclusion (quarantine, inaccessibility, distance)
16. Anonymity (ambiguity, amorphousness)

17. Derangement (volatility, substitution, the thorn, the turn, the twist)
18. Shock (crisis, awe, the exception)
19. Anti-shock (indifference, calmness, the rule)
20. Repetition (ritual, the circle, the spiral)
21. Viscerality (sensation, the flesh)
22. Speed (acceleration, frenzy), Slowness (deceleration, entropy), Stillness (inertia)
23. Hallucination (induction)
24. Forgetting (neglect)
25. Allegiance (configuration)
26. Corruption (violation)
27. Misguidance (endangerment)
28. Prophecy (vision, fatalism, the emissary)
29. Metamorphosis (reversal, paradox, contradiction, hyper-similitude, transition)
30. Objectification (alienation, animism, the impersonal, the automaton, the thing)

DIAGRAM 5:
DECEPTIVE SPACES/OBJECTS/BODY PARTS

SPACES
- The Card Table
- The Masquerade
- The Interrogation Room
- The Sideshow

EPILOGUE: BOOK OF THE LIAR

- The Carnival, The Circus
- The Stage
- The Labyrinth
- The Drug Den
- The Alley
- The Spectacle
- The Black Market
- The Spiderweb
- The Trapdoor (false architecture)
- The Pirate Haven / The Underground (zones of expected deception)

OBJECTS
- The Mask (surface)
- The Veil (anti-faciality)
- The Distorting Mirror (formlessness)
- The Magnifying Glass (proportionality)
- The Crystal Ball (destiny)
- The Box (harbouring)
- The Capsule (preservation)
- The Cosmetic (façade)
- The Costume (dress)
- The Screen (virtuality, occlusion)
- The Decoy (automation)
- The Robe, Scroll, Wand (magic)
- The Vial (alchemy)
- The Talisman (shamanism)

- The Improvised Weapon (martial artistry)
- The Trap (hunting)
- The Hook (death, chance)

BODY PARTS
- The Eyes/Eyebrows/Eyelashes (hypnotist)
- The Smile (guest)
- The Mouth/Lips (seducer)
- The Hands/Fingers (illusionist)
- The Fist/Chest (fighter)
- The Feet (athlete)
- The Hips (dancer)
- The Teeth (animal)

UNREAL PLAYERS: INVENTORY OF GIFTS

We are not quite done yet, for two arguments require further elaboration in connecting mania, doom, and deception: (1) that the omnicidal figure must effectively fuse the talents of all deceptive beings; (2) that omnicidal will embodies the ultimate measure of unreality.

The omnicidal figure must appropriate the ways in which elemental forces lie (geography, nature). The forest is permeated by mist, fragile branches, pathlessness, and pits; the jungle is known for its entangling vines, camouflaging creatures, and quicksand; the desert teases with its sporadic breezes, all-irritating granular sands, and complex assortment of mirages; the mountain subtly deprives one of oxygen, rains avalanches, and offers unsure footholds; the island feigns escape or rescue, leading one to eventual madness; the cave offers false shelter while concealing its other winged or raptorial inhabitants; the sea harbours predatory species of whales, sharks, jellyfish, eels, and stingrays, the arcane intelligence and untranslatable communicative signals of the octopus, tidal undertows and irregular wave patterns, and the vicious subterfuge of calm before storms; and outer space itself is populated by the unpredictable catastrophes of dying stars, meteoric showers, black holes, and dark matter.

The omnicidal figure must appropriate the ways in which gods lie: the hermaphroditic unassignability of the angelic ranks (perplexing quality), the micro-malicious whims of jinn races who hide their interventions behind the inconspicuous cover of accident, and the prankster or fool gods who speak untruths at will. Furthermore, even the binary monotheistic conventions of good and evil deities provide a selection of deceptive traits: for God lies by withdrawing, deferring, breaking promises, double-speaking in parables, cloaking, and mystifying (works in mysterious ways); whereas the Devil lies by taking the role of choice-giver, desire-tempter, and wish-granter, manipulating humans' basic self-misunderstanding of their own soul by mastering both causality (trajectivity, sequence, succession) and miraculous contingency (emergence, spontaneity, deviation, will).

The omnicidal figure must appropriate the ways in which designers lie—seamstress, perfumer, cosmetologist, pyrotechnician: those who understand deception as gradual mood-construction (production of atmosphere) and utilise arsenals of accessory items (adorning the surroundings). Control of climate (coldness, warmth, open or closed perimeters), lighting (dimness, radiance), colour (chromatic, achromatic), tactility (textures of softness, smoothness, hardness), scent (fragrance, sterility), sound (sonic arrangements, acoustics, audition). They thereby cater to decorative assemblages and detailed practices of enhancement, becoming behind-the-scenes guarantors of the aura. Like those earlier-referenced doctors of mesmerism who built large mirror rooms filled with outstretched lounge beds and the notes of lone string instruments, hypnotising with their eyes or with light touch across foreheads, necks, and shoulders, such designers understand those precise aesthetic provocations that bring about belief in what is not necessarily there.

The omnicidal figure must learn to appropriate the ways in which criminals and spies lie, their talented grasp of simulation (false aliases, alter egos) and dissimulation (anonymity) to acquire non-disclosed sources and confidential information. Their grace under pressure while reading rooms, targets, and adversaries (intelligence

EPILOGUE: BOOK OF THE LIAR

gathering), their sleek movements between accents, apparel, and roles (agent, informant, confidante), their capacities for both asceticism and luxury (deprivation, squandering, prestige, waste).

The omnicidal figure must appropriate the ways in which animals and machines lie (fusing primal and futuristic models). Animality employs tactics of biomimicry (owls, seahorses, chameleons), skin-shedding (snakes, scorpions) and organ-regeneration (starfish, spiders, worms, mice), the grim idleness of those scavenger species known for ambush, lying-in-wait, and consumption in the aftermath (the jackal, the hyena, the vulture, the coyote), and those insect colonies whose members share collective memories or hive cognition impossible to experience individually. Machinism, on the other hand, is based on controlling symbols and syntax without recourse to any intrinsic knowledge or semantic framework, although it may conceivably involve adding improvisation to the machinic skillset, in addition to a heightened finesse for copying (impersonation, imitation, recitation) and counterfeiting (signatures, artifacts, documents, jewels). In this partial sense, the liar is the perfect subjective realisation both of the beast and of artificial intelligence.

The omnicidal figure must appropriate the ways in which warriors and mystics lie: to conceptualise deception as War is to uphold language, thought, tongue, and body as training grounds or battle grounds for martial artistic conflicts, including techniques of feinting, jabbing, throwing combinations, flying lunges, and concealed weapons, along with the entire complicated spectacle of posturing and boasting that threatens opponents with well-simulated rage (the fists/blades lie in air). To conceptualise deception as Mysticism is to uphold lying as a discipline of total absorption into the hidden, to procure altered states through ecstatic release of the unapparent, including techniques of induction, dance, incantation, hyperventilation, trance, curse, sympathetic magic, numerology, intoxication, fainting, possession, forgetting, or premonition alongside rituals that simultaneously rivet together the viscerality and ethereality, focus and disorientation, passion and coldness, of the initiate who plays both creative god and dead god. One lies to kill the other, one lies to kill the self; one lies to win a materially-present finitude (glory, plunder); one lies to win the alternative, withheld infinity (adoration, annihilation).

Having noted just a few of the options in the deceiver's deck of cards, we must now commence a philosophical conversation about the many potential standings of the unreal itself. Where does the unreal come from, and what is the nature of its confrontation with the so-called real?

Method: We must lie our way into the lie. If zero comes from the Arabic *sifr*, which also means cipher (a secret message), then to embark upon this study of

EPILOGUE: BOOK OF THE LIAR

deception, we must construct a code, enigma, or puzzle as its point of origin. We must tell a story, or rather several stories, and thereby make phenomenological choices that propel us toward one intricate posture or another. All are valid, in that all render effectual stances at one time or another.

1. What is the unreal? Breaking point, opening, threshold, limit, border, mirror image, nexus, unrelated universe. If the unreal constitutes the breaking point of the real, then its relation is one based in collapse, mourning, haunting, intolerability, or even hatred. If the unreal constitutes an opening within the real, then its relation is based either in escape (emergency, survival), liberation (resistance), or transgression (indulgence, forbidden pleasure). If the unreal constitutes the threshold bridging the real, then it perhaps traverses states of reversibility (the fable's homecoming, the dream's waking, the intoxicant's withdrawal, the trance's resumption of consciousness) or enters the irreversible lair (madness). If the unreal constitutes the limit of the real, then its relation is based in excess, monstrosity, and horror. If the unreal constitutes a border with the real, then we encounter a strenuous relation of clashing, fortification, barricade, or rivalry. If the unreal constitutes the mirror image of the real, then they exist in antithetical resemblance, either as diametrical nemeses or mutual

shadow-worlds. If the unreal constitutes a nexus with the real, then their opposition is a ruse meant to cover their conspiratorial alignment, claiming disparity while they actually work together as allegorical complements or arch-simulations of one another. If the unreal constitutes a universe entirely unrelated to the real, then their occasional intersection can bring only bafflement, indifference, or sheer misrecognition.

2. Where is the unreal? Edge, boundary, beyond, portal, corner. If the unreal forms an edge, then its spatial configuration is experienced as vertical depth, hole, or cavern (fallenness). If the unreal forms a boundary, then its spatial configuration is experienced as horizontal expanse (wildness). If the unreal forms a beyond, then its spatial configuration is experienced as cosmological outside (extraplanetary travel). If the unreal forms a portal, then its spatial configuration is experienced as interdimensional passage (slippage). If the unreal forms a corner, then its spatial configuration is experienced as hidden recess, fold, angle, pinpoint, or pocket (seclusion).

3. When is the unreal? Past, present, future, transitional time, hypothetical time, non-time. If the unreal occurs in the past, then its temporality belongs to the domain of myth, memory, lamentation, or obsolescing fantasy

EPILOGUE: BOOK OF THE LIAR

(the ancients forsaken) and is therefore something to be avenged, resurrected, grieved for, or nostalgically retold. If the unreal occurs in the present, then its temporality belongs to the domain of instantaneity, submersion, or momentary flux (the decadent's night of exception) and is therefore something caught between the quickening and the vanishing. If the unreal occurs in the future, then its temporality belongs to the telescopic domain of anticipation, speculation, hope, expectation, evolution, approach, struggle, or projection (throwing some desire or fear into the vague infrared of the impending) and is therefore something to be avoided, stalled, accelerated, or longed for. If the unreal occurs in a transitional time, then its temporality belongs to the twilight, midnight, dawn, split second, last minute, meanwhile, or eleventh hour as something that accompanies, consorts, or (mis)guides between daybreak and nightfall. If the unreal occurs in a hypothetical time, then its temporality belongs to the phantom-domain of parallelism, potentiality, regret, reset, or wastedness and therefore looms accusingly between the foregone and the foretold option (the sometime, the once-upon-a-time, the time-to-come). If the unreal occurs in a non-time, then it abandons temporal measures for some floating, lawless isle of oblivion, standstill, or freneticism and therefore breaks through the hourglass's walls through over-accentuation of the never (scarcity, rarity, unlikelihood, immateriality, the inopportune, the seasonless) or the always (immortality, perpetuity, endurance, agelessness, deathlessness, return).

4. Who is the unreal? Partner, guardian, orchestrator, slave. Manifold answers have already been provided above, in Diagram 3's elaboration of deceptive figures including the charlatan, the courtesan, the hypnotist, and the eavesdropper, as well as in the duplicitous modes of animals, deities, designers, and machines noted in the preceding section. Nevertheless, what remains undetermined is the particular strategy of transferral or conversion between these deceptive states (i.e. how one juggles propensities) and also the overall disposition of the deceptive player toward the unreal (i.e. the roles implicit to their concord). The first proposition—the sequence, arrangement, and selection of masks at any given moment—must almost always follow a schematic of the most effectual perpetrator: one must dip into one's bag and switch casually from heretic to ringleader, siren, or hypocrite depending on the specific demands of each environment (the scene itself decides whose arsenal of underhanded skills will prove relevant). Thus the rotation between characters or postures is derived by attunement to the sector alone. And yet, once back in the solitude of one's study where thoughts reset to their zero degree, what is the

governing pact between the liar and the unreal? The partner perceives an equivalence or mutual benefit to be had by sustaining the unreal (reciprocity); the guardian perceives a protective obligation, which implies the unreal as something superior yet fragile (siege); the orchestrator perceives an opportunity for manipulative influence, innovation, or experimentation within the unreal (laboratory); the slave perceives captivity, labour, devotion, service, or even worship as the base criteria of its actions within the unreal (whether by voluntary or involuntary bondage).

5. Why is the unreal? Incompatibility, journey, test, fate, solace, archive, eternal substrate, catastrophic event, necessary abstraction. If the unreal arose out of pure incompatibility with the real, then its separation would follow the same logic as the heaven-hell division or consciousness-unconscious division (severed for the sake of making creation, identity, and sanity possible), but which then always conceals a hostile fault line or ultimatum beneath. If the unreal arose as a journey, then its critical disjoining from the real would serve only to establish a terminus for expedition, venture, and heroic stamina (to make striving possible). If the unreal arose as a test, then its counteractive purpose would be to furnish adversity, trial, obstacle, and challenge (to make overcoming possible). If the unreal arose as a

fate, then its original schism from reality would serve to enable an alternative decree or horoscopic prospect (to make inevitability, becoming, and revelation possible). If the unreal arose as a solace, then its schism would convene a safe haven for the amnesty-seeker (to make sanctuary, secrecy, and healing possible). If the unreal arose as an archive, then it would follow the intricate organisational systems of the collector who takes surpassing pleasure in isolation and compartmentalisation (in order to make savouring and difference possible). Moreover, it matters whether one storytells the initial bifurcation between reality-unreality as an eternal split (both having existed in endless detachment) or as being linked to a particular catastrophic event (like those floods, earthquakes, and ruptures in old theological stories) that tore a prior unity asunder. Furthermore, is it an intentional vivisection, failure, accident, or internal rebellion that results in this cleaving of planes? Is the unreal born simply to provide a crucial outer layer of abstraction for the exceptional will: the dissenter who joins the suspicious community of the carnival in order to master insane acrobatic feats, the vigilante who devises the mask to defeat overwhelming enemies, the tribal warrior who coats themselves in paint or animal furs to hasten pulse and heartbeat, the magician who crafts the wooden staff as an aestheticised conductive appendage to their own hand, the lunatic/artist who somehow wrenches into manifest impression what is not there and has never been? For all of these traces to fulfil themselves into delirium, there must first occur a grand rift (genesis of the outside) which will serve later as comprehensive justification for the chimerical and the otherwise.

6. How is the unreal? Does one access it through thought, drive, imagination, spell, device, charm, offering, or quest? Is one chosen to enter its inner circles or is it stumbled upon unwittingly? Should one be guided or won over after some magnificent inquisition? What compelling qualities must be possessed in order to walk upon its fine dust: intelligence, cunning, humour, courage, ruthlessness, purity, brokenness?

DECEPTION AS WILLED DESTINY

If one does indeed find extreme nobility in dishonesty (honour among thieves) and extreme intimacy in dishonesty (thick as thieves), then we must understand Deception as a destiny that eternally opposes ideology. We must never confuse these definitional realms of power: the political universe's opportunistic ploys of mass control share not a single drop of the same substance as the liar's enchantments documented here. They are bound together only by an ageless mutual hatred confirmed by the long line of visionary poets, musicians, sculptors, artists, and philosophers killed by regime after regime across time and in every human civilisation on record. The countless unmarked graves of those whose creative charms bought them only poverty, exile, surveillance, imprisonment, torture, excommunication, censorship, alienation, illness, and untimely death establish these two forms as incompatible spheres of untruth. Anathema. One imposes tired clichés of significance and propagandistic replays of subordination (meaning 'to ordain below'); the other trades in inventively worthless thoughts and original tones of subterfuge (meaning 'to flee beneath'). One demands of its recipients an increasing weakness to mirror its own neurotic anxiety, as best embodied by its heavy militaristic marches, arguments, and anthems; the other inspires increasing strength from its collaborators to mirror its own enthralled complexion, making them lighter, livelier, quicker, more sensitive, perceptive, eloquent, charismatic, and daring in the deceptive episode than ever before (albeit against their conscious or unconscious choice). One seeks bleak universality and permanence while promising utopia; the other ensures delicate partiality and transience while gifting only a single evening or hour of amusement/refuge. The rulers of nations (myth) versus the architects of fabricated lands (fairy tale): archetype versus prototype. Yes, we might even conceivably forgive these interchangeable leaders

EPILOGUE: BOOK OF THE LIAR

their constant violence if not for the two unforgivable sins of all sadisms: (1) that they have no style; (2) that they take no pleasure in their work. The great liar, though, is the thing of meteoric ephemerality that awes a tired world. They breathe back into the void of pale realities to remind us that there are neither rights nor oaths to constrain our most agile machinations, theories, night-songs, inveigling games and ingenuities. The liar has always been party to this wisdom of the extraction of the slightest possibility from inside a false and dying existence. Their words freeze time and make the end never-ending, a synthetic diamond shot right through the temple of Psyche. For the liar has always been the world's best last chance.

Select Bibliography

ADONIS. *The Pages of Day and Night*, tr. S. Hazo. Evanston: Northwestern University Press, 2000.
— *A Time Between Ashes and Roses*, tr. S. Toorawa. Syracuse, NY: Syracuse University Press, 2004.
— *Victims of a Map*, tr. A. al-Udhari. London: Saqi Books, 2008.
— *Selected Poems*, tr. K. Mattawa. New Haven: Yale University Press, 2010.
BACHELARD, GASTON. *The Poetics of Reverie*, tr. D. Russell. Boston: Beacon Press, 1960.
BENSMAIA, RÉDA. *The Year of Passages*, tr. T. Conley. Minneapolis: University of Minnesota Press, 1995.
BLASIM, HASSAN. *The Madman of Freedom Square*, tr. J. Wright. Manchester: Carcanet Press, 2010.
— *Iraqi Christ*, tr. J. Wright. Manchester: Comma Press, 2013.
DARWISH, MAHMOUD. *Unfortunately, It Was Paradise*, tr. M. Akash, C. Forche, S. Antoon, and A. El-Zein. Berkeley, CA: University of California Press, 2003.
— 'I Am Yusuf', tr. A. Amireh, <http://www.naseeb.com/villages/journals/1-palestinian-poetry-oh-my-father-i-am-yusuf-68387>.

FARROKHZAD, FORUGH. *A Lonely Woman: Forugh Farrokhzad and Her Poetry*, tr. M. Hillmann. New York: Three Continents Press, 1987.
— *Sin: Selected Poems of Forugh Farrokhzad*, tr. S. Wolpé. Fayetteville, AR: University of Arkansas Press, 2007.
— *Another Birth and Other Poems*, tr. H. Javadi and S. Sallee. Washington, D.C.: Mage, 2010.

HEDAYAT, SADEQ. *The Blind Owl*, tr. D.P. Costello. New York: Grove Press, 1957.
— *Sadeq Hedayat: An Anthology*, ed. E. Yarshater. Boulder, CO: Westview Press, 1979.
— *Three Drops of Blood*, tr. D. Miller Mostaghel. London: Alma Books, 2013.

KONI, IBRAHIM AL-. *The Bleeding of the Stone*, tr. M. Jayyusi and C. Tingley. Northampton, NY: Interlink, 2002.
— *The Seven Veils of Seth*, tr. W. M. Hutchins. Reading: Garnet Publishing, 2008.
— *The Puppet*, tr. W. M. Hutchins. Austin, TX: Center for Middle Eastern Studies, University of Texas, 2010.
— *A Sleepless Eye: Aphorisms from the Sahara*, tr. R. Allen. Syracuse, NY: Syracuse University Press, 2014.

MANSOUR, JOYCE. *Screams*, tr. S. Gavronsky. Sausalito, CA: Post Apollo, 1995.
— *Essential Poems and Writings*, tr. S. Gavronsky. Boston: Black Widow Press, 2008.

SELECT BIBLIOGRAPHY

Michaux, Henri. *Darkness Moves: An Henri Michaux Anthology, 1927–1984*, tr. D. Ball. Berkeley, CA: University of California Press, 1997.

Mohaghegh, Jason Bahbak. *New Literature and Philosophy of the Middle East: The Chaotic Imagination*. New York: Palgrave Macmillan, 2010.

— *Inflictions: The Writing of Violence in the Middle East*. London: Continuum, 2012.

— *The Radical Unspoken: Silence in Middle Eastern and Western Thought*. New York: Routledge, 2013.

— *Insurgent, Poet, Mystic, Sectarian: The Four Masks of an Eastern Postmodernism*. New York: SUNY Press, 2015.

— *Omnicide: Mania, Fatality, and the Future-in-Delirium*. Falmouth and New York: Urbanomic/Sequence Press, 2019.

Negarestani, Reza. *Abducting the Outside: Collected Writings 2003–2018*. Falmouth and New York: Urbanomic/Sequence Press, forthcoming 2023.

Samman, Ghada. *Beirut Nightmares*, tr. N. Roberts. London: Quartet Books, 1976.

— 'The Swan Genie', in *The Square Moon: Supernatural Tales*, tr. I. Boullata. Fayetteville, AR: University of Arkansas Press, 1999.

Shamlu, Ahmad. *Majmu'eh-ye Asar-e Ahmad Shamlu* (*The Collected Works of Ahmad Shamlu*). Tehran: Zamaneh Press, 2002.

— *Born Upon the Dark Spear*, tr. J. Mohaghegh. New York: Contra Mundum Press, 2015.

URBANOMIC/SEQUENCE PRESS TITLES

The Concept of Non-Photography
François Laruelle

Fanged Noumena: Collected Writings 1987–2007
Nick Land

The Number and the Siren: A Decipherment of Mallarmé's Coup de Dés
Quentin Meillassoux

Synthetic Philosophy of Contemporary Mathematics
Fernando Zalamea

From Decision to Heresy: Experiments in Non-Standard Thought
François Laruelle

To Live and Think Like Pigs:
The Incitement of Envy and Boredom in Market Democracies
Gilles Châtelet

Intelligence and Spirit
Reza Negarestani

On Logic and the Theory of Science
Jean Cavaillès

Pleromatica, or Elsinore's Trance
Gabriel Catren